To Fran

Love & Best u

from

Jennie Shurmer

The
Forgotten
Chariot
by
Jennie Shurmer

The Forgotten Chariot

A novel based on the life of Dick Ripley.

Author: Jennie Shurmer

Published in Great Britain by Cormorant Publishing Hartlepool

Copyright © Jennie Shurmer
1st Edition

First published in 2008 by
Cormorant Publishing Hartlepool.
5 Teesdale Ave.,
Hartlepool. TS26 9QD
cormorant publishing@yahoo.co.uk

www.riddlewrites.co.uk

ISBN 978-0-9558593-6-6

Illustrated and designed by Cormorant Publishing Hartlepool
Written by John Riddle

Typeset, printed and bound in England by
Connoisseur Crafts Limited
Hartlepool Enterprise Centre,
Brougham Terrace,
Hartlepool. TS24 8EY
Conncrafts@surfree.co.uk

This book is dedicated to my father
Richard Nicholson Ripley
"Dick"

who died on
14th July 1996

He never quite made the gold
but to me he was always a winner!

My book is based as closely as possible
on the real events that took place in my
father's life. I have used not only the
stories that my father told me, but also
the letters and newspaper cuttings that he
left behind, together with my own research.
Even so, many of the characters portrayed
are purely fictional and are not meant
to be an accurate representation of real
people, past or present.

The Forgotten Chariot
Foreword by Ken Lupton

As we look forward to the XXIX Olympic Games in Beijing later this year, with a young woman from Hartlepool taking part, how proud Dick Ripley would have been to see a record of his participation in the VIII Olympic Games, being published.

Richard N Ripley, known to all simply as "Dick", ran in the "Chariot of Fire" Olympics in Paris in 1924. He was a member of the Great Britain 4x400m relay team that won bronze medals. This was without their No.1 runner Olympic 400m champion Eric Liddell, who was a minister of the Scottish Church and refused to take part in any events run on a Sunday. The 4x400m relay final was on a Sunday. Two weeks later the British team at full strength with Liddell, Toms, Butler and Ripley thrashed the American gold medal Olympic Champions.

Dick was a member of West Hartlepool Harriers and London Polytechnic Harriers. When West Hartlepool Harriers went defunct in 1928, Dick joined the Bum Road Harriers club.

I had the privilege of meeting Dick in 1994 when researching the history of Burn Road Harriers for their Centenary year in 1995, and heard from Dick himself of many of the happenings in this splendid book by Jennie Shurmer. In 1995 Dick was Guest of Honour and cut the cake at the Burn Road Harriers Centenary dinner at the age of 92.

Despite Hartlepool's proud record in sport over the past 100 years, Dick Ripley, Medal winning Olympian was perhaps our most successful to date. I hope you enjoy reading this excellent book as much as I did - I just couldn't put it down - and I wish every success to Jemma Lowe as she prepares for Beijing and another chapter in the history of Hartlepool's sporting men and women.

Ken Lupton

Prologue

Josie watched as her father's ashes were swept across Harkerside Moor. It was a very lonely and bleak spot, far above Swaledale, with only sheep, black headed gulls and curlews for company. Josie knew that this was just where Dad would want to be, wandering alone high above his beloved Dales. He was free at last, free to roam the moors he had loved so passionately throughout his chequered life.

The funeral had been a difficult for the whole family. Dick's widow, Mary, had not really understood what was going on until the curtains closed around the coffin and the strains of "Chariots of Fire" had filled the chapel.

"Don't leave me Dick!" Mary had cried as she crumpled into her seat. Josie, Dick's youngest daughter, had tried to comfort her, but felt so lost and alone herself.

As the mourners left the chapel many stopped to offer their condolences. Some of the faces Josie had never seen before, some were like distant memories appearing out of the mists of time.

"He was a marvellous old man." One grey-haired old gentleman remarked. "They broke the mould after they made Dick Ripley!"

"His stamina and determination were an example for us all," another added, "and he never lost it."

Josie agreed with them. Dick was ninety-five when he died and, until he had broken his hip a few years before, he had always been active. Well into his eighties he had worked as the formidable doorman of the local Navy club. He was such a diligent guardian of the portals of that establishment that the committee had even changed the rules, once he had turned eighty, just so they could keep him on. Even then he still found the time and energy to entertain his favourite grandson, Josie's son Richard, with walks, football games and endless stories.

Josie sighed. She realised that she had been lost in her own thoughts, staring down the dale.

"Goodbye Dad" she whispered, as she emptied the rest of the casket.

It had been a Sunday morning when Dad had died, "peacefully, in hospital", as the newspapers had put it. They had informed the papers. After all, he had been a local hero. Mam had drawn the line at allowing the TV cameras to the funeral though. "Dad never liked any fuss," she had insisted and she was right. Dick had been a quiet, unassuming man. Although he had run in the Olympics, with Abrahams and Liddell in 1924, and obtained a bronze medal, he was reluctant to talk of his running days. He had a cabinet full of medals permanently on display, but that was his one and only acknowledgement of his former glory, and glory it must have been.

To Josie her dad was a hero, but not everyone agreed. Dick had ended his days living very modestly. He had no accumulated wealth and was not famous. If you passed him in the street you would not have noticed him. Apart from the medals, all that remained of his past were a few faded photographs hanging in battered and worn frames above the radiators. To many it appeared that Dick had wasted his opportunities. One of his own sons had even referred to him as a loser. Josie knew differently. If there was one thing that her father had taught her, it was that you did not have to be rich and famous to be a winner...

Chapter 1

Richard Nicholson Ripley, "Dick", was born one bright, sunny afternoon, on the 23rd. June 1901. He was not quite a Victorian, the old queen having died in the previous January.

Winifred, his mother, woke that morning to the sun streaming into her room. The sunlight dancing on the ceiling did not reflect her mood. That was more in keeping with the sombre mahogany furniture and dark drapes that surrounded her.

The last few days had left Winifred feeling isolated and claustrophobic. She had started getting bouts of severe pain low down in her back two days earlier and no-one would take her seriously when she said that she thought her baby was coming soon.

"Don't be ridiculous," her husband Richard had said sharply, when she had tried to explain her fears during the previous evening. He had been much more interested in the financial section of his newspaper and was obviously annoyed at being disturbed. The paper was cast aside angrily.

"He is not due for at least another week. Your back is aching because you have insisted on rising. You know that our doctor told you to lie still." Richard was undoubtedly the master of their house and there was no question in his mind that the baby was a boy. After all, he was their first born and therefore Richard's heir. Winifred did not know what he would do if she had a girl. Richard resumed his reading and Winifred knew better than to bother him any further with her fears.

Anyway right now she did not feel like lying still. She actually felt like helping her maid, Martha, to get the nursery ready.

She would love to be able to help launder the sheets for her baby's crib. It was all starting to look so nice now, swathed in Nottingham lace and crisp cotton. Of course helping with such menial tasks as laundry would never do. Richard was always reminding her that Martha was paid very well to take care of "those" duties.

"30 pence a week and her keep is, after all, better than average." Richard had insisted sternly, when she had tried to explain her need to be involved with the preparations for the baby's arrival.

Anyway she had enjoyed the needlework and embroidery needed for the nursery linen. She hadn't seen the harm in sitting in the chair to do this. She did try to reason with Richard, but, as usual, he knew best. She sighed.

Another twinge. Richard's doctor had not been very interested in her backache yesterday. He had agreed with Richard, of course.

When the pains had become uncomfortable during the night Richard had become rather impatient. Didn't she know that he had a very important day at the office tomorrow, he needed his sleep? He had reminded her that the reason that she had such good medical care was down to the fact that he managed The Royal Lyver Friendly Society for the area and therefore had a very good private health insurance.

"Many ladies in our income bracket could not afford such luxuries and would have to rely on female relatives." Richard had snapped. "At least listen to the doctor and stop complaining," he had continued, before removing himself to the spare room. He had not even looked in before leaving for the office this morning.

Right now Winifred wished she had a female relative to help her but her mother lived fifteen miles away and would not undertake such a long carriage ride lightly. The only person she could talk to was Martha. Martha had never had a baby, but was happily relaying advice from "her Ma" when required.

Winifred rang the bell. Martha scurried in. She was barely fifteen but already more rounded than other girls of her age. It didn't stop her working hard though and Winifred had become very dependent upon her. Her round cheery face, always beaming, often kept Winifred from feeling alone or afraid.

"Oh you're awake Miss. Mr Richard said as how I wasn't to disturb you, as you had had such a bad night." Martha said as she set up Winifred's breakfast tray.

"Martha what did your mother say about the back pain?" Winifred asked desperately.

"She says the babby will be here afore long Miss, you're not to worry, it's normal. Ma says she'll come and look at you if you like".

"That's very good of her Martha, but I really don't think that Mr Richard would approve. He holds a very high store by Dr. Grey." Winifred sighed. If the truth be known, she would rather see Martha's "Ma".

"That's as may be Miss, but I doubt Dr Grey's ever had a babby himself. My Ma's had nine. Granted five of them has died but four healthy ones is pretty good I reckons." Martha turned to leave.

"Beg your pardon Miss, I hope I haven't been speaking out of turn."

Another twinge.

"Martha!" Winifred called out fearfully," is your mother busy this morning?" Martha smiled.

"I'll just pop and get her Miss. You try and eat your breakfast. Ma says you'll need all your strength getting babby out."

Winifred didn't really know what Martha meant. Nice ladies didn't talk about such things. She had confessed to Richard that she was afraid and he had asked Dr Grey to speak to her. Dr Grey was an elderly man, with a shock of white hair and well groomed whiskers. He came very well recommended by the gentlemen of Richard's club, but his success with gout hardly filled Winifred with confidence. He hadn't explained anything, but he had told her that since Mr Simpson had introduced chloroform into midwifery, a few years ago, it had been easier if women had problems, and not so many died these days.

"There you are dear", Richard had said, "nothing to worry about."

"It's all right for him," muttered Winifred to herself, "but dying is the least of my worries."

Martha's Ma bustled in half an hour later. Even more rounded than her daughter, Ma was red faced and breathless from climbing the stairs, but still managed a reassuring smile as she entered the room. Martha was close behind.

"Now lass," Ma puffed brightly as she pushed Martha gently from the room, "you keep a look out for your master while I sees to your mistress." She took charge immediately.

Very soon she realised how little Winifred understood and set about explaining everything.

"The first 'un is scary," she agreed, "but after that it's just as easy as shelling peas, nowt to it."

" I think I'd like to get this one over first." Winifred winced as a bad twinge shot through her back.

The birth wasn't fun, but, thanks to Ma's patient instructions and advice, Dick took his first breath without the help of the incredible Dr Grey, or his chloroform. He was a beautiful baby, with a full head of dark hair, just like his father. There was nothing wrong with his lungs either, as he quickly announced his presence to the world.

It was all over before Richard came home from the office. Martha's Ma had left. Winifred was worried how she would explain the lack of Dr Grey, but Richard seemed to assume that she had managed with a little help from Martha. Winifred had instructed Martha to make up a good hamper for her mother, to show her gratitude.

"Ee Miss, there's no need." Martha laughed. "Ma helps lasses all the time." Still Winifred had insisted and managed to amend the housekeeping account later to cover the expense. Richard never knew, but he did grumble a little, that they had not had the full benefit of their health insurance.

Dick was a healthy, lusty baby. Like most, he didn't like to sleep much at nights and Richard eventually agreed to hire a nanny.

Just as well as Dick's brother, Harry, followed fourteen months later. Two sisters, Elizabeth and Gertrude, followed in quick succession. Winifred had no real problems with the later births but never could agree with "Ma" that it was as easy "as shelling peas!"

Dick was almost five years old when Richard came home one night full of excitement. He was to take charge of the Regional Office in West Hartlepool.

Winifred viewed this with some trepidation. Both Richard and herself came from West Hartlepool originally. She knew that it was a new town. Richard's father, and her own for that matter, had made a small fortune from building new houses there and the town was rapidly becoming one of the most prosperous in the North East. Workers had poured into the Stranton area twenty-odd years ago, looking for work on the docks, in ship building and on the railways.

She shuddered. She still had unpleasant memories of going down Stranton with her father, when she was a child. It was horrible then. None of the crowded houses had decent sanitation. The cess pits had been located underneath their dwellings and, because they were rarely emptied properly, the effluent had leaked into the streets. Winifred remembered having to pick her way about on stones, placed so people could avoid walking in it. She knew that all that was history. The Public Health and Artisan's Dwelling Acts of 1875 had put paid to that. That's when her and Richard's father had stuck lucky. There was money in building and lots of brick built terraces were soon erected for the workers. They even had sanitation and at least one pump to a street.

Richard's father had his own firm, her father had joined him as his partner. It was therefore obvious to both families that she and Richard would marry. After all they were both middle class, well educated and of similar backgrounds. Everyone had agreed that they made a splendid couple. Richard tall and dark with sombre good looks. Winifred slim and elegant with a shock of copper hair.

Richard had not wanted to go into the building trade but had done so, at his father's insistence, on leaving school. He had never been happy and had got interested in the insurance business through a friend.

"The future is in insurance," he had told Winifred excitedly. "I have an opportunity to take over an established area around North Ormesby," he had continued.

She had been horrified. Newly married and moving so far away from their families. North Ormesby was after all, fifteen miles away, in Yorkshire. Oh travel was not so bad these days. Carriages were very comfortable, there was a regular railway service between Middlesbrough and West Hartlepool and most people had bicycles, but it still seemed an awful long way from family and friends.

Her reaction was nothing to that of her father-in-law, when Richard broke the news to him. The bitter argument that ensued had been heated in the extreme and Richard had been banned from the family home and disowned.

It had led to some very difficult times but Richard had been proved right and had established a very good income from his new career. They now had an income of £600 per annum and had two maids and the nanny.

How would things go in West Hartlepool now though? Winifred was a little afraid, but also excited. It would be nice to live near her mother and sisters again. Society was better there. They had a Music Hall and a moving picture house. Winifred had read about the new production of "The Great Train Robbery" directed by Edwin Porter. Perhaps she would see it for herself now.

What about the children though? They lived in a village at present and Dick and Harry were quite safe playing their games outside the house. West Hartlepool had electric trams and even automobiles that could travel at more than 20 miles an hour. What if they got run over? What about disease and crowded schools? She voiced her worries to Richard.

"Winifred," Richard said rather sharply, "this is my big opportunity to make some real money. We could buy our own house, even have an automobile. All you can whine about is the children. They have a nanny and you to keep them safe, you are just being difficult!"

Winifred pointed out that they could not prevent disease. She rarely argued with Richard, she knew her place, but this was important.

"What if little Betty gets cholera or smallpox and dies or is permanently disfigured?" Winifred knew that Betty had already

12

stolen a large place in Richard's heart. His face softened.

"You may have a point. I will look for accommodation in one of the nearby villages," Richard conceded quietly.

This was how the family came to be moving to Elwick, a few miles outside Hartlepool, one rather wet and dismal May day. As they had been living in rented accommodation, they only needed one wagon to move their furniture, although Winfred's precious piano did take up a lot of room.

Martha had been persuaded to move with the family. Winifred was very pleased about this, she had become even more of a companion since the children had arrived. Richard had never approved of fraternising with the help, but he did have to admit that they would be hard pushed to find anyone else so hard working or trustworthy. The nanny and daily help had to be left.

"No doubt you'll soon find a replacement from the village," Richard had insisted firmly. "Anyway Dick will be going to school shortly, I am sure that Martha and yourself will cope with the younger children. If we can manage without the staff I should be able to get my automobile quicker."

Winifred did not bother to point out that Gertrude was not a year old yet and that it would be more propitious to save for their own home first. She had once suggested that their own home would be much easier to obtain if the rift between Richard and his father could be mended. She could still remember Richard's violent outburst before he slammed out of the house and took solace at the local inn. He had accused her of being disloyal, siding with his father and of being incredibly stupid. He had finished by throwing the tea pot at the wall and shouting for Martha to clean up the mess.

It had, fortunately, been a silver-plated pot, so it had not sustained any damage. Unfortunately, it took Martha an hour to clean the wall and carpet. Martha never grumbled though, she had seen enough of the master's temper not to be surprised by his outbursts or, as she secretly called them herself, "temper tantrams". "Spoilt rotten" her Ma had agreed, when Martha had told her of the incident.

"His whiskers were all of shake, and his face was so red you could have fried eggs on it," Martha giggled, as she relayed the tale.

The move went well, despite the weather. Probably because Richard had gone to work and left Winifred and Martha to organise everything. Winifred's sister had come across to help with the children and Martha's brother had helped the wagon driver to load the furniture. Thanks to careful planning and packing, nothing was broken and everything was more or less straight, when Richard came home from work.

Dick and Harry had been very excited. They had never been on a steam train before and they had even taken an electric tram from the train station to Grandma's house. Winifred and Martha had ridden in the wagon with the baby girls, whilst the boys had travelled with their Aunty Mary. Mary even bought them sugar candy canes to suck, from the station shop. Dick had wanted some of the Black Bullets instead, but Aunt Mary had said he was too young and could choke. He had pleaded, explaining that Uncle John, Richard's brother, gave him them occasionally.

"Well I'm not surprised," exclaimed Mary, "your Uncle John does not have a sensible thought in his head."

The house in Elwick was quite small, certainly not as big as Winifred had become used to. There were only three bedrooms. Martha had the small room, the boys and Betty had a slightly larger one and the baby had to sleep it a cot in the parents room. Even Richard agreed that it was not ideal but it would do until they found something better.

It was at the end of a small terrace, set back from the green, and was very handy for the village shop, the church and the village school.

Dick thought he had moved to Heaven. As the village was small and safe, he was allowed to wander around the green and he was even allowed to help Mother and Martha to tend their small garden. Uncle John also became a much more frequent visitor and, whenever he called, Dick and Harry had to chase him. When they caught him, he would swing them high and play "getting hot or cold", while they searched his pockets for sweets or candy sticks.

Winifred could never understand why John was so unlike his brother. They did look alike, apart from the hair colour. John was not so dark. The brothers got on very well, although they were very different in their outlook on life. John was still only a clerk in his father's office and made no attempt to improve himself. He maintained that, as long as he had enough money for his ale, his women and his bets on the horse racing, he didn't need anything else. Even after the family row John had always kept in touch.

True, Richard enjoyed the ale and the horses, but his main obsession was undoubtedly making money. He rarely played with the children and Winifred did often wonder if he worked too hard. She had to admit to herself though, she enjoyed having money and not seeing a lot of Richard did have its good points, especially when he was in a bad mood.

The highlight of young Dick's week was Saturday morning. Uncle John would arrive, on his old bike, just after breakfast. After the sweets had been distributed to Harry and himself, Uncle John always took them for a walk along the stream. It usually started with a race to the stile.

"Shall we race then?" John would say, as they closed the garden gate. Dick and Harry would crouch down, on their marks, ready to start the race.

"Ready, steady   - cheater, cheater!" Dick would shriek with indignation as Uncle John sprinted off. The boys would run behind yelling that they had not said go and weren't ready but John knew that, small as Dick was, he would have trouble catching him if he played fair. By the time they reached the stile they would be screeching with laughter and would push and shove, wheezing and gasping as they tousled to be first over the fence.

Dick loved the walk that followed. John knew everything: where the moorhens were nesting; where the best place was to tickle trout; the log that Mr Toad lived under and the song of the Blackbird. Thanks to John, Dick quickly learnt to recognise every tree and bird around the fields near the stream. They would sometimes fish with a net to catch stickle-backs and tadpoles.

Uncle John took nature very seriously. He got very cross with Harry when he reached into a Blackbird's nest and touched her eggs.

"She'll smell you and desert the eggs," he explained.

Carefully, week by week, Uncle John took them back to the

nest to watch how they hatched and how the baby birds grew. He made Dick and Harry promise that they would never smash an egg for fun.

"You will be murdering a baby bird," he said, "and if all the baby birds are killed, then we can't sit in the sun and listen to the beautiful songs they sing."

One day they found a nest bursting with eggs.

"Now," said John, "we can carefully take one of these. They would never all survive." He gently removed one egg, taking care not to touch the others. When they got home he borrowed a pin from Martha, and patiently piercing both ends, he blew the contents on to the grass. He handed the perfectly intact shell to Dick.

"You can start a collection now," John quietly explained, "but be sure only to take eggs from a nest where there are too many to start with."

Dick treasured that egg, and the collection of pressed wild flowers that they also started, but John did not just instil into Dick a love of the countryside. For Dick the highlight of the day was the race. Dick loved to run and his determination to beat John, despite his cheating, fuelled a drive to win that would blaze throughout his career.

Chapter   2

Although Winifred enjoyed the village life herself, she had to agree with Richard that their small house was not adequate for their growing family. Consequently she was quite happy when Richard came home one evening and told her they would be moving into the town. He had found a three-storey house in Kilwick Street, within easy walking distance of the office and the main tram routes.

"Isn't that rather near to Stranton though Dear?" Winifred asked, again remembering the Stranton of her childhood.

"Well yes, but the old rat infested days are long gone," Richard reassured her. "You don't need to fear that area now".

Such it was that Dick's world fell apart shortly after his sixth birthday. Not even Uncle John had thought that the children would need to be told.

Dick awoke early one fine Saturday morning and ran out on to the field nearby, to gather mushrooms, as John had taught him to do. When he returned home carrying his prize, his father was waiting for him by the gate, looking very angry.

"Who told you that you could run off this morning?" He grabbed Dick by the arm and the proudly gathered mushrooms were scattered across the floor.

"I always collect the mushrooms on Saturday," Dick cried, trying desperately to reach them, whilst being dragged into the house. "Get to your room and help Harry and Martha pack up your belongings. The wagon will be here soon and you are wasting time messing around in fields. You really must learn some responsibility Richard." Richard's face was a picture of rage.

Dick was confused and frightened. What was happening?

Why was the house being packed into boxes? He ran to his room and asked Martha what it was all about.

"Bless you Master Dick, we're moving into town today," Martha explained.

Dick was horrified. No more fields, no more birds.

"I'm not going!" Dick clenched his small fists. He ran past Martha and dodged passed his father. He ran as fast as he could, towards the path that led to the stream. "I'm not going!" he shouted back. "Go without me. I hate you all!"

Richard ran after him but, even though Dick was only six, he soon left his father panting behind. John arrived at that point.

"What ever is the matter?" He asked looking at Richard's savage face.

"Of all the times for Dick to come up with a tantram," Richard said, "and now he's run off, just as the wagon is arriving."

"Not to worry," John replied, resting his hand on his brother's shoulder. "I know where he'll be, leave it to me."

John went to the special place, near the moorhen's nest. Sure enough, Dick was laid on the ground, sobbing.

"I can't go Uncle John, I will die in the town." Muddy tears were streaming down his face. "The children at the schools are all poor and they punch you and things. Polly at our school said she had been to school in the town and it was horrible!" Dick caught his breath as his sobs increased. "I'll never see the eggs hatch again or be able to build dams across the stream."

"Well now," laughed John, "do you know what I think? I think that you have been listening to too many stories." He took Dick's chin in his hand and looked him straight in the eye. "We can take our bikes on Saturdays and ride out to this stream. I do it every week and you are a big boy now. Then, of course, you will live near to me, so you can come and visit me as well. In the town you will go to a bigger school, that is true, but you will have more friends, trips to the beach and I can even take you to the big swimming pool on the Headland and teach you to swim properly." John held Dick's tear stained face in his hand and wiped a tear way with his thumb. "No need to cry, you might even like it better!"

"If you say so Uncle John." Dick stood up and gave John a

hug. "I suppose it will be all right if you are there. Please don't ever leave me will you?"

"Don't be silly," John laughed, swinging Dick on to his shoulders. "Where would I go? Anyway, you always find the best mushrooms and I love mushrooms."

Dick started to laugh as John galloped him up and down, back along the path. When he and John returned home the wagons were already packed.

Richard was not amused but John managed to stop him from starting at Dick again.

"You're very lucky that I'm too busy to sort you out young man," Richard told him. "Any further behaviour like this and I will take my belt to you. So you mark my words."

The move did go well after this, but Winifred was not too happy with the house. It was a middle terrace, dismal and, she felt sure, very damp.

"I knew it was too near Stranton," she complained to Richard one evening. "There's fungus on the larder walls and Martha had to prime the pump three times before she could get it to flow properly this morning."

"Oh she's just not used to it, too busy dreaming about that wagon driver she was so taken with when we moved." Richard sighed, as he tried to carry on reading his paper. He had to admit though, he wasn't too happy with this house.

Consequently three months later they were on the move again. This time to Carlton Street. The house was much pleasanter, still a mid-terrace but much brighter and definitely not damp. Richard was still aspiring to owning his own house. He had had to give up the idea of the automobile for the time being. They were still too expensive, but a house, well that was definitely becoming a possibility.

Dick was almost seven when they moved to Bellerby Terrace. Their own house at last. Dick had settled in well to town life, despite his fears. Uncle John had been as good as his word.

Saturdays had still been adventures. Now they were even better. They would pack their lunch and set off on their bikes. They often went to Elwick but now they visited Hart, to see the Meteor

19

bedded into the road side, or Dalton, where Uncle John knew one of the farmers and they were able to help gather hay, bring the cows in for milking and feed the hens. In the Spring Dick had even been able to help with the orphaned lambs. They were so strong when they sucked at their bottles that Dick had almost been pulled off his feet.

Days at the beach had been an adventure too, he had learnt to swim in the massive outdoor swimming pool. He had laughed at the ladies who were wheeled up to the water's edge in their
bathing booths and then started swimming in, what looked like, their night clothes.

One day Uncle John had come into the house clutching some pieces of paper.

"Guess what these are?" He held the papers high and, despite jumping for all they were worth, Dick and Harry could not reach them.

"Please tell us Uncle John!" Dick pleaded.

"Well" John replied, "do you know that Buffalo Bill's Wild West Show was coming to town and I have got tickets for all the family?"

Dick was so excited. He had read cowboy stories and he had even seen a moving picture about Bronco Billy. He could hardly wait.

The show was every bit as exciting as he had imagined. There were gun fights, shooting demonstrations and fancy horse riding but the bit that Dick enjoyed the best was when Sitting Bull led his tribe in a attack against the wagon train and the cavalry saved the day. It was truly a spectacular show. The noise, the smoke, the colours and even the fact that the whole audience rose to their feet to cheer as the wagon train was saved, left Dick with a day to remember for the rest of his life.

Dick had to admit that town life had its advantages. Apart from anything else he saw less of his father. He was always at work now. Dick had learnt to keep out of his way anyway. He did have one memory of his father's temper but he smiled when he thought of it. The family had been invited to Aunt Mary's for tea. Before setting off Winifred had warned Richard to beware of Aunt Mary's angel cake.

"It is inclined to make people sick," she had warned. Dick had over heard this.

Everything went well until Dick was offered a piece of Aunt Mary's cake.

"No!" Dick firmly declined.

"No what?" His father asked sharply.

"No bloody fear!" Dick had instantly retorted.

Needless to say he had been marched away and belted on that occasion. It was worth it though, Harry had had some cake and had been ill for days after!

The children never usually had their meals with their parents. Father had a full dinner each evening, the children usually had dripping and bread in the kitchen. Dick knew they weren't poor but it was accepted that the meat was kept for the "Man of the House." Dick was quite happy, he loved dripping and bread almost as much as Black Bullets.

School had not been as bad as he had expected either. He went to Jesmond Road School and he found that having different classes for different age groups meant that he could understand his lessons without any trouble. He soon became top of his class. They didn't only study the usual subjects either, the school had sports periods where they did gymnastics and ran races. Dick loved those best.

One bright summer evening he had wandered into the back street as some of the big kids were running races.

"Can I join in please?" Dick asked politely.

"Get lost squirt!" A boy, who looked in serious need of a wash, gave him a shove.

"Oh give him a chance," Johnny Gibson retorted. He was one of the older boys. His clothes were a bit worn but they were clean and he had a kind face. Johnny lived at No.1 Bellerby Terrace and he had seen Dick running about with his brother. He seemed OK.

"He lives at number nine, we should try him out for our gang," he continued kindly.

"All right kid, it looks like you're in." One of the girls pulled him into their group. Dick later found out that she was called Freda.

She was tall and slim with uneven pigtails framing her smiling face.

"We're racing to the end of the alley," Johnny explained.

"Shouldn't we give him some start?" He asked the others. "He seems a lot younger than us."

"I'm nearly eight," Dick boasted, pulling himself up to his full height, "and I can nearly beat my Uncle John, so I'll beat you lot, no bother."

"Well I'm nearly eleven, and Freda's ten, but it's your funeral," Johnny replied.

Harry was too small to run but he was allowed to set them off. "Ready, steady, go!" he yelled as loudly as he could.

Dick ran his fastest. He thought his lungs would explode before he reached the end of the alley but he was not going to give in. Johnny and Freda did pass him easily, but three of their friends didn't.

"Well done kid, your in!" Johnny smiled, clapping him on the back. "Freda and I run for the school team and you certainly gave us a good race. I bet you'll make the team one day as well!"

"He won't ever beat me though," Freda said laughing. The other lads that Dick had beaten were not so kind.

"Beaten by a girl," the unwashed boy sneered. "Little sissy beaten by a girl!" Dick could feel his temper rising.

"Not for long," he hissed through clenched teeth, trying not to cry. "At least I don't smell," he snorted as he turned and ran for home.

Every night after that Dick got Harry to start him off in the alley and he ran the distance, time and time again. Even when he was tired he kept running. His desire to win, and knock the smirk off the dirty boy's face, drove him on.

Freda, Johnny and the others often joined him. They were all keen on running. They started challenging kids from other sreets and very soon they became known as "The Bellerby Flyers". Flora, Johnny and Dick could never be beaten. Harry joined in eventually and they discovered that he was nearly as fast as them. Harry preferred to kick a football though.

Dick kept challenging the other two but could just not quite beat them until one day they decided to extend their "track".

"This time we will go twice round the block," Dick insisted. He had been running round the block nearly every night and knew that he could now stay the distance.

"OK," replied Freda, "but I'm not much good at distances."

The race was organised like a proper event. Even Uncle John came out to watch. Father was, of course, far too busy but Dick didn't care. This event was very important and Father would never understand that anyway. To him it would just be kids running in the streets but it was far more than that to Dick.

As they lined up together Dick could feel his heart pounding in his chest. A line of perspiration formed on his brow and his whole body became tense, waiting for John to give the word that would release him.

"Are you all ready?" John shouted seriously. They all nodded and shuffled forward a little, each vying for the advantage at the off.

"Right then," John continued. "Ready, steady...   . GO."

Dick was first off but, by some built in instinct, he did not rush off ahead of the others. This was to be a long race and he did not want to be tired before the first bend. They all ran neck and neck until they came to the home stretch. Now Dick let go of the energy he had conserved. In the last few yards he managed to pull ahead by a few inches.

"The winner." Uncle John declared proudly, lifting Dick's arm high.

"Well I never," Freda gasped. "I never thought that he would have me on a longer distance. Good for you Dick. Maybe we'll all be champions one day!"

Dick could not speak as he struggled to calm his breathing, but his face shone with pride. This was a new sensation. It was better than eating ice-cream and black bullets at the same time. He had beaten the others. He had beaten runners bigger and stronger than he. No-one could take that away. Even if his father was in a temper when he got home, it wouldn't matter, because he, Dick Ripley, was the winner. This was the start of a passion for victory that would drive Dick for more than a quarter of a century.

The friendship continued for many years. As the others were older, Dick continued to develop his speed and stamina. He had to in order to fulfil his desire to win, and to save face with the rest of the team.

All the Bellerby Flyers were destined to become champions, in much more than just the backstreets of West Hartlepool. Freda became champion of the Girl's High School and, as Dick later reported, was the only girl ever to have beaten him. Johnny and Dick were to cross swords again, but in much more important arenas.

Chapter 3

Dick was just eleven when Uncle John called one day to say goodbye. An elderly Aunt had left him a cottage at Low Row, in Swaledale and he had decided to leave town life behind. "It's beautiful Dick." John's eyes shone with enthusiasm.

"If you think the walks we have had in the country around here are good, just wait until you come to spend your holidays with me in Swaledale."

"How will you manage though, Uncle John?" Dick asked. He had overheard his mother and father discussing John's move, while they were taking tea in the parlour, during the previous evening. They had considered it irresponsible in the extreme.

"Fancy throwing away a perfectly good position with a good building company to feed chickens in the back of beyond." He had heard his father say. "He could have sold the place and invested the profits."

"Well Dear, you threw up a position in the same firm and you've done very well." Winifred reminded him.

"That was a sensible business opportunity Winifred. I knew that I could better myself. John is tossing away a good career to become a farm labourer, little more than a vagabond." Richard had replied.

Winifred had not continued the conversation as she knew not to disagree with Richard. She had changed the subject to the suffragettes. They had recently been reported in the newspapers as starting a window smashing campaign at Post Offices and Labour Exchanges. She knew Richard despised the actions of these women and would soon forget about John in his heated condemnation of them. Martha and herself secretly admired these brave and determined women, but neither would dream of admitting this to any of the men they knew.

"I'll manage just fine Dick," John said. "I know your father doesn't approve. I've had enough lectures from him to qualify me for Cambridge! There's enough land with the cottage for me to grow vegetables and keep a few hens. There are hundreds of rabbits on the moors that I can shoot, and one of the local farmers has already offered me a labouring job at a nearby farm. The pay is not very good but it'll help me buy bread, oil for the lamps and other supplies." John smiled and ruffled Dick's hair. "Don't look so worried. What with the dockers strikes and all the unhappiness in the towns these days, I am quite sure that I will probably be better off and certainly better fed, than I would be here.

"Won't you be lonely though?" Dick asked. He was used to being always surrounded by friends now, his worst fear was having no-one to play with or talk to.

"Good heavens, no." laughed John. "I still have my bike. I can peddle to the King's Head in Gunnerside for a pint, and there are several good ale houses in Reeth. I'm sure you and Harry will visit me in the holidays won't you? You can write to me as well. The postal service is very quick nowadays."

"Oh I'll write every day, but can we really visit? Can I feed the chickens?" Dick was becoming excited now. He liked writing letters and his father had an automobile now, even such a long trip was possible. Anyway Dick didn't care if he had to ride his bike all the way to the Dales, he would walk if he had to!

"You can come every school holiday. I'll be angry if you don't." John gave Dick a hug and whispered in his ear, "we'll call the naggiest old hen Martha and the bad tempered old cockerel Richard, and it will be our secret".

Dick did miss John a lot but the gap in his life was soon filled up by his friends and his running.

Not long after John's departure Dick came in one evening feeling rather more tired than usual. His throat was sore and he felt very cold. He went to the kitchen to tell Martha that he did not want any supper, he didn't think he could swallow it anyway.

"Good heavens Master Dick!" Martha exclaimed when she saw him. "You're as red as a beetroot." She felt his forehead. "You're burning up lad".

Martha rushed to find Winifred.

Between them they got Dick to bed and Martha filled the stone bed warmers and piled the blankets on to him.

"Let's hope he just has a chill." Winifred did not like the look of him at all. Some of the ladies taking tea that evening, had indicated that Scarlet Fever was in the town. Several younger children and elderly people had already died of this. The isolation hospital was half full already.

"They say it's terrible in there," one lady had explained.

"People dying all over the place. Not enough staff to look after them properly. Even with all these modern medical techniques they can't do much but wait for the fever to pass."

"Many people do recover though," another had said, "it's not as bad as smallpox or diphtheria."

When Richard came home, much later that night, he found Winifred and Martha in a dreadful state. Dick's fever had increased and his breathing had become erratic. Martha was bathing his head, while Winifred was wringing her hands and sobbing. Richard pulled Martha away roughly and grabbed Dick by the shoulders.

"Come on Dick, stop playing games." He shook him but Dick's head just rolled about and his eyes were not focusing.

"Good heavens woman," Richard snarled at Winifred, "why haven't you sent for the doctor?"

"I, I hoped..." Winifred began to sob uncontrollably. She grasped Richard's arm as though grabbing on to a life line. "Please save him, please Richard, do something."

Richard turned to Martha. "I thought at least you had more sense. Get off and get the doctor and hurry up about it."

"Do you think it is Scarlet Fever?" Winifred sniffed, trying hard not to annoy Richard any further.

"How would I know, I'm not a doctor?" Richard retorted.

"What I do know is that if this boy dies it is your fault. There's no excuse, we have good insurance, you should have sent for the doctor immediately."

When the doctor arrived he examined Dick thoroughly and advised Richard that he must remove him to the isolation hospital immediately.

"The rash is already evident in his joints. The symptoms are classic. He undoubtedly has Scarlet Fever," he announced, almost proudly.

Dick was barely conscious but he had still understood most of the conversation and he was terrified. He was bundled into a wagon and taken to a very large austere building. He was fully awake by now but still no-one explained anything to him and neither his mother or father were allowed to accompany him. He was sure he was going to die. He had never felt so ill in his life. They didn't care, they were getting him out of the way.

Dick started to cry and begged to be taken home again but it did no good. He was bundled quite roughly into a very uncomfortable bed, told to stop making such a fuss and left in the dark.

"Help, oh please help me! Martha, Uncle John, don't let me die. I promise to be good. Please help!" He crocked through his sobs.

A lady dressed in a neat and clean uniform appeared at his side. She spoke softly to him and smoothed his brow with a cool cloth.

"Don't take on so, you'll make yourself even more ill. We don't want that now do we?"

She carefully explained that he was very ill, but that he was fit and not a small child, so the likelihood of him dying was very remote. She also explained that they had had to take him away from his family because his brother and sisters were younger and could suffer even more than him, if they caught the infection.

He soon settled down and slept. During his six week stay in the isolation hospital Dick came to idolize the soft spoken nurse. She was called Nurse Sarah and she ran the ward. The doctor told him that she was a proper "Nightingale Nurse". Sarah had been trained to the standards set by the London Nightingale School for Nurses. Unlike the ordinary nurses, who were little more than maids, Sarah had medical training and was indispensible to the doctors.

Everyone in the ward loved Nurse Sarah, not just Dick, but his admiration was bordering on obsession and he found these new feelings very difficult to deal with.

He was embarrassed whenever she came near, but he lived for the moments when she did. His heart seemed to stop when he caught sight of her hat at the end of the ward, but he blushed when she spoke to him. As his health improved he became her slave, fetching and carrying things for her, hanging on her every word. He thought his heart would break when he found out that she was walking out with one of the hospital doctors. He hated him.

An elderly gentleman in the next bed witnessed his confusion.

"Don't worry lad, it's all part of growing up," he explained. "Sarah is a wonderful, intelligent and competent young lady. It's ladies like her who will get women the vote, not Emmeline Pankhurst and her WSPU. They are nothing but a bunch of cranks and lawbreakers! It's easy to see why you have a crush on Sarah, but you will soon get over it, once you're out of here and mixing with people of your own age again."

When Dick was told he would be going home and that his father would be collecting him shortly, he thought he would die. He would probably never see Sarah again.

She came with him to the hospital door when he left.

"You have a fine son there Sir." Sarah had been giving Richard instructions for Dick's convalescence and had turned to shake Dick's hand. Her eyes were smiling. "He is polite, intelligent and helpful. You must be very proud of him." Richard thanked her curtly and asked Dick to hurry up. He had an appointment shortly and couldn't dally.

Dick looked back to see Sarah waving to him.

"She liked me," he thought "she really liked me!". He felt as though he was floating on air.

The old gentleman had been correct, once Dick was back with his friends, Sarah very soon became nothing more than a fond memory. There was no doubt that Dick would always have a soft spot for nurses from that day forward though.

John had written to Winifred and Richard, while Dick was ill, insisting that he be despatched to the Dales for a good period of convalescence, as soon as he was well enough to travel. Richard had been only too pleased to agree. The last thing he wanted was to be stuck with a sickly and bored child. He had found Nurse Sarah's instructions irritating. Pampering had never done a boy any good, was all he had relayed to Winifred when she had asked if there had been any special advice about Dick's on going care.

Consequently Dick found himself riding in a train bound for Darlington, happily looking forward to a full month in Swaledale.

Uncle John was waiting at the station. He was looking really bronzed and well. Dick had never seen him looking so happy. Although it had only been two months since John had left, it was already clear, even to an eleven year old, that John had made the right move. Dick soon discovered why. As the wagon weaved and rattled it's way along the country lanes Dick could hardly believe the splendour that unfolded in front of him.

First came Richmond with it's magnificent red-sandstone castle, set on a cliff high above the river. John told him of the legend that King Arthur and the Knights of the Round Table were asleep in a cavern, under the castle, waiting to emerge in England's hour of need. He sang of the "Sweet Lass of Richmond Hill", encouraging Dick to sing along to the words of the eighteenth century ballad.

There was also the story of the little drummer boy, sent down from Richmond Castle through a secret passage, believed to lead to Easby Abbey. He was supposed to drum as he went so that those above could plot the route of the passage.

"He was never seen again Dick." John's voice became deep and menacing. "But if it's quiet and you put your ear to the ground on the path between here and Easby, you can still hear him playing, or so they say."

Dick shivered.

"Have you ever heard him Uncle John?" Dick asked seriously.

"Of course I have Dick. Especially after I've visited a few of those fine ale houses around Richmond market place." John winked.

As they left Richmond the true beauty of the Dales started to emerge. First they passed Marske Hall, set in thick woods but dominated by the high moors.

"The family from there have produced two sons that have become Archbishops of York, Dick." John pointed to the building. "Perhaps they were affected by the beauty of Marrick Priory, I'll have to show you that."

Next they passed through Reeth, tucked away in the shelter of Fremington Edge, then Grinton where they crossed the Swale on an ancient grey stone bridge. In the distance the magnificent mountains framed the whole Dale. Great Shunner Fell, Kisdon, Lovely Seat and Rogan's Seat were all to become as familiar to Dick as the back of his hand, during the next four weeks.

At last they arrived in Low Row. The cottage was heavenly. Set at the road side, it was built in the grey stone, so evident everywhere in the dales. It was bigger than Dick had expected and had a large kitchen, with a hugh walk-in larder, a good sized sitting room and two big bedrooms. There was also a very small room set into the roof at the back. The tiny window looked straight on to the Moor. Uncle John had made a bed up in here as he thought it would be warmer, being above the kitchen chimney. He said it had been a smoking room at one time but his Aunt had sealed up the vent as she did not keep pigs and therefore did not wish to use it for its original intention, smoking bacon and ham.

Dick thought it was delightful.

That month, and the many subsequent holidays that Dick was to spend in this cottage, was idyllic. His days were spent wandering the hills, swimming in the peaty waters of the Swale and exploring the lead mines of Blakethwaite Smelt and Old Gang, abandoned by the lead miners not so many years before.

One day Dick was wandering along one of the Coffin roads, high on the moor. He had John's border collie, Lady, for company. Uncle John had been telling him some of the eerie legends of the area, while they had sat contentedly by the kitchen fire, during the previous evening. He wasn't afraid as he marched along, but he was a little apprehensive. The moors seemed to be so full of

31

ghostly memories.

Suddenly, from behind, Dick heard a whirring noise like nothing he had ever heard before. It was above and behind him. He turned round only to be confronted by a huge flying monster, heading straight for him.

He and Lady plunged into a nearby ditch. It was wet and muddy but neither cared, both pushing to be best hidden. The creature turned and came back across. Dick's heart was racing. John had not mentioned such a terrifying monster. As the creature passed again Dick dared to look up. What a shock he got, the creature was nothing more than a huge kyte, with two wings and a propeller at the front. A man dressed in a heavy leather jacket and goggles waved, laughing, before heading off down the Dale. Dick realised that he had just seen his first airplane. He had heard talk of such things. He had learnt at school that Wilbur and Orville Wright had perfected this mode of travel in America, but he did not realise that they had such things in England. He ran home so quickly that he was too out of breath to explain his excitement, or his muddy state, to John. It turned out that the whole Dale has seen this man-made bird and everyone was almost as excited as Dick.

"Going against God!" One of the village ladies was heard to remark, outside the village hall, as many of the locals gathered to discuss the unusual sight. "It'll never catch on, far too dangerous, scared my sheep half to death," she continued, folding her hands over her well developed abdomen. Little did anyone realise what an impact these "Airplanes" would have on their lives in the future.

All too soon Dick's perfect month came to a close. John was sorry to see him go but promised that he could come for every holiday, if his father approved, of course.

The night before he left the two wandered along the field paths to Gunnerside. They stopped on the banks of the Swale to drink in the most beautiful sunset. The reds and golds painting the tips of the craggy mountains, casting deep shadows across the valley.

"This is what life is all about young Dick. Not automobiles and fancy houses." John whispered, not wanting to break the moment.

"Do you think Dad ever watches the sunset?" Dick asked.

"He hasn't time," John sighed. "He's lost all that in his pursuit of fortune."

"I do like having money though Uncle John. It can't be much fun for those families without enough to eat and no shoes to wear," Dick reasoned.

"Well you do have a point, we all need some income in this modern society. I suppose the secret of happiness is knowing when you have enough. As you grow up and try to seek fame and fortune, as all young men do, remember the sunsets and don't be too disappointed if things don't always go as you would wish." John's voice took on a serious note as he helped Dick to his feet.

"Anyway, let's get you home. You have a long journey tomorrow."

Dick returned to school. It was his last year at elementary school. He was lucky. His father considered that it was quite a status symbol to have children attending secondary school and•he was more than willing to pay for the privilege. Dick was to continue in education and complete his "matriculation". Many of Dick's school friends could not afford to pay and had to leave after their twelfth birthday.

Dick continued to enjoy school and, of course ran in the school team. He went on to obtain many athletics trophies, including the school's Victor Ludorum medal in 1916. His zeal for victory growing with every successful contest..

Chapter 4

At midnight on 4th August 1914 Britain declared war on Germany. Dick was still attending school, but was now quite a young man. Tall, dark and slender, very much his father's son, in looks if not in temperament. He enjoyed discussing current affairs with his father. Each morning they read the newspapers together and then set the world to rights before leaving for school and work.

Shortly after Christmas Dick had read that Lloyd George had called the arms build-up in Europe "organised insanity". He had expressed his concerns to his father then and now, although he was reluctant to admit it, he was quite afraid.

There had seemed to be a lot of unrest in Britain recently, despite the many Liberal reforms over the last few years. Even with the introduction of old age pensions, for people over seventy and the National Insurance Act of 1911, many of the working classes were still very poor. Illness was still rife, mainly because people were forced to live in overcrowded slums. Many died of pneumonia, bronchitis and consumption.

In June Dick had read that two million British workers were on strike, railway and mine workers, as well as builders. The suffragettes were becoming increasingly violent, even planting bombs and destroying national works of art. It was the end of that month that the heir to the Austrian throne had been assassinated.

"The country seems to be going mad, Father. Do you think we can handle a war with all this tension and unrest?" He desperately wanted his father to reassure him.

"The government have spent more than £15 million during the last few years, not just helping the working classes, but also reforming our Navy and building those splendid new Dreadnoughts. I should know, my income tax has soared to pay for it all!" Richard sighed. "Don't forget that Britain is the richest and greatest country in the world. Oh I wouldn't worry Richard. The war will be over by Christmas, and even if it is not it will not affect us, these European wars never do." His father, returned to his own newspaper.

The war progressed and to thirteen year old Dick, reading the papers each morning, it became just another adventure story. He was disappointed when the British were defeated at Mons but elated when the British and French armies advanced during the battle of Marne. None of it seemed real. The men dying were just story book characters, in a far away country.

One of his favourite novels, "Twenty Thousand Leagues Under the Sea", became more realistic when he read, in September, that three British cruisers had been sunk by one German U-boat. Although 1500 men lost their lives on the Cressy, Aboukir and Hogue, young Dick felt nothing but excitement when those cruisers were lost. He and his friends chattered merrily about these new "undersea boats". They were not heartless young men, they just could not conceive the true horrors of war.

Dick came home fairly late one evening. He had been to a meeting of Scouts. He had joined the movement earlier that year and enjoyed the outdoor activities that it promoted.

His father was home early and shouting even louder than usual. He was pacing about, screaming about "being ruined". Dick asked what was the trouble.

"It's this damn war Richard. Bloody government!" He stormed out of the room muttering, slamming the door so hard that the whole room shook.

"What's happened Mother?" Dick asked. Winifred laughed.

"It's not the end of the earth Darling. Lloyd George has announced that income tax will double next year, to pay for the war. Apparently it is costing £1 million a day. Your father was all for the war, until he realised that it would hit his pocket. I am just grateful that neither you nor Harry are old enough to fight. I would hate that," she sighed. "Let us hope that the war ends before you get much older."

"Well I wish I was older. I would like to be give the Hun some of his own medicine. How dare the Kaiser sink our ships and even drop bombs on London?" Dick's eyes shone with enthusiasm.

It was only one month later when that light died from his eyes and Dick was to learn that war was not really "fun". Aunt Mary had been visiting friends in Whitby when the shells struck the town. It was unexpected. Mary had been delivering Christmas presents and had decided to spend a few days with her friends, rather than returning the same day. She was one of the hundred people killed by the shells. She had been taking the air along the sea front when the attack from the sea had happened. The family were stunned.

"Why Mary?" Winifred had cried. "She never hurt anyone."

Winifred spent the next few days trying to console her mother. Dick had not been really close to Mary but he watched the distress of his mother and grandmother and realised that the pain of this war was real, not a story in a book. Not only that, but it wasn't just happening in a foreign country, death had called only a few miles down the road.

The war continued. Battles were lost and won but, thanks to the censorship of the newspapers, no-one realised that there was stalemate on the Western Front. Even soldier's letters home were censored so that the true carnage was well hidden.

Kitchener, the Minister of War, was very successful with his recruiting campaign to start with. More than two and a half million men volunteered to fight. It wasn't enough.

By late 1915 the number of men volunteering had dropped. Even with censorship people were beginning to realise that there would be no quick victory. Young Dick could tell from the large lists of casualties being published in the newspapers, that this war as not leading to the glory that Kitchener had promised.

It was just after the New Year in 1916 when the Commons voted in favour of conscription. All unmarried men between 18 and 41 were ordered to fight. That included Uncle John.

John came home to West Hartlepool before joining his regiment. He was far from happy. John had never believed in this war and admitted to Dick that he was afraid.

"The trouble is, I don't believe in what I will be fighting for. So many of my friends volunteered last year and never returned." A tear rolled down his cheek. "If I don't come back, look after Lady for me Dick. Look I haven't made a Will." He gave a little laugh, "poor Mary always said I was disorganised. Anyway I've told Richard that he must keep my cottage until you're old enough, then it's yours. Your dad can be a bounder sometimes, but I trust him to see to that for you."

"Don't talk like that Uncle John. You'll be home soon. I'll see to Lady and I'll write everyday and tell you what she is getting up to." Dick felt the tears starting now. "There will be sunsets in France you know."

"Yes Dick, you're right. I'm just being silly. You get off to bed now. The war will soon be over and we will be back climbing Great Shunner Fell together before we know it." He kissed Dick lightly on the head, squared his shoulders and left the room without looking back.

Dick never saw John again.

It was November when John's name appeared in the list of casualties. He had been one of the 420,000 men lost in the Battle of the Somme. The largest and bloodiest engagement on the Western Front. Minutes before Richard had been bemoaning taxes again.

"They have increased 500 per cent since the start of this stupidity," he grumbled.

Dick wasn't listening. His eyes had rested on the name John William Ripley under the list of men confirmed dead. He didn't usually bother with the lists, but something had drawn him to this. Lady put her paw on his knee.

"Oh Lady!" He cried as he fled from the room with Lady hot on his heels. He left the house blindly and ran and ran.

"No! No! No!" was all he could think off. His head reeled. This can't be true, not John. He heart was crashing against his ribs but still he ran. He couldn't bear this. He just kept on and on driven by a hopeless need to out run the truth.

Eventually he collapsed in a sobbing heap. Lady still at his heels. He hugged her tightly and cried and cried until there were no more tears left.

It was Harry that found him in the nearby park two hours later, still hanging on to Lady.

"Dick aren't you coming home?" He asked. "Father has seen the notice in the paper and knows why you left so quickly. He's not angry. You are to come home and have your supper."

Dick didn't want supper, and he didn't give a damn whether or not his father was angry. Harry looked so lost though that he eventually followed him home quietly.

Winifred hugged him as soon he got in. Even Richard was silent and red-eyed. Everyone had loved John, but no-one felt the loss as much as Dick. Of course there was no funeral but the whole family attended one of the special masses to commemorate those lost in the various battles.

Dick felt empty for weeks. He lost interest in everything, even his running. Winifred began to worry.

One day, several weeks after the notice in the newspaper, a letter arrived addressed to Dick. Winifred recognised the handwriting immediately.

"Do you think we should open it?" Richard shook his head.

"No Dick is old enough to be treated as a adult now. Give it to him. Who knows, it may help him to handle his grief. I was thinking that a little trip up to Low Row might help as well," he added.

Winifred went to Dick's room with the letter.

"Do you want me to stay while you read it?"

"No, if you don't mind, Lady and I will have a walk up the beck and read it alone. Don't worry I'll be all right."

The letter wasn't censored. John had given it to a friend who had been badly wounded and was being shipped home. It had been written just a week before the Battle.

"Don't believe any of the reports that you read about the war being an opportunity for adventure and excitement," John had written. *"The trenches are the worst hell you could imagine. Young boys, not much older than you, terrified and crying for their mothers, blood and mud everywhere.*

We aren't winning this, no one is. Whatever you do, avoid the trenches. If the war is still raging when you are nearly 18 promise me that you will volunteer for the Merchant Navy. Avoid this at all costs."

"Dick, there's no sunset here. Only pain and death and destruction".

"I am sure now that I will never see my precious Dales again. I miss you and Lady and hope that you will look after each other when I am gone. Please don't mourn for me Dick. I am glad I went to live in the Dales, I had real happiness there. The sort that many of these lads here with me have never experienced. I have been privileged and I do not regret my life. Climb Great Shunner Fell for me and when the sun goes down, remember me with happiness, for the way I lived, not the way I died."

The letter was signed simply *"Love John"*.

The letter did help Dick. He realised that John would have wanted him to get on with his life and it wasn't long before he was back entering into the activities of youth again.

It was quite a bad winter and the family were not able to make the journey to Low Row until the following Spring.

Then Dick and Lady did climb that mountain and, just as the sunset kissed the summit, Dick cast the fragments of the letter to the winds. "Bye John" he whispered.

The War continued and everyone was affected. There were not just attacks to coastal areas from the sea, but also a silent menace glided across the English skies. Zeppelins. When they first appeared in 1915 Dick and his friends had been fascinated by them. The destruction they could reek soon became apparent when there were 188 people reported as killed in Zeppelin raids in 1915 alone. Nothing seemed to touch them, they flew so high. It was in September 1916 when Dick and his friends found a new hero to worship. Lieutenant Leefe Robinson. This brave young airman flew his plane right up to a Zeppelin and shot it down.

"They say it looked just like a big cigar. All the bag part caught fire... it was roaring with flames; blue, red, purple. Eye witnesses said that it seemed to come down slowly instead of falling down with a bang." Alfred Harrison had reported in the school hall one morning, just before assembly.

"There were sixty Germans in it and they all roasted to

death!" George Blackett added with relish.

"How terrible." Dick replied sadly.

"Don't be ridiculous Dick, these are Germans we're talking about, not people like us!" George replied.

After that the threat of the Zeppelins did decrease, but in 1917 Germany introduced the long distance bomber plane. On 13th June of that year 594 people were killed and injured in a single raid on London. The government reacted by introducing a blackout throughout the country. Dick and his friends were not happy about that. It was not bad through the summer, but it affected their social calendar during the winter. You couldn't run races in dark alleys!

More important to hungry young men, was the scarcity of food. The Germans tried to starve the British into submission by attacking merchant shipping. By April 1917 Britain had just six weeks of grain left, even though bread rationing had been introduced in February. The trip to Low Row was therefore very opportune. Many of the farmers had "unofficial" grain to spare, as well as eggs, meat etc. Being in the country had distinct advantages. The family car returned to West Hartlepool loaded far more heavily than it left. Richard decreed that the family would return to the Dales whenever it was possible and Dick was not complaining. He soon introduced Harry to the walks and secret places that he had shared with John. During that summer a new bond was forged between the two brothers that would be unbreakable for many years.

Dick also left the Polytechnic that summer but not until he had claimed an impressive array of medals, as a very active member of the Polytechnic Harriers.

Dick was now a man and that, in his father's eyes, meant that he was now an insurance agent! Dick had hoped to go to university but knew that his father would never agree to the expense. He joined the Royal Liver Insurance Office, where his father was the manager, the day after he left school. He had no enthusiasm for the job but at least he now had a steady income.

Chapter   5

Dick and his father were in the office on 11th November 1918 when a telegram was received. It was quite a surprise to them to hear that the Armistice had been signed.

Richard closed the office immediately and sent everyone home to celebrate. The atmosphere was electric as Dick walked home. Bells were ringing everywhere and flags were being raised on buildings wherever a pole or post could be found! Strangers were hugging and kissing and every where people were smiling.

Dick thought for a moment of John. It was exactly two years since the notice had appeared in the paper. Britain and the Empire had lost almost one million men. Was it worth it Dick thought?

The party was in full swing in the street by Dick got home. The anti-alcohol measures introduced during the previous years had obviously been forgotten.

"Here you are Dick, grab a glass of ale and let's drink to victory." One of his friends shouted from across the road. It didn't take too much persuasion. Although still only seventeen, Dick was soon as merry as the rest. He didn't remember much of the party but he must have had a grand time, judging by the resulting headache!

Celebrations continued for several days throughout the country. Dick had to admit that he had quite enjoyed his introduction to the pleasures of alcohol. Oh, the first few glasses had been a touch bitter, he hadn't admitted this to his friends, of course! It was amazing how the taste improved after four or five though. The headache wasn't much fun either but a good hard cross country run soon settled that as well!

Life soon returned to normal. Johnny Gibson came to the

door one evening. Dick hadn't seen much of him recently.

"Some of the athletics clubs are re-forming Dick, and I'm helping the recruitment drive. How about it?" Johnny was so excited that he hardly paused for breath. "I'm going along now. A few of the old members of the Christ Church Harriers and the West Hartlepool Harriers are trying to get it off the ground. Unfortunately they disbanded during the war and a lot of the old members are gone, of course. They're meeting at the Greyhound Stadium."

Dick didn't need a second bidding. Grabbing his spikes he left at once.

The newly formed group kept the name "West Hartlepool Harriers". Their training consisted of short sprints, followed by one long sprint and then lots and lots of laps. They warmed up and cooled down with gymnastics and various exercises.

It was a very hard regime and Dick loved every minute of it. It quickly replaced the school sports that he missed so badly.

One evening the club had a visit from the members of the "West" Rugby Club. They all trained together and organised a few races, just for fun. One of the professional footballers was also a top sprinter and Dick was very excited when they were introduced. Laurie Kessler had just been piped by inches for the Professional Footballers 100 yards Championship, in a time of 9.9 seconds.

"Bad luck." Dick commiserated as Laurie explained his near miss.

"No it wasn't bad luck, I just wasn't quite good enough," Laurie explained. "The experience was something else though Dick. To actually run in a national championship, along with the best, and get second place, I just can't explain the feeling. It's like everything you ever wanted happening at once!"

"I would love to feel that," Dick longingly replied, "but I doubt that I will ever be that good."

"Don't be so hard on yourself, young man." Laurie laughed. "You already have an impressive array of school championships under your belt, from what I have been told. Get yourself entered into a few of the local race meetings and get yourself known. I wouldn't mind betting that you have a good career in front of you."

Dick didn't agree but what Laurie had said did stick in his

mind. The two became close friends and Laurie pushed Dick hard to get himself noticed in athletics circles.

Unfortunately Dick was rapidly approaching eighteen and would have to serve his king and country. Athletics would have to be left on hold.

It was the beginning of April in 1919. That day at the office had been particularly boring. Whilst eating his lunch Dick had been reading, in the "Daily Express", of the continuing food shortages and of the need for merchant seaman, to man the ships bringing the much needed supplies into the country. He remembered Uncle John's letter. True the war was over now but conscription was not and somehow the army did not appeal. Merchant navy service does count as National Service, the article informed him.

Dick did not stop to think. He contacted the Board of Trade immediately and was surprised at how quickly they arranged to assign him to the "Rhoda" as a cadet. The ship was to set sail from London on 25th April and was bound eventually for Australia. It was to be the voyage of a lifetime.

Dick hadn't decided how to break the news to his parents but he had confided in Harry from the start.

"Just think Harry, I can travel round the world and be paid for it. No more insurance policies or grey haired old gentleman wanting impossible medical cover. This is a new start for me."

That was fine when he had first gone through to Middlesbrough to sign the papers, but things had happened so quickly since then. Somehow he had expected a few months to get used to the idea, and more importantly, to get his father used to the idea. Well he would have to take the train to London in two days time, so he would have to break the news soon.

He resigned himself to taking the plunge that evening. Martha had just brought in the vegetables and Father was carving the joint. For once the whole family was present.

"I have an announcement to make." Dick stated, rising to his feet. "No don't go Martha, I want you to hear as well." Martha had turned to withdraw from the room.

"I sail for Australia in three days time. I leave for London the day after tomorrow." He decided the short, sharp, brutal approach was best.

Richard dropped the carving knife, fortunately. Dick could almost imagine the steam coming out of his ears.

"You what!" Richard shouted."I hope this is some sort of joke. It is very poor taste if it is."

"No, it is not a joke," Dick confirmed. "I will be eighteen in June and the government would assign me to some squalid army unit in Germany. I am following Uncle John's advice. I have made my own choice, the Merchant Navy seems like an excellent alternative to me."

Richard actually paused to consider this. Winifred rose from her chair and threw her arms around Dick. Tears were pouring own her face.

"Steady on Mother," Dick offered her his handkerchief. "The war is over, I won't be sunk by a U-Boat now you know."

"But you are so young to be leaving home," Winifred sobbed.

"Don't be ridiculous Winifred," Richard snapped, "and do stop that snivelling. You are quite right Richard, and very sensible for once. I do think you may have given more notice though. How will I manage at the office? You have really made things awkward for me."

Dick was relieved that his father had taken things so well. He agreed to return to the office that evening to help sort his case register out. Winifred and Martha dashed about washing, ironing and baking. Martha was convinced that he would not be fed correctly on a boat.

"It's a ship Martha. It weighs 4638 tonnes and has it's own cook," Dick reassured her. Still, when the whole family assembled at the railway station two days later, Dick could hardly carry his kit bag and the parcels of various extras that Winifred and Martha had been convinced that he could not possibly survive without.

Harry hugged him and told him to take care and hurry home. Betty asked if she could have his bedroom and told him not to forget to bring her a good present back. "Typical," he thought. Winifred and Martha could not stop crying.

"I'll be back on leave in October." Dick reminded them as he waved from the train window. The whistle went and he was on his way.

London was quite an experience. His father, in a moment of uncharacteristic generosity, had given him sufficient money to take a taxi cab from the station to the ship, but he asked the driver to take him around some of the main sights. Much of the city still had bomb damage but Buckingham Palace was still very much intact. Dick remembered reading that King George V had been some relative of the Kaiser and that the palace had been avoided because of this. Standing proudly in the middle of the ravages left by war he could well believe it!

Embarking on the voyage was terrifying but also exhilarating. The other lads on the ship were very friendly, though some were a bit rougher than Dick had been used to. It wasn't long before he looked forward to the nightly rum ration and the tall stories that followed.

During the first part of the voyage Dick was also introduced to his first pipe. The older sailors told him that he would need to get used to smoking this.

"It's the only way you'll keep them damn mosquitoes away when we get to Africa," they warned. It didn't take him long. A few coughs and splutters and he was soon puffing along with the best of them and puffed merrily for almost the next eighty years.

Dick took to the Navy as a duck takes to water. He was teased though. Many of the lads kept fit, but the sight of Dick pounding the deck, lap after lap, whenever he was not on duty, was the talk of the ship. Even the Captain noticed.

"Doesn't matter how fast you run lad, you'll not get there any quicker." He remarked laughingly, as he passed him one day.

The voyage far exceeded Dick's expectations. The work was fairly mundane but not difficult and the countries he visited and sights he saw stayed with him for the rest of his life. Not only did he come to love his rum and his pipe but he rapidly became aware of how sheltered his life had been. When calling at one of the islands he had seen native women rolling cigars, using their thighs as a rolling board. Having come from post Victorian England, where women had only just started wearing trousers and occasionally showing ankles, this was quite astounding. He just had to try those cigars. Although the manufacturing of them was fascinating he found that they were even more fun to smoke Definitely better than his pipe. He bought a huge box full. He had to give these out when he got home. Think of the stories he could tell while his friends were sampling them!

Dick was standing on the deck one evening, with a couple of the other lads, just as the sun was starting to slip into the ocean. He felt like he could lean over a touch the silver, shimmering rays left on the water, as the sun gently slipped away.

"This is just the best life!" Breathed Dick quietly, frightened to break the spell.

"Aye! If you can avoid those blasted mosquitoes!" Laughed one of his mates, slapping his neck hard, as an insect tried to turn him into lunch. "Pass me one of your cigars, before I get eaten alive!"

Unfortunately, despite the smoking, Dick also fell foul of the mosquitoes. The ship was homeward bound and called at Cape Town. It was particularly hot and the crew went for a swim to cool off. When they were getting dressed several of the crew felt sharp nips.

"Damned mosquitoes." One of the lads retorted. Dick was one of the many to be bitten but one of the few to develop the illness. At first he thought he had caught a chill. Before long his body was shaking violently and sweating so badly that his bunk was soaking wet.

He didn't know a lot after that. He understood that he had a very bad attack of malaria, and probably would have died, if he had not been so fit.

Soon after he returned to duty he was summoned to the Captain's cabin. Unsure of what he had done, Dick couldn't help but feel uneasy.

"I'm sorry lad," the Captain said, rising from his chair, "these attacks will recur, you will not be able to sign up for another voyage. I am sorry to lose you, your work and conduct has been excellent but I am afraid that your naval career has ended."

"Oh God, No!" Dick slumped into a nearby chair, all thoughts of standing to attention forgotten. The Captain's voice took on a softer tone.

"Look on the bright side lad, you can concentrate on that running of yours now." He clasped him on the shoulder before returning to his seat, shaking his head sadly. Dick left the cabin slowly, feeling as though he was leaving his whole world behind.

Dick returned home after being discharged on 25th October 1919.

Chapter   6

As Dick arrived in West Hartlepool station, his feet felt like lead but they were not as heavy as his heart. He had loved life on the ship. Six months was not enough, yet here he was, his naval career all washed up at the ripe old age of eighteen!

The ship's doctor had explained that he had been lucky. He had not had Blackwater Fever, if he had he would almost certainly have died. However there was a very strong possibility that Dick would experience chronic relapses into the disease, there was nothing the doctor could give him to prevent this. Not a happy prospect at his age.

The station looked drab and dark as he alighted from the train. Even the pigeons roosting in the canopy over the platform were puffed up and unhappy looking. The steam and smoke from the train was lingering above like a heavy storm cloud, matching Dick's mood exactly. Then through a broken pane of glass a ray of sunshine filtered on to a small group of people standing near the exit. Suddenly, giving an excited bark, a dog yanked away from it's owner and dashed towards Dick. Before he realised that this was no stranger's dog, this was Lady, he was almost knocked on his back by the enthusiastic greeting. Lady just could not contain her excitement. She squealed and squealed, jumping and licking.

Dick dropped his bags and threw his arms around her, the tears pouring down his face. He had been very ill and his life had become a disappointment but at least he was home and Lady still loved him! Winifred ran up and threw her arms around him. He looked thin but better than she had expected. A little broken perhaps, but nothing she and Martha couldn't mend.

"I'm so glad you are home Dick, we have missed you terribly." She sobbed and laughed at the same time.

Harry stepped forward, looking extremely well and fit.

"The lads at the Harriers will be glad to see you back," he said, a little shyly. "You've got all winter to get fit again before next year's events. I've done well this summer and have taken lots of prizes for the club, but racing and training without you has not been much fun."

Dick hugged Harry and was surprised to find himself still crying. He had forgotten just how important all the family were, especially Harry and Lady. Then of course there was the running, but would he ever get well enough to run again? How could he face the Harriers when he felt weak just rising in the morning?

Lady would not calm down.

"She's just not been herself while you've been away," Harry explained, rubbing her ears. "The two of you could do with a spell in the Dales by the look of you."

"Your quite right Harry," agreed Winifred, "but not until Martha and I have put some weight back on him. I thought you said they had cooks on those boats."

Dick laughed weakly.

"It was a ship Mother," he corrected, "and the food was unbelievable. I have never tasted anything like the curries and casseroles that our cook produced. No disrespect to you and Martha but Mrs Beaton's cook book can hardly compete."

"Curries and foreign spicy rubbish. We'll soon get some good Spotted Dicks and Yorkshire puddings into you!" Winifred retorted.

Dick managed to survive exactly two weeks of the care inflicted upon him by his mother and Martha.

"I know they mean well," he confided to Harry, "but I am starting to feel smothered. I think I'll take Lady and escape to Low Row tomorrow. Do come with us, it will be like old times."

"I'll come for the weekend but I do have work remember?" Harry reminded him. He was father's latest recruit. "We haven't all got six month's Merchant Navy pay to survive on you know."

The pair managed to persuade father to lend them the car and set off early next morning. The cottage was cold and felt damp. It

49

had been a very wet Autumn and it had not been used much while Dick was away.

"Betty complains that she has no friends in the country, she can't see "The Keystone Cops" at the picture house here either," Harry explained, "and you know Father always panders to her every whim! I brought Lady up a few times but I find it a bit quiet on my own."

"They soon had a roaring fire going and left it to warm the place up while they had a run further up the Dale to the Farmers Arms at Muker. The fire was blazing well as they entered the dark bar. There were settles pulled up beside the fire and a couple of the old farmers were playing dominoes in the corner. They hardly looked up as the two ordered a jug of ale. Dick settled by the fire and lit his pipe. Puffing contentedly he realised for the first time in weeks that life wasn't so bad after all.

The sun had been setting as they had driven down the Dale. The red sky seemed to feed down the mountain and kiss the river, turning it to a river of blood. The scene had immediately reminded Dick of John and a momentary sadness had swept over him. Then he remembered what John had taught him of life and he knew that here he would start to live again.

"Life is good Harry. I was somewhat depressed when they threw me out of the Navy, but I did see a lot of the world and at least I had that opportunity. Now I must start again." He blew a smoke ring towards the fire.

Next morning Dick was up and out with Lady before Harry had turned over for the first time. It was misty as he ran along the river side. He kept a steady pace but covered six or seven miles before breakfast. Harry had the kettle on when he came in and the smell of bacon frying filled the air. Dick inhaled deeply.

"It's good to be alive Harry. We're starving!" He laughed, throwing Lady a rasher of bacon. Harry was glad to see the old Dick rapidly emerging from beneath the despondent waif that had first alighted from the train.

"You'll soon be showing them your heels again at the Harriers, if you keep this up." Harry smiled, as he threw a couple of eggs into the pan.

Dick spent two weeks increasing his speed and stamina by running the paths and tracks that he knew so well. The weather was kind considering that November was well under way. Frosts were holding off but there were many heavy morning mists. They did not bother Dick, he kept to the coffin roads to ensure that he didn't get lost. He didn't give it much thought until he was seated by the fire in The Kings Arms in Gunnerside one evening. He leaned forward to tap his pipe out on the hearth and couldn't help but overhear three of the farm lads deep in conversation.

"Well I weren't drunk this mornin' an I see'd it agin." One of the lads was saying. "It were down at t'moor edge, all ghastly and bloody, and runnin' like devil were after it. I thinks it were ole Nick hissel!"

"I saw it an all," said another of the lads, "but I were down by the river, along near Rolleth Bottoms. It 'adn't been dark long and I weren't drunk. A white, ghostly figure emerged from the darkness at incredible speed, passed me quick, like and were gone. My legs fair turned to jelly I can tell 'e."

The landlord entered the conversation.

"Well why has it just started appearing in the last two weeks?" He asked. "Do you think there has been some dastardly murder committed and the spirit is earthbound because the poor murdered body hasn't been discovered yet?"

"Rubbish," one of the farmers replied, "your ale is too strong, that's all."

"Well if ye doesn' believe us, ye gan and see for theself," the first lad challenged. "It'll be on t'old coffin road about 'alf seven in t'morning. Let's us all gan, then us 'll be sure."

They all agreed to meet the next day and the conversation changed to stock prices and bad crops.

Dick was intrigued. He ran along the coffin road at seven thirty, very often and he hadn't seen anything, certainly not a Will O' the Wisp with a bloody patch where it's heart should be. Still it had been very misty most mornings.

"Sounds a bit like my Harriers shirt," he thought to himself, "that has a red emblem on the chest and my running kit is white. I wonder?"

Dick was soon to solve the mystery. The next morning was dark but not misty. He had only gone a few miles when Lady stopped and started barking. Sure enough the farmers lads and Farmer Spencer were spread out across the track, with shot guns pointing.

"No need to shoot me lads, I'm only trying to get fit for next years Northumberland and Durham Championships." Dick held up his hands. He was a little worried by their gruff faces.

Farmer Spencer started to laugh, it was the heartiest laugh Dick had ever witnessed.

"Well Amos is this thy ghost?" Tears started rolling down his cheeks. "Sorry we startled thee lad, these Jessies 'ere was sure thee were a murdered soul. Can't wait to tell the cricket team on Sunday!"

With that they turned away and headed down the hill. Dick laughed and carried on. A different greeting waited him that night at the King's Arms. Dalesmen are naturally reserved around strangers and Dick had found difficulty breaking through that reserve. Not that night though and never on his future visits.

"'Ere 'e is, ghost of Old Gang!" One of the farmers shouted, as he entered the door "Bring 'im yer best ale Landlord."

Several shook his hand and no-one would let him buy his own beer all night. It was a story that would stay in the Dales for many a year and the Dales farmers became his biggest fans during his running career.

Dick returned home two days later and he also soon returned to West Hartlepool Harriers. There he was to discover that Johnny Gibson was now firmly established in athletics circles. Now known officially as J.W Gibson, he was already Northumberland and Durham champion at 100, 220 and 440 yards.

Dick threw himself into his training. Despite his running in the Dales he was surprised to find that he still experienced periods of weakness. He was reluctant to start racing again but the continued encouragement from Harry and Laurie definitely helped and he was soon challenging the best of them. He even developed some light hearted rivalry with Johnny.

"Don't think you are keeping those titles." Dick teased him

one evening. "I'll soon be fit and then your reign will be over!"

Johnny playfully punched his shoulder.

"Any time Rip, I wasn't the one who sailed half way around the world to avoid racing against me!"

That was a good winter. Dick's health continued to improve. He now had a new job as a book keeper with a firm of accountants. His father had been most apologetic on his arrival home.

"I just could not keep your post available Richard. After all I expected you to be gone for two years at the least."

Dick had been secretly relieved. Working constantly under his father's eye had been very wearing, and the job had not been very exciting either. He found a new job very easily, through friends at the Harriers. He enjoyed the company of the other men in the company, many of whom enjoyed athletics and shared Dick's enthusiasm for most sports. He did not enjoy being desk bound but you couldn't have everything!

Home life was quite good too. Father still spent most of his life at work. Mother, Martha and his sisters had started taking more of an interest in politics and current affairs and held far more interesting conversations. Women had been granted the vote in the previous year and Lady Astor had taken her seat as first woman in the Commons on the first of December. There had even been an Act, just before Christmas which meant that many professions were now open to women. The Sex Disqualification Removal Act. Even Dick's sisters thought that this was exciting. Gertrude announced that she would probably become a barrister or something. Dick thought it highly unlikely as she hated studying but decided to refrain from voicing his opinions.

Father would not listen to this talk. He was determined that no daughter of his would work. He was still firmly convinced that a woman's place was in the home!

As winter gave way to spring, Dick's athletics performance and stamina were regained and Dick's spare time became totally involved in training and racing.

By then nineteen year old Dick was entering all the sporting events he could. It was then that he entered the Northern Championships, in Jarrow, one Saturday in 1920, not long after his birthday.

Dick, Johnny and Harry travelled to Jarrow together. Harry was taking part in the youths' relay team. A new event at this years sports. Dick had encouraged his younger brother to enter. Athletics was definitely a family event these days.

Dick couldn't help teasing Johnny all the way there.

"Remember when you let me win that time in the back alley? Well you better give it all you've got today, as I'm not going to be so generous." Johnny laughed. Dick was a challenger to Johnny's title in the quarter-mile flat. Although he was on top form, and had already won five lesser events that season, Dick did not really think he had a chance.

The race was reported afterwards as "the outstanding feature" of the sports.

"The crowd, certainly, could not withhold their appreciation of the performance of Ripley." The newspaper declared.

A dual had been expected between N. Barnes of Darlington and Johnny, but "Gibson was finished at the half distance, Barnes soon receded to the rear... .Ripley shot into the lead," the report continued, "the victor by three yards.".

Dick could not believe it. Laurie and Johnny had been telling him he was good. He had never dared believe it. Now he was Northumberland and Durham Champion. It wasn't long before Dick had stripped Johnny of all his titles and was also acknowledged as Northern Counties champion.

The Ripley's had reigned supreme that day in 1920, as Harry's team also won the youths' relay team race. Even father was impressed with their achievements!

"Don't forget though Dick," Richard added after congratulating him on his achievement, "athletics can only be a hobby, it is not a respectable profession, and probably never will be. Do not let it affect your work."

Despite his father's warnings Dick's athletics career went from strength to strength. He retained the 440 yards title easily in 1921 and 1922 but, not content with one championship, he also took the 880 yards in August 1921 and helped to win the 1mile relay on his twenty-first birthday. No runner had ever won more than three of these Championships consecutively, but Dick was now equal to that record and he was just starting!

It was July 1922 when Dick received a letter from Harry J. Barclay, the Secretary of the Amateur Athletics Association.

"I have pleasure to advise you that you have been selected to represent England in the 400 metres (reserve) against France at Stamford Bridge, on Saturday 29th." Dick read. At last he had been recognised as good enough to represent his country. Yes, it was only a "Reserve" selection, but at least the Amateur Athletics Association had picked him!

This was it, he was on his way!

Chapter 7

Dick could hardly contain his excitement as he read the letter. He was invited to attend the games with a guest. He rushed into Harry's room.

"Get packed Harry!" He shouted, pulling his blankets off and shoving him out of bed. "We're off to Stamford Bridge to witness the International between England and France and, who knows, if I'm lucky, someone will break a leg and I might even get to run for England. Just think of it Harry, me in the England vest, parading with the England team, I can't wait."

Harry looked up from the floor and held his hand out for the letter.

"This says you will receive the tickets and information on the 25th.," Harry complained, "it's only the23rd. today, I didn't need to get up for hours yet."

"Oh shut up lazybones," Dick rushed on. "We need new clothes. Betty was telling me just the other day that all the young men about town are wearing Oxford Bags now. We haven't got any, we must get to the tailors fast. Come on move it."

"Can't I have a cup of tea first?" Harry laughed. Still he was as pleased for Dick as he could be. He was sure this was just the beginning and he could not help being affected by Dick's excitement.

The games were on the Saturday, 29th July. Dick and Harry decided to make a short holiday of it and spend the weekend enjoying London. They travelled down on the Friday and managed to get last minute tickets for a Beethoven recital at the Queen's Hall. Both had learnt to play the piano, thanks to Winifred's tuition and Dick loved Beethoven above all others. For him the night was magical and "The Moonlight Sonata" was an incredible finale. Already emotional from the whole occasion Dick found tears coursing down his cheeks.

"I will never forget this night and," he confided to Harry later, "even if I'm not needed tomorrow this weekend will always be part of my special memories."

Harry did agree but he was also missing a young lady he had met recently. A student called Eva. He could not get her out of his mind. He confided this to Dick.

"Well you kept her a secret, you dark horse." Dick chided. "Why didn't you tell me, I would have understood if you had not wanted to come?"

"Don't be ridiculous Dick! I have got all of my life to get to know Eva. I would not have missed this weekend for the world. I hope I'll always be able to be there for you Dick, and I hope you don't forget your poor little brother when you are rich and famous!"

Fortunately for the team, and Dick, no-one broke a leg that weekend, but Dick and Harry were allowed into the L.A.C. dressing room with the England team and the atmosphere was electric.

They watched the whole event from stand "D" and made themselves hoarse from shouting and cheering.

After the races an Official approached them with dinner tickets.

"We would be pleased if you would join the Team and Officials this evening, at the Cafe Monico, in Piccadilly Circus". He handed Dick the tickets. The brothers were delighted.

They had a wonderful evening, swapping stories with the athletic greats and participating in a meal fit for kings. Before the night was completed Dick was on first name terms with the best and Harry Barclay, the Amateur Athletics Association secretary had Dick's name and address firmly imprinted on his brain.

Next morning the pair slept late and had a walk to London Tower to help clear away the residue of the previous nights champagne. They passed a poster for the Alhambra Theatre. Marie Lloyd was appearing.

"Isn't she that music hall singer who does those naughty songs?" Harry's eyes twinkled.

"A little of what you fancy does you good." Dick sang. "Yes I wouldn't mind seeing her but I bet we have no chance. I wouldn't think she would be performing on a Sunday anyway."

"You never know," insisted Harry, "nothing is going to mar this weekend."

Sure enough the lads were lucky enough to enjoy her cockney humour that evening and spent most of the train journey home, the next day, singing their own version of "Oh Mr Porter". Until the guard offered to put them off the train at the next station if they did not temper their enthusiasm, that is!

Marie Lloyd collapsed and died on that very stage less than three months later. The lads had not realised at the time just how fortunate they had been to obtain those tickets.

A wonderful weekend but when the pair arrived home there was an air of gloom about the house. Mother had obviously been crying and Martha bustled them out of the room quickly.

"It's just your Pa again," she explained to Dick. "The neighbours are tittle-tattling about his mistress. Your Ma could handle it as long as he was discreet, but he has set her up in a house over in Eamont Gardens. He never turned up at home at all yesterday. Ladies over the road were gossiping about it."

Dick was horrified. The shame and scandal was one thing but how hurt must Mother be, her heart must be torn apart.

A hatred, that had been building up in him all his life, came to the surface. All the times he had been beaten for nothing serious, the hundreds of times he had heard the shouting and seen his mother belittled by his father. The tears he had seen her shed and the tears he had shed himself. Richard had never been a real father to him. All he ever did was bully, critise and humiliate. He didn't know or care what his victims felt like, the pain and hurt they suffered. With Richard as your father you were even terrified if you had an accident. Dick almost trembled as he recalled so many fearful events, like the time he had fallen off his bike. An accident, he had hit the corner of a bush and fallen badly, hurting his arm, scrapping his knees and banging his head. He was young then but the bike had fallen against the precious automobile. Automobiles cost money and father made it very plain that this one must not be touched. Although Dick had been quite badly hurt he remembered only too well, that his pain was nothing to the pure horror that he felt when he saw the small scratch on the vehicle. Betty had taken delight in telling father and the explosion was unbelievable. Dick tried to hide in a cupboard, he was so afraid. Father's temper was even worse than Dick had feared. He cared nothing for the fact that it was an accident or that Dick had hurt himself. His face twisted with rage and Dick was dragged from his hiding place. He was convinced that he was dead and pleaded with his father for forgiveness. Father would, no doubt have beaten him very severely but Mother, in a rare moment of bravery, grabbed him and pushed Richard away. Even after all these years the terror of this incident came back in full force.

That was just one of many similar occasions, The man had ruined almost every special event with his anger and ridicule.. Christmases, holidays. Whenever anyone was happy he seemed to delight in destroying the moment. Now he had publicly degraded mother and spoilt one of the most special weekends of Dick's life. Well enough was enough!

"Dick what are you thinking?" Harry shook him slightly, he was concerned over the silence and the black cloud that was gathering across Dick's face.

"What number Eamont?" Dick asked between clenched teeth.

"Number 20 I think." Martha mumbled reluctantly.

Dick was out of the house so fast, he was out of sight before Harry had time to react. He had no chance of catching him.

Dick did not bother to knock. There was no need to guess where his father would be. He headed straight for the bedroom. Twenty-one years of pent-up passion burst forth that day. His father was lucky to still have his long johns in place, as Dick dragged him down the stairs and threw him into the street.

"You bloody scoundrel!" Dick shouted as he smacked his fist firmly into his nose. He actually enjoyed the crunch that he heard on impact. "Give me one good reason why I should not kill you now?" He screamed as his fist contacted with his abdomen.

Through his rage Dick noticed that his father was not fighting back. He was in a quivering heap in the road, actually trying to crawl away.

Dick gave him a shove with his foot.

"You're not worth hanging for, you're pathetic." He started walking away.

Just then Harry, Martha and Winifred ran up.

"Oh Dick what have you done?" Winifred cried. "What have you done?" She was wringing her hands in fear.

"Pack your bags Mother." Dick implored. "We will find a hotel until I can find somewhere for us to live."

"Don't be silly Dick. I could never leave your father, it would not be proper. I like things the way they are. You must leave though, your father will never forgive this!"

Dick did not understand her reply. He had released his mother from this man's oppression and yet she was chasing him away and kneeling beside this animal. What was the point? Had she no pride or self respect?

Dick turned and walked away. He knew now that he could no longer be a member of this family. He had had his revenge, but he felt no glory. His father was no more than a cruel, contemptible coward, but he had won again and now Dick was alone.

As he approached "home" he realised that he must leave immediately. His bag was still just inside the door from their arrival home earlier. He hurriedly packed another and left. He knew that the mother of one of his friends at the Harriers ran a neat little boarding house and he made for that.

His mood was heavy as he was shown to the pretty little attic room. Again he felt that life was not fair. He looked out of the window across the fields and was surprised to see that the sun was setting. A beautiful glow lit up the sky and spread into the room, touching everything with pink and gold.

"Remember the sunsets!" John had said and here again was John reminding him that he was not alone, or that was how it felt to Dick.

"Are you hungry young man?" His landlady shouted. Dick realised that he had not eaten for hours.

"Yes starving," he replied.

The landlady, Mrs Johnson, had explained that they usually

ate in the kitchen.

"It's not so formal as the dining room," she explained, "but if you ever want to bring a young lady to take tea I can get the china out with the best of them." She laughed.

As Dick entered the kitchen he was instantly taken by the homely feel of the place. Although it was July, there was still a fire in the range. There had to be, the food was cooked in the ovens along side. A copper kettle sang away on a hob which had been swung across the embers. The floor was stone but had been stained dark red and was well scrubbed. Raggy mats were scattered around, making blotches of bright colours everywhere. Herbs hung in bunches to dry at various point around the room, giving the whole place an out of doors smell. This was mingling with an exciting aroma of baking. The doors had been thrown open to keep the place cool and a pleasant breeze kissed Dick's face.

"Sit yourself down. I'm sorry you'll have to eat alone but we all ate earlier," Mrs Johnson explained. "There's only one other lodger at present and he is walking out with a young lady, so we only see him at mealtimes. I do allow ladies to visit in the parlour, but not in the rooms."

"No fear of that," laughed Dick. "I don't seem to have much time for lady friends. I'm hoping to run for England one day and I like to spend most of my time training."

" My Jack told me about you," Mrs Johnson smiled, "but remember, all work and no play makes Dick a dull boy! Come on anyway, eat up before it gets cold."

Dick sat down to a steak and kidney pie, creamy potatoes and home grown cabbage and carrots, all covered with a thick savoury gravy. A huge slice of home made apple pie followed.

"Delicious but I'll never run in the Olympics if you feed me like that everyday".

"Don't be daft love, I know you athletes, you'll soon run that lot off. Don't ever go hungry in this house. There's always cakes in the larder. Just help yourself." Mrs Johnson beamed. "My Jack just loves his Victoria Sponges. I pride myself on my cooking. You just let me know your favourites and I'll see they are on the menu. Don't be slow to ask now. Treat this as home."

"Home," Dick thought,"I hope that is one place this won't remind me of." He felt a momentary sadness but it soon passed.

"Have a brandy and a cigar in the parlour if you like." Mrs Johnson instructed."Jack will be home shortly, he is going to try and get his new wireless to receive that new radio station 2L0 later. Perhaps you would like to help him. There's one of them phonograph things in the corner as well. Just wind it up if you want some music."

Dick was impressed, his house had never been one for new fangled inventions, as his mother called them. He had always had a fancy for a phonograph himself. Now he had access to music without having to play the piano.

The parlour was as comfortable and welcoming as the kitchen had been. Heavy velvet curtains lifting slightly in the draft from the open windows. A small table held a huge vase full of honeysuckle which filled the room with it's fragrance. A grandfather clock ticked rhythmically in the corner. Dick had to smile when he saw a badly carved sailing boat displayed in the centre of the mantle.

"Jack made that at school," explained Mrs Johnson. "I'll always treasure it." Dick remembered making one too. He had run home with it, so excited. His father had promptly pulled it apart, "to show that shoddy workmanship is a waste of time" and thrown the remains in the fire. Dick sighed. What a difference, their mantle had been full of Wedgewood and silver, anything that could be shown off, of course. He had no doubt that Jack's ship was far more valuable to Mrs Johnson, but his father and mother would never understand that. Dick accepted the glass Mrs Johnson was offering. Not crystal, but who cares. This is much more "real" somehow.

"This is the life," he thought, "and if this is what being homeless is all about then I should have done it years ago. I think I will survive after all."

Dick sipped the splendid brandy and blew a smoke ring, relaxing into an enormous arm chair, the pleasant strains of Chopin issuing from the corner. "Yes I will always survive!"

Chapter   8

Dick soon settled into life with the Johnsons. Mrs Johnson was a widow. Her husband had been in the Royal Navy and had been drowned when his cruiser was sunk by a U-boat in 1914. Dick found himself even more spoilt once she knew of his short naval career. Better still Mrs Johnson made a wonderful curry, it had been her husband's favourite!

The other lodger, David, was a banker and only ever seen at mealtimes. As Mrs Johnson had remarked, he was always in a hurry to call on a Miss Hill and rarely hung around for polite conversation.

Dick had known Jack for years, through the Harriers. Jack was a couple of years older and ran a small timber company. He had started it with a small legacy left by his father and was doing very well. He had won a contract to supply pit props to the local collieries and sleepers for the rail tracks. When he wasn't running, he was working, but did not seem to be obsessed with making money, as Dick's father has been. Jack was always laughing. His workers loved him, as did the rest of the Harriers. He and Dick soon became firm friends.

Dick's main concern, after he left home, was that his friendship with Harry would suffer. He was very fond of his little brother. He need not have worried. It was his habit to run each morning before getting ready for work. He had explained this to Mrs Johnson and assured her that he would be very quiet leaving the house at 6.30am. He therefore set out the very next morning, following his usual route through the Burn Valley gardens. To his surprise it was not just the familiar Peter Pan figure that he found at the pond. Sitting despondently on a rock was Harry.

"Good heavens Harry," Dick laughed "have you wet the bed

or something?"

"It's not funny Dick." Harry replied seriously "Martha and I have been worried sick. Just dashing off like that without a word. Where did you get to?"

Dick explained about his new accommodation and assured Harry of his safety and comfort.

Harry told Dick that Father had been very humble since the incident.

"He's even promised to buy Mother that huge house she wants in Hutton Avenue. He is even arranging for electric lights!" Harry sighed. "I don't fancy living there without you though. Betty was her usual pleasant self, fussing round father like a mother hen and condemning you for your actions. Oh, Father has disowned you by the way."

"What a surprise. At least you might benefit from his death one day. I hope you don't have to wait too long!" Dick scowled.

"I don't think you should talk like that and I certainly am not after his money," Harry retorted. "I doubt very much that I'll stay at home too long now. I might ask Eva to marry me and get out while the going is good."

"Don't go rushing into anything, just because you're not happy. You're much to young to marry, Father would never allow it and I thought you said Eva was a student. Surely you would not want to stop her studying. Just keep calm, things will settle down. I'll still see you at the Harriers and, now you know where I am, you can come and see me whenever the atmosphere gets too bad." Dick advised.

They had been running together as they chatted. Now their ways parted.

"Look after yourself," called Dick, as Harry turned away.

"Oh I almost forgot," Harry came back pulling a letter from his pocket, "there was a letter at home for you. I couldn't help but notice the Northern Counties Athletics Association emblem on the back. I hope it's good news."

Harry sprinted away.

"See you tonight at the rugby ground." Dick shouted as he opened his letter. He had applied to be part of the Yorkshire relay team in the Yorkshire V Lancashire inter County Games taking place on Bank Holiday Monday. His friends had laughed.

"We don't live in Yorkshire Dick. How can you be Durham champion and run for Yorkshire?"

Dick had a secret weapon, he had been born in North Ormesby, in Yorkshire. That meant in his eyes that he could run as a Yorkshire man by birth and as a Durham man by residence. Would the Yorkshire committee agree though?

The letter, signed by the Hon. Sec. J Lawrenson, was more than pleased to accept him, even stating:

"If you are willing to be one of the Yorkshire team my committee would be very pleased."

The race was to run at the Leeds Hospital Gala. Winners were to receive gold medals and badges. Dick was over the moon. He would be able to fulfil another ambition, to enter any future North Yorkshire championships. What if he could become North Yorkshire Champion as well as Northumberland and Durham Champion?

He didn't think anyone had ever held both titles before. Now that would be an achievement! Dick could not contain his excitement.

He ran into the kitchen to find Mrs Johnson cooking breakfast. He ran up and kissed her on the cheek.

"Jack is very lucky, you are a wonderful woman," he laughed as he ran upstairs to get washed.

"Go away with you." Mrs Johnson flushed. She was pleased to see the young man so happy, so soon. She had really worried when he had arrived the previous evening, he looked so like a man who had the weight of the world on his shoulders.

"Still, that's the young for you," she thought. "One minute down, the next flying high like a kite. Well good luck to him!"

That night Dick threw himself into his training with a renewed vigour. Harry, normally able to keep up with him reasonably well, found himself left behind.

"Steady on Dick," he panted. "Where's the fire, we usually take the first few sprints easily?"

Dick explained about the letter and his ambition to prove

himself in Leeds.

"I've slacked all weekend and then with the family trouble, I haven't slept so well," Dick explained. "I just want to get back on course now."

"Well all you'll get like that is a strained muscle." The coach chided. Dick wasn't standing still, he started his exercises immediately; running on the spot, touching his toes etc. During the long sprint after he left everyone standing.

"If Dick keeps this up he's odds on for selection for the '24 Olympics." Laurie said to Harry. Both had given up but Dick was still sprinting.

"It's like he's got a fire in him tonight." Harry agreed.

"But please don't mention the Olympics. If he gets fired up like this for a local derby in Leeds, I dread to think what he would be like if he thought he was to run against the world!"
It was the talk of the bar later.

"Well Dick, you're a Yorkshire tyke now are you?" One of the team teased. "No wonder your so stingy about buying your round."

"You know the Yorkshire saying, don't you George?" Dick asked. "Hear all, see all, say nowt. Take all, supp all, pay nowt and if thee does owt for nowt, do it for thee sen. So hurry up and get the ale in, you wouldn't like me to break with the tradition would you?"

Dick spent the whole of August training hard at every opportunity. It had been an epic year for him. He had already won the district championships at 100, 220, 440 and 880 yards.

The newspapers had proclaimed it as a gallant achievement, "a record which I doubt will ever be beaten", the "Evening World" reporter, Mercury had later called it. Dick may not have run for England yet but now he was running for Yorkshire, not even his father could deny that he was a champion now.

Bank Holiday Monday arrived and he set off, with Harry and the beautiful Eva. Dick had to admit that she was a lovely girl, both in looks and nature. Harry had introduced him to her a few days after he left home. He actually brought her to the Johnsons' on the following Saturday morning. It was a beautiful day and they had decided to walk down to the beach for a picnic. Dick had declined to join them but had agreed to find them later in the day. Mrs Johnson had invited them to return and take tea later. Despite their protestation that they did not wish to inconvenience her, she insisted and the tea party was duly arranged.

Mrs Johnson had exceeded her usual brilliance. Having baked all afternoon, the dining room table almost groaned under the weight of home made pies, cakes, and sandwiches. Dick offered to pay something for the banquet but she would not hear of it.

"I get a real thrill from seeing people enjoy what I've cooked. I just wish my Jack would bring a young lady home. I would really show off then." She sighed. "Too much like you, if it's not made of wood or wearing spikes he doesn't want to know!"

Dick laughed. "I don't think Jack will escape the young ladies' attentions much longer," he confided. "There is a very attractive sister of one of the club members who can't take her eyes off him."

"Would you run round and invite her to tea?" Mrs Johnson pleaded.

"Mrs Johnson!" Dick feigned shock. "That would be highly improper." Jack walked in at that point.

"Why is everyone looking at me?" He asked innocently.

"Your Mam would like you to invite Daphne Foster to tea." Dick joked.

"Oh I never said any such thing." Mrs Johnson scurried out of the room, turning bright scarlet.

"Dick, that was really unfair." Harry scolded, but none of them could help laughing. Still it must have got Jack thinking because at the very next meeting of the Harriers Jack asked Daphne's brother if they could be introduced. Within two weeks Mrs Johnson had her wish and yet another tea party was arranged, Daphne being the guest of honour. Things looked definitely promising. Jack had even missed two Harriers meetings to walk out with her, and he had taken her to see Charlie Chaplin in "The Kid" at "The Palace". Dick had never known Jack to visit a picture house before.

Jack and Daphne also insisted on accompanying Dick on the outing to Leeds. It was quite a merry party. Dick was almost sorry to leave them all, when it was time for him to join his relay team members. This feeling soon left him as he entered the dressing room and was greeted heartily by the other athletes.

"We have read a lot about your achievements," one of the lads said. "We are very honoured that you have come to help us today. We've no doubt now that the opposition will be left well behind."

Dick felt somewhat embarrassed by this welcome.

"It's me that's honoured lads. By accepting me in your team you have fulfilled one of my dearest wishes. To run for Yorkshire. Now my next ambition is to run for England." Dick explained, "so come on, lets give it all we've got today. I need this medal, it will not only be another feather in my cap, it will go a long way to getting my name noticed where it counts."

Even though it was little more than a local derby, there was a big crowd at Leeds on that warm September day. The race did go as well as expected and Dick took home the gold relay race medal that he so desired. His medal collection was growing fast, but this was special, this was a Yorkshire medal!

After the race their group were all invited to join in the teams celebrations. It looked like it was shaping up to be quite a party. Regrettably they had to leave at 6 o'clock, to catch the last train home. After all, they all had work to go to next day!.

It had been a very special day and, as Dick turned into the Johnsons' gate later that evening, he couldn't help but feel that life had just taken an upward turn. Nothing could improve the way that he felt right at that minute.

Just then the door opened and Dick heard a sharp bark before being hit by a wriggling tornado.

"Lady, where on earth have you come from?" Dick laughed as he struggled with the excited bundle.

"Oh, I heard she was missing her master, so I persuaded her owners to let me have her." Mrs Johnson smiled from the doorway. "Hurry up now, your tea is getting cold!"

Chapter 9

Autumn started to set in very shortly after "The Wars of the Roses", as Dick affectionately called his first Yorkshire V Lancashire competition. The training continued, Dick had never been one for letting a little frost or rain hold him back.

Nights were cosy at the Johnsons'. Huge fires in the kitchen and parlour, the heavy curtains drawn against any draughts. Jack would get his wireless going and this became the focal point of the evening's entertainment. Early in December that year the BBC started broadcasting the daily news and it became a tradition for the whole household, which very often included Daphne now, to cluster around the set, after their evening meal to listen to the happenings of the day.

Dick was particularly interested in a report that a young English archaeologist, named Howard Carter had discovered the tomb of an Egyptian king, Tutankhamen. The tomb had never been robbed and the treasures that Carter uncovered were spectacular.

"I would really have loved to be there, when they opened the tomb." Dick said, as they listened to a report of the opening, a few weeks earlier.

"It would smell dreadfully and be full of dust and creepy crawlies." Daphne shuddered. "Even the young king's preserved body was there. How spooky, an eighteen year old, who died 2,400 years ago. They think it might even be cursed. Oh I just can't bear to listen, please turn it off!"

"Perhaps we should take a turn in the garden," Jack laughed, "and leave Dick to the gruesome commentary! I trust you won't be cursed just for listening Dick?"

"It is very cold outside, remember your wrap Daphne." Mrs Johnson called after them.

"I've no doubt Jack will keep her warm." Dick smiled..

There was no doubt that these evenings were very pleasant and Dick definitely felt that he had finally found a true "home".

Christmas came and went. He had thought that he would miss his family but the Johnsons insisted that he share Christmas Day with them. Mrs Johnson had even knitted him a sweater. The goose was the best he had ever tasted. They played silly games, sang carols round the piano and drank far too much mulled wine. Jack had bought him some excellent cigars and as he was enjoying one of these, with a final glass of the spicy warm drink, when he suddenly realised that he had not given his mother and father a second thought all day. He really hoped that the day had gone well for Harry though.

He had met Harry on their usual circuit first thing in the morning. He had been glad to give him a Christmas hug and give him the bottle that he had bought. Harry's favourite brandy. Mrs Johnson has beautifully wrapped it the evening before. Harry had a special present for him, not gift wrapped but carefully chosen.

"It's for the Olympics," he said, as he handed Dick the plain black case. Dick opened this to reveal a silver trowel, carefully engraved "To Dick, the winner. Merry Christmas, Harry"

Dick had felt a lump in his throat. He could hardly find the words to thank him properly.

"My bottle seems rather lacking in thought. Oh Harry. I will really treasure this." A sob caught in his throat. "It's only eighteen months before the next Olympics though, and I'm not even running for England yet. Don't hold your breath. A Northern lad like me will never be selected, but thanks for this and the faith you have in me." Dick ran off. After all grown men don't cry and he had felt very near to it.

1923 was a very busy year for Dick. He trained more intensely than before. The Olympics were to be held in Paris in July 1924 and he was now burning with a determination to be part of the England team. He listened carefully to the sports reports on the wireless. There were many good runners, Toms, Butler, Abrahams and Liddell were names that started to appear in broadcasts and on the newsreels on the picture houses. He was sure he could match their times and he had the added joy of knowing that Abrahams and Liddell both specialised in 100m, not 440m, his preferred distance.

A letter arrived in April inviting him to run for the Amateur Athletics Association. Mrs Johnson was glued to the radio, listening to the preparations for the wedding of the Duke of York to Lady Elizabeth Bowes-Lyon, to be held in Westminster Abbey on the 26th. Dick was once again full of excitement.

"I am really going to run for England this year Mrs Johnson." He waved the letter under her nose.

"Very nice dear. Will you be in London in time for the wedding?" She asked.

"No, I'm running at the end of June," he replied, a little crestfallen. Mrs Johnson could never understand how important his running was. Jack and his other friends were very pleased for him however, and their enthusiasm more than made up for Mrs Johnson's apathy.

"This is the start Dick. I told you." Harry was delighted.

"I won't be able to come to Stamford Bridge this time though. I'm getting married in June."

All thoughts of running were temporarily forgotten. Dick clapped Harry on the back.

"You kept that quiet," he cried. "Congratulations, but what date, I don't want to miss that?"

Fortunately the wedding was a week after the race. Dick represented his country as part of the relay event and counted well for his team. He did not have time to enjoy the celebrations afterwards, as he was in a hurry to return for his brother's big day. Harry insisted that Dick was his best man despite his father's objections. Dick had offered to stay away from the occasion, to avoid problems, but neither Harry nor Eva would agree to this.

The weather was beautiful on the morning of the wedding. It was to be held in St.Paul's church, with the wedding supper being held in the new house in Hutton Avenue. Dick did not know what to expect. He had not set eyes on his mother or father since the previous July when he had left so hurriedly.

He arrived early at the church. Mrs Johnson, Jack and Daphne went with him. He therefore did not see his mother and father arrive. Harry stood beside him and the ceremony went well. They had even hired a photographer to record the occasion. Father just ignored him afterwards but Martha and Winifred dashed to see him at the first opportunity.

"I've missed you so much Dick." Winifred said, throwing her arms around him. "Your father has promised not to mention the incident today. He says he will never forgive you but I am allowed to contact you if I wish. He has heard that you ran for England. We even saw your team on the picture house."

"Hang on a minute." Dick held her away. "I didn't do anything wrong, remember. Father was the scoundrel who was mistreating you. Let me get this right. He likes having a son on the newsreels, presumably because he can brag to his friends about me, so you can talk to me and he can acknowledge me, but I'm still not fit to be received in his circle! Well just forget it!" Dick turned on his heels and started striding away.

Martha caught him up. She quickly reminded him that it was his brother and his new wife that counted today.

"Surely Master Dick," she pleaded, "you won't wreck your brother's wedding day? That temper of yours, you always had to be right! Think of the young ones, it's their big day."

"You're right Martha." Dick calmed down. "Just keep Mother away from me."

Martha changed the subject quickly. The photographs being completed, the party walked round to the house for an "adequate" meal. Dick sat with Mrs Johnson.

"Food is not up to your standard," he whispered. "I bet Jack's spread puts this to shame."

"Is Jack getting married?" Mrs Johnson asked eagerly. "Has he said anything to you?"

"No he hasn't, but perhaps this will give him ideas." Dick winked, his eyes twinkling with mischief. "Hey, Jack, when is your big day?" Dick shouted across the table. "Your mother needs to make the cake well in advance you know?" Daphne blushed.

"You need talk Dick," Jack laughed. " You've been living with us for almost a year now, and I haven't so much as seen you pass the time of day with a young lady. Isn't it time you ran a little less and talked a little more?"

"Oh I've done plenty of talking," Dick replied. "I was talking to Harry Barclay last week and he has told me that, if I win the Northern Counties 440 yards title again this year, I will almost certainly be in with a chance of selection for the 400 metres in the Paris Olympics. Even if I don't get selected for that, I will almost certainly earn a place on the British team with Liddell, Butler and Toms. I met those men last week Jack. We'd be unstoppable!"

"Well you've certainly kept all that quiet," exclaimed Harry, who had come up during the conversation.

"I thought you would have other things on your mind," Dick explained. "But I am almost assured of a place on the team now. Let's face it, the Northern Counties is in the bag. I've won it twice already and I wasn't as fast during the last two years as I am now. Just keep tuned into that wireless. My name will be on there a lot in the next couple of years."

"Did you meet Abrahams down at the meeting last week. They say he's a nice chap. Probably even faster than Liddell?" Jack asked.

"No, he seems to be having trouble getting selected," Dick explained. "Apparently he is Jewish and, even though no-one is admitting it, it's even harder to get noticed if you're a Jew, than it is if you are from pit-yakker country, like me. I met Liddell though. He is certainly fast and fit but I can't stomach the man myself. He is so full of self righteous bunkum, sorry ladies, but he affected me that way. What an arrogant man! It's a good job he is the best, I can't imagine anyone giving him the time of day, if he wasn't. Of course he is a Minister of the Church of Scotland, so I suppose you can expect him to be a bit pompous and I have to admit, he's an excellent athlete. I will actually be glad that he'll be on the relay team, we would be a little bit weak without him."

"What's all this athletics talk?" Eva scolded, as she approached the group. "Not allowed today. Come on Dick, let's do a duet on the piano."

The party was quite lively after that and Dick managed to avoid further confrontation with his family. His sisters were polite but cool towards him. Martha did her best to be as friendly as possible and to make allowances for her mistress.

Dick let it all wash over him and excused himself, once all the pleasantries had finished. He could not wait to pound the roads again and purge himself, once more, of a family he preferred to forget.

Dick's confidence in his abilities were not misplaced. He did, for the third time, retain the Northern Counties Championship. That summer was a very busy one. Dick entered everything possible, local derbies, sports days, galas etc. Rarely beaten, always entering any distance from 100 to 880 yards. His stamina became almost legendary and he pushed himself to his limit on every occasion, but his speed could never quite match up to Liddell.

The Autumn came again and Dick came home one evening sweating profusely but shivering violently. He assumed he had a chill. Mrs Johnson ordered him to bed and gave him an infusion of tea made from the feverfew plants that she grew in her garden, just for treating such ailments.

Dick deteriorated during the night. The bed was ringing wet and he started rambling, talking to someone called John and shouting for Harry. Mrs Johnson sent for the doctor. Jack said it didn't matter what he charged, he would pay, if Dick couldn't.

The doctor was confused by the symptoms. It certainly was not the flu or any chill he had ever experienced. Mrs Johnson remembered that he had left the merchant navy because of malaria.

"I think he did say that he had been warned that it could recur," she explained to the doctor, "but he has never had any trouble and that must have been four years ago. He is usually so fit."

The doctor was a keen sports follower and knew of Dick's summer achievements.

"He has probably pushed himself too hard. These tropical diseases are so difficult. We just do not have anything to treat them with. Just keep bathing him and pray." He left, explaining that hospitals in this country were not equipped to handle such cases.

"Wonderful!" Jack was disgusted. "Modern science fails again".

Jack and his mother tended Dick carefully for several days and eventually the fever diminished. Harry and Eva came to help as often as they could. Even Martha managed to become a regular visitor.

The doctor did call from time to time and recommended a long rest to complete the recovery. Dick thought it was about time he returned to the Dales. The problem was, father now virtually owned the cottage. It was still legally grandfather's but, as the old man had no love of the Dales, he had given the keys and the deeds to Richard. Richard had not agreed to Harry's request to loan the keys to Dick for a few weeks.

"Even father knows that John wanted me to have that cottage," Dick pointed out to Harry. "Surely he can't object to me using the place for two or three weeks. No-one ever goes up there anyway, do they?"

"Not really," agreed Harry. "Eva and I use it occasionally, but you know father's attitude towards you. He did agreed to Martha visiting and Mother even called when you were very ill, but he's being stubborn about this. I don't know what to do. I could get the key and you could go without his permission, I suppose."

"Buggar that. I'll not stoop to that." Dick felt too weak to argue any further. "Just tell him to keep it and I hope he rots in Hell!" He sighed, before drifting back to sleep.

Harry and Eva had an idea. They had a run up to the cottage that weekend, and explained the problem to some of the farmers.

Many of them followed Dick's career, especially since the "phantom" episode, several years earlier. They soon came up with the offer of a cottage in Gunnerside, "Debra Cottage". It was a tiny doll's house of a cottage. Almost built into the bridge, it was constructed from huge grey stones, with walls at least two feet thick. It even shared it's entrance yard with the King's Head. Couldn't be better situated. It was basic, one up and one down, with a tiny kitchen under the stairs. Harry didn't doubt that Dick would love it. With the soothing sound of the river just outside and the pub, literally within falling distance of the front door. No-one was living there at present and the farmer who owned it was more than happy to have it used for a few weeks, for a very small fee.

Harry accepted the place immediately and couldn't wait to

tell Dick what he had found.

Dick was rather annoyed. "You don't understand Harry, John got father to promise that the cottage would pass to me. Father has no right to refuse me admission to my own place. I do appreciate your efforts but I can't help but think that you are sucking up to Father by shipping me to another accommodation."

"Oh hell Dick! It's alright for you, just lying there, expecting me to fight your battles. I've done my best. Eva even got the farmer to let her in to clean this place out. It was an old shepherd who used to live there and it wasn't exactly savoury. You aren't just making things awkward for me, you are belittling her efforts. Well fine, if that's how you feel, do your own dirty work." Harry turned on his heel and started to march out of the room.

"I'm sorry Harry, don't go," Dick pleaded. "I do appreciate your efforts and I will go to this "Debra Cottage", but I will not let this rest. Father is not depriving me of my memories of John and I will not let him ignore John's wishes. I just need to get my health back first."

Debra Cottage proved to be perfect for Dick. Right in the centre of the village, handy for eggs and milk from the farms and, as Harry had said, within falling distance of the pub. Most of all, a little path led down to the Swale where Dick could fish, watch the wildlife and, most precious of all, watch the sun as it rose, or set, behind the wonderful mountains. Once again Dick found the peace and tranquillity that only the Dales could truly provide.

Chapter 10

Following doctor's orders, Dick refrained from training for the first week. Instead he explored the Moors with Lady. He had read of first century Britons who had dwelt on these Moors. Their circular dwellings, made of stone or timber, hollowed out in the earth then rising to conical roofs of thatch or turf. The idea of these peoples, surviving the worst of winters, high on the highest, wind swept Moors, fascinated him. The farmers told him of many earthworks and barrows throughout the area and Dick now took time to investigate. He was surprised how easy they were to spot and he spent many hours sitting, smoking his pipe and listening to the "Curly, curly, curly" song of the curlews, while sheltering from the wind in the hollows left by these ancient farmers. It was easy to imagine the smells of the skins drying and the smoke curling around the homesteads before escaping through a hole in the centre of the roof. The peoples had been conquered by the Romans. Dick even found the earthworks relating to a Roman Fort, Maiden Castle, on the Moors above Low Row.

Mist started to roll in as Dick started his trek back to the cottage. He shuddered, remembering the many ghost stories that John had told him many years before. He almost thought that he could hear the screams of the women and children as the Romans attacked. He quickened his pace, very pleased to see the village lights shining through the gloom below. The pub had never been more welcoming. Dick made very sure that he came down from the Moors much earlier after that!

Their walks certainly soon put life back into Dick but he also noticed that Lady seemed to enjoy the gentler pace. She was old now and when, at the start of the second week, Dick found himself back into full training, Lady seemed to prefer to stay curled up by the fire. One day, on his return from an early morning sprint Dick found that he could not wake her.

"Oh Lady, how could you leave me as well?" Dick could not hold back the tears. "At least you had one last visit to the Dales, and now you need never leave your favourite haunts again!" Dick buried Lady high on the moors, beneath the heather that had been her favourite bed.

Dick sadly returned home and threw himself into his work. His job was even more important now that his running was taking him further afield. Athletes normally had to cover their own expenses, and Dick was no exception. He therefore kept his sick leave to a minimum. In any case the Dales seemed empty without Lady.

1923 ended on a wild note. The Johnsons had a small New Year Party. Big Ben's chimes were to be broadcast by the BBC at midnight, so all the friends gathered to listen to this new event. Daphne insisted that they must all try the new dance craze, The Charleston, first introduced by a musical "Runnin' Wild". Dick soon got the hang of the frantic arm movements and sidekicks but Jack didn't fair so well, finally crashing into Harry and sending half the party sprawling in a heap. Dick could not remember when he had laughed so much.

After the Big Ben's chimes had stuck midnight they all crossed hands and sang Auld Lang Syne. Harry proposed a toast, "May 1924 see a wedding for Daphne and Mrs Johnson, I'm not hinting Jack, you understand! A new home for Eva and me, and a gold Olympic medal for Dick!"

"Hear, hear!" They all cheered as they emptied their glasses.

"Alright," Jack laughed, falling on one knee, "Daphne will you consent to be my wife? This will be subject to your father's permission being correctly sought, of course."

Daphne didn't get time to answer. Mrs Johnson let out a loud cheer. "You had better accept," she instructed Daphne, "I'm not getting any younger and I need grandchildren before I get too old to enjoy them."

"That's settled then," replied Daphne. "I would not dare to go against my future mother-in-law's wishes."

Dick and Jack both kissed Daphne and just about shook Jack's hand off. Everyone was so delighted. The dancing started again and this time it didn't seem to matter whether they got it right. The party continued into the early hours. Neighbours joined in, bringing in the traditional offerings; a new coin for wealth, evergreen for health, a piece of coal for continued warmth and food to ensure that no-one went hungry during the year. Dick was sure that, as long as Mrs Johnson was running the home, none of their household would ever want for the last two.

Full of perhaps a little too much warmth, Dick led a final toast: "To good friends!" He announced, as he slid into a chair.

Dick's training was intensified as the year progressed. He was sure that he now had the fastest time in the country over 440 yards.

"They just have to pick me," he insisted to Harry. "The letters are supposed to come out in May, that seems like forever." It was only April.

The bomb shell dropped very shortly afterwards. Dick had heard "unofficially" that he was definitely in line for the 1600 metres relay, and definitely "in with a chance" of the 400 metres. He accompanied Mrs Johnson to the picture house one evening. She was desperate to see Rudolph Valentino in "Blood and Sand", but Jack had promised to take Daphne and Mrs Johnson didn't like to intrude.

"I really can't go without an escort," she explained to Dick.

"I can't understand why you haven't got escorts queuing at the door," Dick insisted. However he did have a fancy to see what all the fuss was about, with this Valentino fellow, so he agreed to be her escort for that evening.

The newsreel featured Eric Liddell training for the 400 metres. The storyline was that Liddell had been informed that the preliminary for the 100 metres was to be held on a Sunday. He had changed his plans and was now determined to take the gold in the 400 metres. Abrahams was named as the probable 100 metre entrant.

Dick felt as though he had been kicked in the chest. His worst nightmare had come true. There was no way that he would be selected for the 400 metres now. Even he had to admit that Liddell was the obvious choice. Even in training he was passing Dick's fastest time over that distance. He felt that he could not breath. He excused himself from Mrs Johnson, explaining that he felt a little unwell. She was very concerned but he managed to persuade her that she must still enjoy the picture.

Once outside he just walked. He wasn't aware of the direction he took, or the distance covered. He was full of so many emotions; bitterness, anger, sorrow, disappointment. He suddenly just didn't want to have anything to do with athletics again. He had worked so hard and now a pompous preacher, with a university degree, had stolen his dreams because of his religious beliefs. What about considering his fellow man?

Dick didn't know how long he had been walking. It seemed late when he turned up outside Harry's home. He couldn't bring himself to knock but just collapsed on the step and sobbed. He knew he was wallowing in self pity but he didn't care.

Eva had been talking to a neighbour and found Dick on her return. She ran in to fetch Harry and together they brought Dick in and revived him with a small sherry. They did not question him, they knew he would tell them soon enough, what the problem was.

"I've wasted my time Harry." Dick said eventually. "All that training, all those championships and I'm not good enough. I'll never be good enough." His shoulders sagged and he sighed deeply.

Harry eventually got to the bottom of the matter. "That's just the race you weren't sure about anyway, you still have the relay!" He reminded Dick eagerly.

"To hell with the relay. That scoundrel will probably mess that up for me as well. Religion, who needs it!" Dick said furiously. Harry decided to let Dick alone. He would have to accept this in his own time, there was nothing he could say to help, especially with Dick in this mood. Eva made some tea and they let Dick talk when he wanted to, until he had calmed down.

Dick was back on the usual circuit the next morning. Harry had hung around the Peter Pan statue, having arrived ten minutes earlier than usual. He breathed a sigh of relief as he saw Dick approaching at his usual speed.

"Morning Harry," greeted Dick cheerfully. "Beautiful Spring morning isn't it?"

"I could kill you!" Harry exclaimed "I've been worried sick all night about you, and here you are, fresh as a daisy."

"Well it's down to you and Eva. You were right. I never really did think I would be good enough for an individual event. I guess I just hoped too much. I do still have the relay and I'm almost certain of selection for that, but not if I let the training slip, so come on, get a step on there." He laughed and ran off. Harry just looked after him shaking his head. That was one thing he always admired about Dick. He took things on the chin and felt them deeply but, once he had accepted what had happened, he just shook himself off and got on with it. "Good luck to you Dick." Harry thought. "You'll get the 1928 event, I'm sure."

Dick had not got over it as much as his appearance would indicate, but he had accepted the disappointment. One good thing had come from Liddell declining the 100 metres, Abrahams was now the only possible alternative and Dick was sure he was a better chap for that distance anyway. At least it made him feel better to consider it from that point of view.

The hoped for letter arrived at the beginning of June, dated 30th May1924. It started:

"I am instructed by the General Olympic Committee to advise you that you have been provisionally selected to represent Great Britain at the Vlllth Olympiad, to be held in Paris from 5th to 13th July next ... It is proposed to assemble the team as from the 28th June, possibly at Uxbridge, to enable the Coach to get into touch and give final advice, as well as to enable the various representatives to meet and become known to each other and thus go over as a united party and engender "esprit de corps."

The letter went on to request measurements for the uniform and three photographs for identification cards etc. It also pointed out that final selections still had to be made. At the foot of the letter were listed the events for which Dick had been selected. The typed post script said :

"400 metres.,   1600 metres Relay.,"

Dick did not allow himself to look at this too closely. He was not deluding himself into the belief that he would take preference for this event over Liddell!

Dick passed the letter around the breakfast table. He was bursting with excitement but managed to keep a straight face as he handed it across to Jack.

"Well done Dick, you've done it!" Jack was delighted.

"What, what?" asked Mrs Johnson, "Let me see". Jack passed the letter across.

"It says at the bottom that you are running the 400 metres Dick." Mrs Johnson pointed out. "See, they do know you are as good as that Mr Liddell".

Dick laughed. "Not exactly," he explained. "They do have to pick more than one for the events if possible. There will be heats before final selection and, of course, people do fall ill etc."

"Well then, he could fall ill, with a bit of luck." Replied Mrs Johnson folding her arms firmly across her ample bosom.

"I really don't think we should wish that on him," Dick replied. "After all, he is a preacher and has friends in very high places." He turned his eyes upwards. "Still he is the best and should take the gold for Britain. I'm not sure that I would have been good enough to beat Fitch, from the USA. Anyway, if I'm honest, Guy Butler also runs the same distance and he has beaten my time over that distance. He will be in our relay team. He's a grand fellow. I wouldn't mind betting that he has been selected for the heats over that distance as well. I will give it my best shot but I am determined not to worry about that. It's the relay that I'm building my hopes on. Our team should consist of myself, Liddell, Butler and Toms. There just isn't a choice on that, as far as I can see. There is another man called Renwick, but he really is nowhere near fast enough. I dread to think what would happen if one of us fell out of that line up!"

The telephone rang and Mrs Johnson rushed to answer it. Jack had only recently had it installed and she was very nervous when she first picked it up. Her determination to conquer her fears was shown by her insistence on answering it first, every time.

"Who is speaking please?" She asked in a very trembly voice.

"Yes Mr Ripley is a guest at this residence." She beckoned to

Dick. "Who is it?" he mouthed to her. She put down the receiver.

"A Mr Toms wants to talk to you," she answered urgently. "Hurry up, it's long distance and must be costing a fortune.

"Ripley here. It's a pleasure to hear from you Mr Toms. I have just been telling my friends that our team will slaughter those American fellows." Dick was laughing but the smile quickly faded. "Tell me that this is a bad joke. I haven't read anything in the papers and there was plenty enough about the 400 metres."

Dick paused to listen. "Well we will have to see what happens when we all meet up on the 20th and 21st. for the final selections. Surely he can't let the whole team down?" Dick listened for a while longer, the others trying very hard to signal for information but Dick ignored them. "Well thanks for telling me. It is a shock, I'm going to need a few days to accept that this is happening. See you on the 20th." He returned the speaker to the cradle and sat down with a thud. He stared almost uncomprehendingly around. His eyes stopped at Jack.

"Why?" He asked. "What type of person can kick three team mates out of the chance of a gold medal, whilst making sure that his own is safely in the bag, and then insist that he is doing it in the name of God?"

Jack didn't have a clue what he was talking about, but it was very clear that he was very upset.

"What's happening Dick?" He asked gently.

"Liddell has dropped out of the relay team. Guess what? Dick snarled bitterly. "The bloody heats for that are on a Sunday as well. The press and news people haven't considered that worth mentioning. How come Liddell has found out all these dates when the rest of us don't even know if we've definitely been selected yet? Has a bloody phone line direct to God I suppose!" Dick rose quickly and left the room, muttering an apology to Mrs. Johnson as he left. His dream of a gold had once more been dashed and once again, by the same man!

Chapter   11

As Dick left the Johnsons' home and headed for work his feelings were mixed. Yes, he was angry and upset, but even his disappointment could not totally overshadow his excitement at being selected to run for his country in Paris. His thoughts were in turmoil. At that moment he hated Liddell, that could not be denied, but he had less than three weeks before he left to join the team and they would have the chance to beat the world. Butler and Toms were excellent chaps. He had met Renwick at Stamford Bridge last year and he seemed to be a good chap too, he had a lot of heart but hadn't learn to pace himself right. Perhaps since last year he had improved. Anyway the great Sam Mussabini was to coach them beforehand. Perhaps he could weld them into a gold standard team without Liddell. Yes, perhaps they could save the bacon after all!

Dick felt the spring come back into his step. To hell with Liddell, he thought, we can do it! Then he giggled to himself. Perhaps "Hell" wasn't an appropriate place to wish the man to, in the circumstances, but he wasn't the only decent runner in Britain and Dick and the other chaps would show him!

Life was quite hectic over the next few days. Dick went to his tailor to have a new suit made and to obtain all the measurements required by the firm of outfitters for his Olympic uniform. He had his photograph taken and made all his travel arrangements.

There was not just the travel to Uxbridge, the whole of July was to be hectic. First the Championships at Stamford Bridge on the 20th.and 21st., where the final selections were to take place, then Uxbridge and departure for Paris on July 2nd. He was determined to return home in time for the Northumberland and Durham Championships in Darlington on the 17th and then he was to return to Wembley to run for England again, this time in the British Empire Games on the 19th July.

Making sure he had all his travel arrangements co-ordinated, and his accommodation arranged, took up quite some time. His training was even more important now that he was determined to show Liddell that he wasn't the only decent runner in Britain and he still had to work everyday. After all, this all had to be funded somehow! There was certainly no time to dwell on what might have been.

The 19th June arrived in the blink of an eye. Once again Dick was at West Hartlepool station, waiting for the over night sleeper to Kings Cross. The station seemed to be crowded, indeed it was. Not only were the Johnsons there to see him off but Harry and Eva, Martha and his mother and the whole of the West Hartlepool Harriers! Dick could not believe the good wishes and good luck tokens he received. There was one person he had not expected to see though and he had mixed feelings as he saw him making his way through the crowd. His father stepped forward and offered his hand. Dick looked at it and momentarily felt the old anger. No nothing could spoil this day. Not even his father. He took the hand and shook it enthusiastically.

"We haven't always seen eye to eye Richard," his father said, "but I must tell you that you are making me very proud today." He handed him a five pound note. "I know all this is costing a great deal. I would be honoured if you would let me help."

"Thank you." It was all Dick could say, his immediate reaction was to hurl it right back. He didn't trust the man but why look a gift horse in the mouth. Five pounds was an awful lot of money and there was no doubt that it was useful right now. The Olympic committee did cover the Paris costs but all the other Championships were down to himself and it was just about wiping out his savings. Anyway he owed it to him. "We will have to have a talk on your return." His father's words cut into his thoughts. He stuffed the money into his wallet as he nodded his agreement.

The whistle blew and Dick climbed on board. This was it, the start of the most important journey of his life!

Chapter 12

The train journey was a long one and Dick found sleep elusive. He had hardly settled into a deep slumber when the steward knocked to bring breakfast.

"No need to rush Sir, you do have an hour before you must alight from the train." The steward assured him.

Dick felt like death. Today he had to run in the 440 yards and it would determine the final selections for Paris. Not the relay, that was tomorrow. He looked out of the window at the gloomy station. In the early morning light everywhere looked dismal and dirty. A fine rain was falling.

Dick had a feeling of impending doom. He hated a soft track and knew the lack of sleep would take it's toll.

"Why didn't I come down a day earlier and spend an extra night in a hotel?" He thought miserably. He knew why, funds had been dwindling and he had had to cut his cloth accordingly. Again he felt a bitterness towards his father. If that five pounds had been readily available earlier, it would have made the difference.

"Well, it will serve him right if I don't succeed. Then he'll have nothing to brag to his posh friends about." Dick thought resentfully.

The tea and toast, plus a good wash, soon revived Dick's spirits. This was the start of the day he had been working for for the last four years. "Never say die 'til your dead," an old sailor had once told him. He fastened his suitcase and left the train singing.

The heats at Stamford Bridge did not go well on the first day. Liddell did not even bother to turn up but was automatically selected. Butler beat Dick by seconds but those seconds cost Dick his selection for the 400 metres. He shook Butler's hand and congratulated him sincerely. Butler was a good man and deserved to win.

The next day went much better. The sun was shining and Dick's spirits were high as the relay race began. The relay team had been selected as Dick had predicted. Butler, Toms, Renwick and himself. They won easily but it was obvious that Renwick was not used to the distance. He had a lot of spirit but burnt himself out far too early.

"We've got a lot of work to do Dick." Guy Butler was agreeing with Dick in the hotel bar, after the selections had been announced. "It is still a great honour to be part of the team though and, even if we don't achieve a medal, I'll be glad to be part of it all. I must admit that my thoughts of the incredible Mr Liddell are not exactly Christian right now either!"

"What's all this talk of not obtaining a medal?" Harold Abrahams approached the bar with Sam Mussabini. Dick had not had the pleasure of meeting their new coach and was surprised to find a thin, wiry little man, with a white moustache and a shock of white hair protruding from beneath a grubby looking trilby. A huge cigar protruded from his lips. He was totally dwarfed by the immense size of Abrahams. Introductions were made.

"Well Mr.Ripley, I have heard of your stamina," Sam said, shaking his hand. "Perhaps you should concentrate on one or two races, instead of trying to win them all." He chuckled. "The pipe doesn't help either you know." He removed ash from his cigar.

"Would you recommend a cigar instead?" Dick asked cheekily. Sam laughed. The conversation swiftly moved on to the problems the team had, now that Liddell would not be part of it, and they all agreed that all was not lost. Perhaps they would not make the gold, but a medal would almost certainly be within their grasp.

"Aim for a gold anyway." Sam insisted. "The Americans are not gods and Liddell is not the only runner in Britain. I am surrounded by Britain's best right now. Think positively gentleman. We will mould you all into such a perfect team that no one will dare to beat you!"

It was a splendid evening. Sam certainly knew how to lift morale. Dick also discovered that he shared an interest in music with Abrahams, they both loved Chopin and Beethoven but also delighted in Gilbert and Sullivan. They soon found a piano and had the whole room singing extracts from "The Pirates of Penzance" and "The Mikado".

Next morning Sam gathered the whole team together for a de-briefing. Liddell had finally arrived. He had apologised for his tardiness, explaining that his church commitments had kept him in Edinburgh.

"I wonder if we would have had automatic selections if we hadn't turned up?" Butler whispered to Dick as they took their seats in the hotel conference room.

"We don't know the right people!" Dick remarked bitterly.

"That, whether you like to believe it or not, is more true than I care to admit," commented Sam Mussabini. Dick had not realised that he was standing near by and felt very embarrassed. Sam smiled. "Don't worry Mr Ripley, I'm no fool. Sometimes the club you belong to, or the people who support you, can be far more important than skill. It is not really the case with Mr Liddell. That gentleman has a very great talent, he's just got his wires badly crossed when it comes to considering his fellow men. Abrahams, however, has an equally great talent but has had tremendous problems in his selection. That is also down to religion, but in his case he follows the wrong one. It doesn't pay to be Jewish, even if you are a Cambridge don! You on the other hand, Mr Ripley, are not fettered by religion but by the place of your birth. Most of the main race meetings are in the South, you live in the industrial North. People down here see that as the back of beyond, still in the dark ages, full of morons and miners. Certainly not the area that gentlemen athletes are found."

Dick was rather annoyed by this. "This country could not survive without the "morons and miners" of the industrial North." He cut in. "We are not all uneducated and poverty stricken you know."

"Please don't take offence. I am not giving my opinion," Sam hastily pointed out, "merely explaining why you have not been running in more national competitions despite your obvious talents. You would do yourself a lot of good by joining the London

Polytechnic Harriers and running for them, rather than a small club like West Hartlepool Harriers. Unfortunately no-one has really heard of them and they do not carry much standing with the selectors. I have seen you run and I know what you can do. Your performance in the 400 the other day was not a true reflection of your abilities. With the right training and the right club behind you, I have no doubt whatsoever that, inside twelve months, you will be giving Mr Liddell a run for his money. Anyway we must get started. See me later, we must discuss this."

Dick could not help but feel excited. The great Sam Mussabini had seen him run and thought he had potential. Suddenly his recent disappointments didn't matter. He would enjoy this great occasion and accept that it was not the end for him, just the beginning. Who knows, perhaps this would just be a practice for the 1928 games!"

The training started in earnest. Sam was a hard task master but a great inspirer. He started with a moving picture show. He had compiled a moving dossier of all their techniques and explained, in depth, all their strengths and weaknesses. Using the moving film to illustrate his opinions was a stroke of genius. Seeing their faults on screen, no one could deny that they had room for improvement.

A discussion of their main opponents' attributes and how they could be counteracted also followed. Sam would not tolerate any defeatist talk. Yes the Americans were excellent athletes, with advanced training techniques but old Sam had a few good methods up his sleeve as well! The Americans were masters in public relations and the importance of presenting fearsome reputations.

"Don't be fooled by their seemingly godlike qualities." Sam stressed. "They have Hollywood and an awful lot of money behind them. We all know that Hollywood exists entirely on make believe, and the one thing that they have not got is the British spirit." Sam paused to emphasise his point. He pulled himself up to his full height. "We are the greatest nation on earth. No-one can match us for stamina, fortitude and determination under pressure." He swept his arm across the listeners. "You are the greatest athletes of that great nation. You are British and proud of it. Get out there and blow those Hollywood myths away!"

Dick felt so proud that he felt as though his heart would burst. The training that day went better than anyone's wildest dreams. Yes, Sam was a hard task master but no-one could deny that he was the best. Every man gave his all. Nor did the moment pass. The training covered a ten day period and Sam kept the spirits high throughout the entire time.

The team moved from Uxbridge to Broadstairs after a couple of days. It was Sam's idea. He wanted a beach to train on, as he felt that the sand and sea would help build up stamina.

Dick knew all about beach training, many of his weekends had been spent pounding the dunes from Seaton to The Blue Lagoon and he felt especially at home in the new environment. Some found it quite hard, but none complained.

Everyone enjoyed the evenings. Sam and the other Olympic officials knew only too well that the "esprit de corps", essential to keep the team together, was not just forged by hard work but also by hard play. The evenings started with an intense massage and a shower. After a few hours rest there was always an excellent dinner, followed by assorted outings. They were taken to the theatre, concerts, even moving picture shows.

The team was to embark for Paris on Wednesday the 2nd July. A grand ball was to be held in their honour on the Tuesday evening. The excitement was already mounting and the splendour of the evening was to be a wonderful culmination to the most unforgettable ten days of their lives. This was only the start!

"Well everyone, this is it." Sam stood up, after the superb banquet, before the dancing began. "The training is over and I want to thank every last one of you for your outstanding efforts." Sam paused to sip the excellent port. "I have every confidence that you will all bring honour and satisfaction to your country."

The Toastmaster stepped forward.

"Gentlemen, please raise your glasses." Everyone stood and glasses were held high.

"Gentlemen, the King!"

"The King!" The shout was full of excitement and jubilation, as the entire company acknowledged the majesty of the occasion.

To Dick the night was magical, like a dream. Chandeliers

twinkled above his head, an orchestra was striking up a waltz and everyone seemed to be chattering at once. All Dick could think was that this was it, it was really happening. He, Dick Ripley, was going to the Olympic games to represent his country. Thanks to Sam, he was even half convinced that they might get a medal. If they didn't it would not be for lack of team spirit, or for want of trying. The rest of the evening passed in a sort of trance. Dick remembered dancing with some very beautiful ladies, smoking some excellent Havana cigars and drinking some excellent champagne. (At least Guy and Harold told him that it was excellent, if he was honest, he would have preferred a decent pint!)

The evening ended at midnight and everyone drifted to their rooms. Very few slept that night, despite the champagne, and Dick was no exception. There was fear and there was tension but most of all there was excitement and pride. Sam had done his job well, the team were convinced that they could beat the world!

Chapter   13

There were some very weary team members embarking for Paris the next day. It wasn't a problem, there would be plenty of time to rest on the journey. Dick loved the sea. As the land disappeared far behind them Dick stood on the deck, enjoying the spray in his face and the rush of the waves along side the bow. His thoughts turned to his Merchant Navy days and he smiled, realising just how far he had come since then. He had thought that his world had ended when the malaria had forced his discharge. Dick laughed to himself. He knew that he would not be standing here now if things had gone as he wished back then.

"Every cloud has a silver lining." He mused to himself. "This is the life!"

"Never a truer word spoken." A voice said from nearby. Dick was quite startled. He hadn't realised that he had spoken his thoughts out loud. He looked around. Eric Liddell was the only person standing further down the deck, gazing out to sea. Most of the team were nursing their heads, or loosing their stomachs in their cabins, regretting the previous night's champagne.

Liddell had been at the ball, but had remained very much alone. He did not drink, smoke or dance. Dick almost felt sorry for him. There was no doubt that he had given his all during training, except on Sunday, of course, but still he was not quite one of them somehow.

Watching him now, Dick could understand why he was a minister. He had an air of tranquillity about him. Some kind of inner strength and determination, nothing to do with running. Dick smiled but Liddell merely raised his hat and turned away, walking off down the deck without a backward glance.

"I wonder how he got involved in all this anyway?" Dick mused.

"He is a rugby player you know, played for his university." Harold Abrahams had appeared by Dick's side. "They"ll take you away for talking to yourself you know." He laughed and punched Dick playfully on the shoulder. "Liddell was so fast on the field that he was persuaded to try a few races. He won them all!" Harold sighed. "I did think that I would run against him sooner or later but it never happened. We just don't mix in the same circles." Harold chuckled. "Probably just as well really, I'm not sure that I would have beaten him. There is no doubt that the man is fast!"

"I have no doubt that the man has many admirable qualities," Dick replied, "but I'm afraid that I am only human, and I find it very hard to reconcile the idea that he runs his life by Christian standards, but is prepared to totally disregard the feelings and efforts of the rest of the team, letting everyone down because of the date on the calendar." Dick took his pipe out and started packing the bowl furiously.

"He can't go against his principals. Bah!" Dick turned from the wind to light his pipe. He continued through clenched teeth as he struggled to get the tobacco to catch. "I won't say I dislike the man. No, a few moments ago I almost felt sorry for him. He seemed so solitary somehow. Anyway, I don't even know him. I can never forgive him though. I consider that he has destroyed my early career." He took a deep pull on his pipe. "We could have got a gold with him on our team. Now it's up to Guy and myself to pull the fat out of the pan." Dick paused and turned to look out to sea again. "Oh Sam says we're good enough and we will give it our best shot, but if we don't get a medal, that man is to blame. He won't care, he'll no doubt run off with at least one gold, one he doesn't have to share! He doesn't give a damn about Butler, Toms and myself." Dick gave up on the pipe and knocked it out angrily on the ship's rail."

"Principles! I know what I would like to do with his principles!"

"Come on Dick, don't let him spoil all this for you." Harold rested his hand on Dick's shoulder. "Let's get a beer and go and tickle some ivories. There's a splendid piano in the state room."

Dick's spirits quickly lightened. The rest of the trip was spent singing, laughing and telling silly jokes. The excited atmosphere was restored and Dick gave no more thought to Liddell.

Paris was an adventure to Dick, even without the added bonus of being part of the Olympic Team. Dick and the rest of the team were soon ensconced in their lodgings, within sight of the Columbes Stadium. The hotel was adequate but a far cry from the splendour of Broadstairs. Dick didn't care. He just couldn't wait to explore, but first duty called. Once they were settled they were summoned to a meeting. The Chairman of the British Olympic Team welcomed them and explained procedures and protocols.

"Firstly Gentlemen, remember at all times that you are ambassadors for Great Britain." His speech started as soon as they were all seated in the dining room. He continued

"Paris has many delights to offer and I hope that you will all take full advantage of the next ten days that you will spend in this wonderful city. All I ask is that your conduct is above reproach, particularly when you are wearing your splendid Olympic outfits. Please do not wear these openly until after the Opening Ceremony." The Chairman looked around the gathered assembly.

"You may or may not be aware that the Prince of Wales and Prince Henry will be joining the team on Saturday." He paused as a gasp and excited mutterings passed round the team. He held his hand up for silence. "One thing that you do not know is that His Highness has notified me that he intends to select four members of the team to accompany him on Monday, as his Guard of Honour, when he makes his official tour of Paris." He raised his hands again for silence as everyone appeared to start asking questions at once.

"It is no good asking who this will be. It is not yet known. All that I am sure of is that this will be a very great honour and the persons selected will be informed on Saturday evening."

"Well we have no chance." Dick whispered to Guy. "What's the betting Liddell is amongst the chosen few?" Guy just nodded and smiled in agreement.

"What an honour that would be though Dick." Guy added. "I think I would forego a medal to be one of those selected. That is really something to tell the grand children. Not only did I run in the Olympics, but HRH The Prince of Wales chose me to be part of his Guard of Honour!" He grinned shyly. "Well even us lesser mortals can dream!"

The next day saw not only the recommencement of their training but also their social life lifted to new heights. Friday night was a very special treat. The whole British team had been invited to the Folies-Bergere, as special guests of honour. Dick had heard that the presentations were unbelievable, although somewhat risqué. Certainly this was to be yet another memorable experience!

The team had a table right in front of the stage. The meal was excellent and the free flowing wine very soon removed any embarrassment that any of the lads felt when the curtains drew back to reveal a picture of loveliness. Several ladies posing, dressed as Greek goddesses. Their shimmering robes clinging to their very ample breasts and long curvy legs like cobwebs kissed by the morning dew. The scene was breathtaking and very beautiful. Although the costumes left very little to the imagination, the lads were silent, as though sharing a sacred moment.

Suddenly one of the lads rose to his feet clapping and very soon the whole team were clapping, whistling and shouting their admiration. Dick was silent. He only had eyes for one "handmaiden". A small redhead kneeling to the side of the main tableau. She was quite modestly dressed and carried an urn.

Dick gasped. He had never seen anyone more beautiful in his entire life. She turned her head towards him and her penetrating green eyes seemed to look right at him. The tableau remained totally still and Dick felt as though time had stopped. Then the centre ladies bowed their heads in acknowledgement of their audience and the curtains closed.

The applause was deafening, then Dick realised that he was on his feet shouting and clapping with the rest. It was not long before the curtains reopened, this time to a nautical theme. The ladies were mermaids, dressed only in brilliantly coloured fish tails, their long flowing locks interwoven with flowers and sea shells. Dick was disappointed that he could not see his redhead amongst them but he did not have to wait for long.

The curtains closed again and the orchestra struck up a lively number that Dick soon recognised as the "Galop" from "Orpheus and the Underworld". With a loud scream a long line of dancers ran onto the stage. They were dressed in multi-coloured, silk dresses with close-fitting bodices, nipped in at the waist and then flairing out over numerous petticoats. Before Dick had chance to catch his breath, the dancers were throwing themselves into a wild, high-kicking, skirt-whirling dance. Dick had read about the Can-Can but had never in his wildest dreams, imagined the excitement that it could generate. He felt as though he could hardly breath. Strange feelings were coursing through his body and, when dance had ended, he felt exhausted. Dick looked about and realised that his friends felt exactly the same. Their faces were glowing and many were loosening their collars. Throughout this excitement Dick could remember only one dancer. A redhead whose flashing eyes were matched only by the flashing highlights dancing on the skirt of her emerald silk dress.

As the evening came to a close the manager presented himself at their table.

"Pardon Messieurs." He bowed politely. "Would you gentlemen care to meet my dancers?" He smiled as everyone shouted acceptance at once and started rising to their feet. He raised his hands "Patience mes amis." He gave a sharp clap and the girls rushed from behind the curtains and started to greet the men, who by now had left their seats and were rushing forward excitedly. Dick stood back. He was a little afraid that his redhead would be plain, away from the clever lighting, or worse still, would make a beeline for one of the other men. He looked about but could not see her. Suddenly she came from behind the curtain and, to Dick's surprise and embarrassment, headed straight towards him. He need not have worried. She was breathtaking and her eyes seemed even more alive away from the lights. She approached him, smiling. Her skirts swishing with the motion of her hips.

"I am called Nanette and I am very pleased to meet such a world famous athlete." She held out her hand to Dick and he kissed it politely. He assumed that the speech was given under instruction, as her English was perfect. As he spoke very little French he was unsure how to reply.

"I am very pleased to meet you." Dick eventually replied, giving up her hand reluctantly. "I am afraid you must be confusing me with someone else." He continued, "I would hardly call myself a world famous athlete. My name is Richard but my friends call me Dick."

"Are you not a runner then?" Nanette asked. Her voice was very pretty, she spoke with only the hint of a French accent.

Dick quickly explained that he was a runner but not in the same league as Abrahams and Liddell.

"Your English is excellent." Dick couldn't help but comment.

"Ah, my mother was English." Nanette laughed. "She came to Paris for a holiday and fell in love with the city and my father! That is the magic of this city, you had better beware, many fall under her spell!" Dick felt that it was already too late to "beware". Very soon the two were in deep conversation and Dick asked if she could advise the places that he should not miss during his stay in the city.

"There are so many wonderful places, which shall I tell you?" Nanette thought for a moment. "Non, I can do better than that. I am not working tomorrow, as the whole of Paris will be at the Stadium for the opening ceremony. Perhaps after the festivities are completed I could show you a little of our wonderful city?" Nanette suggested. Everyone was starting to leave and Dick could not believe his ears. "Come on Dick, we're leaving." Guy shouted, pulling at Dick's sleeve as everyone was disappearing. Dick gathered up his hat and gloves.

"I will be delighted." He shouted back, "How will I find you?" Nanette blew a kiss.

"Don't worry, mon cherie. I will find you." She turned and ran back to the stage, laughing.

Dick hardly slept that night. He was no longer excited about the opening ceremony. He just wanted it to be finished so that he could see Nanette again.

The next day burst open to the sound of a song thrush just outside the window, heralding the new and glorious day. As Dick opened his eyes he could see the sun dancing through gaps in the heavy dark red, velvet curtains, breaking through the gloom to dispel the darkness of the night and start a bright and wonderful day.

Dick jumped out of bed with excitement. Everything started today, including his time with Nanette! Firstly though, the team was to meet to attend a service in Notre Dame Cathedral and Dick wanted to be extra smart for the occasion. This was their first public appearance in full Olympic uniform. He did not rush out to pound the streets in his running kit this morning, he had much more important matters to attend to. An hour and a half later Dick emerged from the bathroom sweet smelling and fully groomed, ready to face the most exciting day of his life!

Chapter 14

The service in Notre Dame was led by the Archbishop of Paris. He praised sport as a modern form of chivalry and told the competitors that they should be proud of the talents that God had given to them. He charged them to use their skills well, and to the best of their abilities. The sermon was very rousing but Dick's mind was elsewhere.

Finally the service closed with the Athletes' song and the "Te Deum". As they were leaving the Cathedral, Harold, Guy and some of the chaps fell into a conversation about the previous evening's entertainment and the gorgeous ladies they had met.

"I think I'm in love." Dick admitted. "I can't get Nanette out of my mind. I couldn't even sleep most of last night for thinking of her!"

"Probably not exactly love, old chap." Harold teased. "Be careful though, the ladies of the Moulin Rouge are not exactly ladies, if you know what I mean?" He nudged Dick and winked.

"Oh I don't think Nanette is one of those." Dick protested immediately.

"Well, perhaps not, but at the very least she is a dancer." Harold stopped teasing now and concern came into his voice. "These girls like to be seen with the rich and famous and right now we fit the bill. Take care Dick, whatever she is she is no lady you know." He laid his hand patiently on Dick's shoulder and squeezed it gently. "Have fun Dick but don't get too involved, we're here to run, remember?"

"Oh I know that," Dick replied. He was quite touched by his concern but wanted to make him understand. "I have worked too hard for this chance not to give it my all, but Nanette was not like the others. She has hair like a sunset on the mountains and eyes like emeralds," He sighed "I don't care about her breeding."

"Oh dear Dick, you are smitten, aren't you? Just as well we will only be here for a few days, and very busy for most of that time!" Harold clapped him on the back. "Come on we've got training to do."

Even Dick had to forget about Nanette during training and then the preparations for the Opening Ceremony. Despite his overwhelming attraction to Nanette, nothing could detract from the splendour of the occasion or the elation felt when marching through the stadium as part of the British team. The Prince of Wales and Prince Henry were sat with President Doumergue and Dick's pride was complete as His Royal Highness stood as their team passed the podium.

On returning to the dressing room after the ceremony, Dick heard that the Prince of Wales had invited the whole team to dinner that evening. They were to assemble, in full uniform, at a nearby hotel, at 7.30 for dinner at 8 o'clock.

"Great," Dick thought, "I can still see Nanette for a couple of hours before then!"

Nanette was waiting outside the Columbes Stadium. The crowds had long since disappeared and she must have been waiting a long time. She looked wonderful. Her clothes were the height of fashion. She was dressed in an almond green Crepalga tunic, decorated with silk braid to match and worn over a pleated under-dress of the same material. A large, elegant hat rested on her long red hair. As she stood before him Dick couldn't help but smile. Dressed as she was Nanette would easily pass for an elegant society lady.

"So much for your determination that she is a call girl, Harold." He thought to himself. "I wish you could see her now!"

Dick explained that he only had a couple of hours now, but, as his race was not until Sunday 13th, he hoped that he would find a lot more free time during the following week.

"Do not worry, mon cheri." Nanette laughed. "We have all the time in the world."

The pair explored the back streets of Paris, talking to the street artists in Montmartre, sipping stong bitter coffee outside the street cafes and enjoying the real side of Paris, behind the tourist areas. Dick had never enjoyed a lady's company so much before. They laughed and talked and the time passed in the blink of an eye. All too soon Dick was saying goodbye outside her apartment. She leaned forward to give him a swift kiss on the cheek.

"You must come in next week, when we have more time." Her eyes sparkled as she turned and blew a kiss before disappearing inside the door. Dick returned to his hotel on cloud nine. He did not even remember getting ready for the evening with the Prince until he descended into the lobby to join the others at 7.30.

Spirits were running high and the speculation was rife as to whom the Prince would select for his Guard of Honour.

The evening was very pleasant. The Prince had obviously done his homework and he chattered to every member of the team about their achievements, their hopes and aspirations, as well as their disappointments. Dick was surprised to find that he was fully aware of the relay teams' disappointment that Liddell would not be able to compete. "Liddell is a splendid athlete and I commend his principles." The Prince was speaking to Butler, Toms, Renwick and Dick. "However, whilst I applaud his commitment to his religion I feel that his team spirit, and commitment to his country, leave a lot to be desired." He paused to take a sip from the superb apperitif. "I actually admire you chaps for carrying on with such determination after such a set back. You deserve to win, but if you do not, I for one, will not belittle your efforts. It is a brave effort that you are making gentlemen, and that type of effort deserves some recognition." He paused and looked round the group." Gentlemen, I would be proud if you four would accompany me, on Monday, as the British part of my Guard of Honour, during my official duties in this lovely city."

The four were thunderstruck. Butler muttered thanks and the others quickly remembered their manners and followed suit. The Prince sat back, enjoying the effect his announcement had generated.

"Perhaps you would consult with my secretary concerning your duties, timetable etc." He then rose from his seat, smiled and walked away, leaving a sudden uproar of excited chatter behind him. Dick felt like a school boy who had just been told that he had been made head boy. The four were all talking at once. Harold rushed over to congratulate them and even Liddell shook their hands and seemed genuinely pleased for them. All thoughts of Nanette were temporarily forgotten. This was even more important!

"You've certainly got something to tell your grandchildren now Guy!" Dick laughed as they all shook each others' hands.

The Prince's secretary approached and presented each of them with a written agenda for the events on Monday. He informed them that a car would take them to Notre Dame early in the morning, so that they could be instructed in their duties before the Prince arrived. Basically they would simply stand to the side of the Prince during the ceremonies and form part of the Guard of Honour as he left each of the venues. Their duties would end at midday, when the Prince would join General Gourand, the Military Governor of Paris, for lunch at the new headquarters of the British Legion. This was situated at the Boulevard L'Annes, at the edge of the Bois de Boulogne. They would attend the Prince here, until he entered the building, then the car would return them to the Games.

The rest of the evening took on a dreamlike quality. The meal was a gastronomic delight and the superior French wines flowed freely. Harold resisted the wines though. He could not afford to run the risk of a hangover tomorrow as it was to be his big day. In the morning Abrahams was to represent Britain in the 100 metres. As the evening wore on his nerves began to show.

"I'll never beat the Americans, and what about the Fins? They have got some pretty swift chaps!" Harold said worriedly. Douglas Lowe, another team member, replied with a laugh.

"The two fast Fins are Paavo Nurmi and Ville Ritola and neither of them would even consider themselves warmed up on your distance." He raised his glass. "You have no competition Harold. I bet you ten shillings that you win Britain's first gold tomorrow."

"Get that in writing." Dick laughed. "You would win twice in one race then Harold." Dick's voice took on a serious note. "Seriously though, you, Liddell and Douglas here are our best hopes for gold, so you better just accept that you are going to win.

You haven't any choice in the matter!" He raised his glass.

"Gentlemen, to Harold!" He announced. They all stood up and raised their glasses towards Harold.

"Harold!" They said in unison. Harold was touched but he excused himself shortly afterwards. Liddell also left, but the rest remained until the early hours discussing tactics, rivals and prospects and just having a jolly good old time!

Sunday would see the start of the Games in earnest and though all were eagerly anticipating the event, they were petrified too. For many this would be their last chance to relax.

Harold was not alone with his pre-race nerves. This was it. The moment they had all been training for. The 1924 Paris Olympic Games were about to begin!

Chapter 15

The whole of the British team were there next day to cheer Harold on. The poor lad looked pale and Dick was not convinced that his early night had done any good. Who could sleep just before such a momentous occasion anyway?

The tension mounted as the runners used their shiny new trowels to prepare their starting blocks. The starting pistol sounded and they were off. It was all over in 10.6 seconds. Harold had not only taken the gold for Britain but had set an Olympic record into the bargain!

The team rushed onto the track to congratulate Harold and Douglas pushed a ten shilling note down his neck.

"Worth every penny." He grinned as he, and the rest of the team surrounded Abrahams.

What a start! The Prince himself came forward to shake Harold's hand and then they all stood to attention as the Olympic Band stuck up "God Save the King".

Dick felt that his chest would burst with the pride. One of their team had done it, others would certainly follow. Who knows, perhaps they could even pull the relay off after all. At that moment every team member was totally convinced hat they were the best and unbeatable. That win did more for morale than all Sam's lectures and training schedules!

The day turned into a full scale party. Dick felt quite guilty later that evening when he got ready for bed. What with the training first thing that morning, then the excitement of Harold's victory, followed by the impromptu party that lasted for most of the day, he had not given Nanette much thought. Now she came flooding back into his mind. As he drifted to sleep he could almost smell her perfume and feel the soft silkiness of her hair. His dreams were very pleasant that night and he awoke the next day full of excitement. Nothing to do with Nanette though, she had again been pushed back to the back of his mind. This time it was an appointment with HRH the Prince of Wales. Yes, this was it, today was to be the proudest day of his life!

After an early breakfast the car was waiting as promised. The teams' uniforms had been specially pressed and their shoes had been polished until they reflected the sun. They were well instructed long before the Prince's convoy approached Notre Dame. As the car approached they were ushered into position by the Prince's Aide. The Prince was accompanied by Prince Henry. Dick was surprised to see that he was dressed in Khaki, but he quickly realised that it was part of the Prince's way of acknowledging that one of the main points of today's events was to honour those who died for The British Empire in the Great War.

Dick was surprised to see such a large gathering outside the Cathedral. The crowd obviously consisted of British and French spectators, but also included many Allied officers, all in full dress uniform. Flags were flying everywhere. The whole scene was awe-inspiring. On the steps of Notre Dame the Prince met President Doumergue and the clergy of the cathedral. The team had been told that the Prince was to unveil a tablet commemorating those who gave their lives in the Great War. This tablet had been placed on a pillar in the corner of the south transept.

The party entered the church and proceeded up the central aisle until it stopped before the Union Jack veiling the tablet. Dick and his friends stood to either side of the tablet as the Prince stepped forward. A hush fell over the packed cathedral.

His Royal Highness lowered the flag and placed a spray of lilies against the pillar. He remained motionless, with head bent, until the great organ of the Cathedral broke the silence with the strains of the National anthem. Dick, once again, felt his chest ache with pride. He was trying to commit every little detail to memory, so that he could recount every moment to Mrs Johnson in his letter to home. The colours, the flowers, the tremendous atmosphere. He did not believe that he could ever explain this in words. He then tried to make a mental note of the words on the tablet. It had been erected by the Imperial War Commission, as representing the whole Empire. It bore the inscription:

"To the glory of God and to the memory of one million dead of the British Empire, who fell in the Great War, 1914 to 1918, and of whom the greater part rest in France."

"That includes you too John." Dick thought. He felt a lump in his throat. Now was not the time to allow himself such thoughts. "John would have been so proud of me now." He felt a tear start to escape down his cheek.

"Concentrate!" He told himself firmly. He looked above the inscription to where the arms of the United Kingdom had been placed, surrounded by the arms of various Dominions. Below the tablet other wreaths had been placed from the War Graves Commission, the British Army and the Ministry of Pensions.

Dick turned his attentions to those attending the Prince. All were decked in their finery and medals. They made a marvellous sight. Amongst those present were Lord Crewe, the British Ambassador, Lord Ypres, General Sir Fabian Ware and Generals Nollett, Mangin, Gouraud and De Castelrau.

It was soon time for the Prince to leave the cathedral and the team discretely left by the side aisles in order to re-form their Guard of Honour again, at the great doors of the cathedral.

A great cheer went up from the crowd as His Royal Highness emerged into the sunshine. The Garde Republicaine was drawn up in front of the steps and the Prince reviewed these splendid men before climbing into his car for the next venue. Dick could still hear the hearty cheers of the cosmopolitan crowd two streets away!

Their next stop was the Arc de Triomphe, where the Prince laid a wreath on the tomb of the Unknown Warrior. By now Dick was totally overawed by the whole event and people were starting to become a blur.

"You'll just have to read about it in the newspapers, Mrs Johnson." He thought to himself. "I'll never remember all this in a million years."

His Royal Highness next proceeded to Boulevard L'Annes, the final stage of the official tour. This part of the tour was to be informal but it was no less an impressive ceremony. Yet another large crowd was assembled outside, again giving proof of the Prince's popularity in Paris. Dick and his fellow team members formed part of a larger Guard of Honour drawn up in front of the building. They were accompanied by a band of French Industry.

The Prince was received on arrival by General Gourand, the Military Governor of France, who, in the name of the French Government, handed over five Army huts which were to form the headquarters of the British Legion in Paris. A gift from the French Ministry of War.

As the Prince and Prince Henry entered the building for lunch and the speeches etc. Dick and his friends were told that their duties were ended. They were returned to their hotel. Most of the other team members were having an impromptu game of cricket on the hotel lawn, whilst waiting for lunch to be served.

"Come on then." Guy said to Dick, quickly removing his jacket and tie. "Let us take this lot on. I quite fancy myself as a rival for Jack Hobbs!" Dick laughed. He loved cricket as much as the rest and greatly admired the legendary Mr.Hobbs. After all, it had only been in May last year that Mr Hobbs had scored his hundredth century in first class cricket. Right now though, Dick was eager to write home. He had to write to Mrs. Johnson about today's events before he forgot something.

"Good luck to you Guy, but cricket isn't high on my list of priorities at present. I'll join you at lunch." Dick shouted as he turned back into the hotel.

As Dick was handed his key at reception, he was also handed a note. He did not recognise the hand writing and hurriedly tore open the envelope. It was from Nanette. Dick's heart skipped a beat. She had called that morning and had heard of his "duties" with the Prince of Wales. She had hoped to see him, as she was not working at all today, but understood that he was not available. She suggested that he call at her apartment at 7.30 for dinner that evening. She advised that, if she did not hear from him she would expect him. She begged him to let her know if he was otherwise disposed. The note finished by hoping that Dick had not forgotten her in all the excitement of today's ceremonies.

Dick was delighted and hummed merrily as he returned to his

room. He had definitely not forgotten Nanette. True he had put her to the back of his mind but she was definitely at the fore front again now! Well he would write his letters, have lunch and then join the team to watch Douglas win the 800 metres this afternoon. (He was sure that Douglas would win). Then he would have plenty of time to bath and change before taking a stroll to Nanette's home in time for dinner. This week was certainly exceeding all his expectations!

Douglas Lowe did win another gold for Britain. He cleared the distance in 1:52.4, beating the Swiss competitor, Martin, comfortably. Dick and his friends were delighted to see that the United States, represented by Enck, could only manage a silver.

"See", Guy pointed out happily to the others, "these Americans aren't gods after all. Both Harold and Douglas have wiped the floor with them now! Eric only has to show Scholz how tomorrow, in the 200 metres, and we'll have them well and truly worried!"

"I'm afraid that 200 metres is not my best distance." Liddell commented, "but I will do my best. Britain is certainly not being disgraced by us in these games." He clapped Douglas on the back.

Once again the afternoon degenerated into an impromptu celebration, but Dick did not forget to excuse himself in time to change and prepare for his dinner with Nanette.

"Don't expect too much Dick." Harold whispered as Dick said his farewells. "Just enjoy yourself!" Dick gave a thumbs up sign as he headed back to the hotel.

It was a pleasant evening and Dick enjoyed the walk to Nanette's. The stroll gave him another opportunity to sample the many sights and sounds of Paris, and also time to calm down and collect his thoughts. He was full of excited anticipation but also very apprehensive. He found racing in the Olympics far less frightening than visiting a beautiful young lady in her home!

Dick had convinced himself that Nanette was a lady. Oh he knew that ladies did not dance and remove their clothing in public, even in a high class establishment like the Follies, but he was certain that Nanette had been driven to this by hard times, like some heroine in a novel. When he had left her outside her home on Saturday, he had only had eyes for her and had been in a hurry to get back to the hotel to prepare for the Prince's dinner. He was not prepared for the rather squalid rooming house that now confronted him as he arrived at the door. He wondered if he was mistaken and checked the address on the note. No, this was it. He knocked on the door and a young lad, dressed in rather dirty clothes, answered. Dick asked if Nanette was home. The boy just stared and uttered "Comment?"

Dick realised that he did not understand English. "Mademoiselle Nanette?" He tried. His own French was very limited. The boy just pointed up some rather dirty stairs and stood back to let Dick pass. Why did Dick get the feeling that the lad was used to gentlemen callers? He started to feel rather uneasy. Was Harold right after all? Nanette's voice broke into his thoughts.

"Just come up Dick." Her voice twinkled down the stairs. "I asked Claude to let you in. I don't always hear the door from up here."

Nanette had two rooms at the top of the building. One served as a bedroom and the other had a small table and chairs and a large sofa. It was shabby and dark, but spotlessly clean. The table was neatly laid with a white cloth and sparkling silver cutlery. There were two large wine goblets. They did not match, in fact they were very reminiscent of those used in the Follies. Dick felt annoyed with himself for even thinking that they may not have been obtained legally. He had to admit though, that again Harold had been right with his warnings, especially when he looked at Nanette. She wore an emerald green robe, similar to that worn by Mrs. Johnson when she was retiring. There was a marked difference though, this one was much more decorative, edged with feathers and fine lace. It was made from a very fine fabric. In fact when the light was behind it, as it was now, you could see right through it and there was very little beneath.

Dick's emotions were mixed. Initially he was disappointed. He had convinced himself that Harold had been mistaken in his assessment of Nanette. Now he knew the truth. Then he was excited and a little afraid. He had no real knowledge of women, perhaps a lady who was not lacking in experience was just what he needed! He decided to try and relax and just see what the evening held.

He was not disappointed. The meal was a simple salad, with the delicious French bread that Dick was growing to love. The wine was excellent and, after a few glasses he totally forgot his fears that Nanette was not quite a lady. It had not been long before Nanette had realised that Dick was not exactly a man of the world and she had been delighted.

"Oh mon cheri," she purred as she started to remove Dick's tie, "you must not look so afraid. I think it is a new and special experience that I will give you."

Dick started explain himself. "I've been a bit tied up in my running. I never had the time... ." Nanette stopped him by placing a finger on his lips. Slowly she peeled back her robe and let it slip from her shoulders. Her rounded breasts were now revealed, her nipples standing proud in anticipation. Dick forgot his fear as he reached forward to touch her. Nanette stopped his hand and reached forward to kiss him savagely before leading him to the bedroom...

As Dick walked back to the hotel later that night, he felt on top of the world. Well true, Nanette was probably not to be the love of his life, but she certainly knew how to make a lasting impression!

Dick slept well that night and was eager to get back into training first thing next morning. It was another beautiful day, and, as he was up early, he had a run through the streets before breakfast. He was surprised to see the American team already under instruction from their coach. He recognised most of their faces from newspapers and newsreels. They included Cockrane, Helffrich, MacDonald and Stevenson. The USA 4 x 400 metres relay team. They were certainly an impressive bunch and Dick felt himself doubting his own teams ability to beat them. He knew that, with Liddell, they would have stood a chance, without him, who knows?

Jackson Scholz was also there, training alongside Paddock. Dick knew they were both running against Liddell today and he really hoped that Eric would show them how. Their trainer was obviously not happy. He was positively ranting as he reminded them that Abrahams had beaten them already and that the honour of the USA was on their shoulders. They must not fail today!

"Well he's certainly giving them hell." Dick smiled to

himself. "I hope Eric has got his prayer mat out this morning. He'll need it."

When Dick went into breakfast the rest of the team were already assembled. The excitement was high, everyone convinced that today would see a third gold for Britain. The fact that the USA already had four was incidental.

"They have far more resources at their disposal." Douglas was saying. "Let us face the facts. We are all working lads, mostly financed by our own efforts. Oh I'm not suggesting that the Americans are not amateurs, just better supported than we are."

"There is no doubt that some of their training methods are different," Sam commented, "but that doesn't necessarily mean better. Let's just wait and see. Mr.Abrahams beat Mr.Sholz on Sunday, I don't see any reason why Mr Liddell can't do the same today!"

"Could we talk about something else please?" Eric pleaded."I really have not been pacing myself for the 200 metres, I have been working all out for the 400 metres on Saturday. How did your evening go with Nanette Dick?"

"Very well thank you, but I didn't realise that everyone knew about it!" He threw a dirty look at Guy and Harold.

"Don't worry old chap, we kept it quiet. There's only us, the Americans, the Finns and the Swedes know. Oh and the French of course." Harold teased.

"Well that just about covers the world. Thank you very much!" Grinned Dick turning very red.

Eric seemed very agitated on the track later. Dick actually felt a little sorry for him. Everyone expected Liddell to succeed. Abrahams, Butler, Lowe and himself were just expected to "do their best" but Liddell was the best and was treated accordingly. He was allowed no margin for error.

The runners assembled under starter's orders and a hush fell over the stadium. The starter's pistol fired and Jackson Scholz took off like a bat out of hell. He covered the distance in 21.6 seconds, with his team mate, Paddock, hot on his heels. Liddell lost something at the start and never recovered. He came in third. A Bronze. Still a good result but not what you would expect from the best!

The team was silent, they were devastated. Suddenly Bill Nichol, one of the 100 metre relay team members, ran out to congratulate Liddell and the rest of the team followed. A bronze was, after all, a good result. Liddell shook their hands but there was no joy on his face and he left the field as soon as he could.

The other team members enjoyed the rest of the day, despite their disappointment. They were to witness an unprecedented display of running by Paavo Nurmi, later to become known as the "Flying Finn". Running with a stopwatch on his wrist, Peerless Paavo captured the 1500 and 5000 metre finals within an hour of each other and set Olympic records in both.

Dick found a new hero, whom he watched closely throughout the rest of the games. Sure enough, two days later, Paavo blew away the rest of the field in the 10000 metre cross country. It was an unusually difficult course and the sun was blazing relentlessly but while other runners fell by the wayside, Paavo made a respectable time of 32:54.8 and won his third and fourth gold medals. (Finland having also won the team gold in the same event.)

Finally, just one day later, he led the Finns to victory in the 3000 metre team race, making a total of five gold medals.

His performance was the sensation of Paris, the only other athlete coming anywhere near his achievements was his team mate Ville Ritola, who also achieved four gold medals for Finland.

Chapter 16

Dick was starting to feel the tension now. Only another four days and he would be out there facing the world's greatest. Although they had trained consistently, the relay team members virtually lived together now. Training, eating and practising until they operated as a well-oiled machine.

Guy was in an even worse state than Dick. After all, he was running in the 400 metres on Saturday, with Liddell, then on Sunday, as part of their relay team.

"I thought that I was really just a pace setter for Eric," Guy confessed to the others, "but after Tuesday I'm not so sure."

"Don't be like that." Renwick replied. "We can all have off days and Liddell has certainly been pushing himself since."

They could see Liddell exercising vigorously, on the other side of the field.

"Come on lads, standing around gossiping won't win you the gold." Sam shouted as he approached from the changing rooms.

Dick began to feel almost relieved that he had not qualified for the finals of the 400 metres, when he saw the state that Guy got himself into as the week progressed.

Saturday was to prove all their fears unfounded. Britain regained her glory, thanks to the stalwart efforts, not just of Liddell, but of Guy Butler as well. Liddell set a new Olympic record for the 400 metres, taking just 47.6 seconds to complete the distance. Guy, to the absolute delight of his friends, came in third, landing a bronze for himself and his country!

The week had not been all training though, the lads still had some time for relaxation. In fact, despite his slave-driving, Sam insisted that they play as hard as they train.

Dick managed to see Nanette several times during the course

of the week. Although both of them accepted that they had no future together, they enjoyed the short time they had. Dick was not concerned about Nanette's lack of breeding or suspect reputation. She was a beautiful, amusing and exciting woman and he enjoyed her company.

It was not just a physical relationship, although there was no doubt that that side of things was a new and enjoyable experience for Dick. He had not just found a lover, he had found a friend, someone easy to talk to and laugh with. Someone who made no demands.

Nanette made sure that Dick grew to love Paris and to understand it's magic, just as she did. They watched the sunsets on the Seine, admired the Mona Lisa in the Louvre, climbed Gustave Eiffel's now famous tower, all 300 metres of it, and walked the cities many boulevards and parks. Usually hand in hand, always happy. Dick had to admit to himself that he would miss his lady with the sunset hair but he would never regret a moment of their time spent together!

Sunday arrived all too quickly. It was the thirteenth and the whole team was feeling very superstitious. Dick had hardly slept that night and he could see from the faces of his friends, when they all assembled for breakfast, that he was not the only one. There was hardly a word passed between them during the whole meal.

The temperature had been rising over the last few days and the heat was oppressive now. As the team made their way to the stadium Dick could feel the sweat trickling down his neck. He loved the uniform but the stiff collars and dark blazers were not designed for this heat.

Changing into their kit did not help either. As the team gathered for the start of the race the sweat was running from them all and every man felt as though his strength was being drained from every pore. Dick could not believe how cool the Americans looked. Perhaps they came from the warmer states and were used to it. Dick couldn't remember.

The track looked endless. Dick, who was renowned for his stamina, and who was also used to the greater 800 metres, had never found 400 metres a problem, now it looked like a marathon.

114

Sam was giving last minute instructions; remember not to look back, grasp the baton firmly etc. etc. Then to Dick, who was to be the fourth runner, push yourself forward as you approach the finish tape.

Dick watched Renwick as he dug out his starting block. He looked very tense. Dick hoped that he would remember all that Sam had taught him over the past two weeks, especially, not to start too quickly and burn himself out.

"Take your marks please gentlemen." The Starter shouted.

The pistol shot almost made Dick jump, he was so lost in his own thoughts. Renwick left the starting block like the Devil was after him and quickly took the lead, but he was not half way round the distance when the pace began to tell. First he was passed by the American, Cochrane, but then four more runners quickly left him behind. By the time he passed the baton to Toms Dick could see that he was almost in tears. Dick felt sick. They could never do it now. Toms ran as though his life depended on it. Dick's spirits lifted slightly as he watched him pass one of the other runners.

Guy would be next and he had a lot to make up. Would he be able to save the day? Dick knew that he was still on a high from the previous day's race, but winning the bronze in that event had taken a lot out of him.

Toms passed the baton and Guy gave it his all. He had recovered a lot of distance and had almost made up another place when he passed to Dick. Dick knew that it was all down to him now. He ran as he had never run in his life before. The heat did not help. He felt as though his lungs would burst and his legs were covered in lead. Everything seemed to turn to slow motion.

He passed someone, he did not know who. He was gaining on the next person. If he could take him, they would get a bronze. His determination took over. He could see the finishing ribbon and he pushed for the final sprint. As he approached the line he sensed more than saw that he had passed into third place. Throwing himself forward, as Sam had taught, he hardly dared hope that he had made it!

Dick collapsed and the world started to spin. Butler, Lowe and Renwick surrounded him and helped him to his feet. "Did we do it?" Dick asked as he staggered to an upright position. "Did we really get the bronze?"

"No doubt about it," Renwick answered, "but it was not due to me, I panicked. I'm really sorry." Not your fault in the least." Dick assured him. "We all know who let us down in this race." He looked over Renwick's shoulder to where Liddell was approaching to congratulate them.

"Let them have their moment," Liddell said as he raised his hand in salute to the American team, "They set a new world record of 3:16.0 but they won't keep that for long. I won't let you down next Saturday gentlemen, when we meet them again in the Empire Games, on our own soil. We'll show them what a world record really looks like. I know that none of you were pleased when you found out that I was not going to be out there with you today, but you have still achieved a splendid result for Britain. Believe me, I will do everything in my power to set matters straight next week." He turned and walked away.

"Well of all the pompous, arrogant, condescending..." Guy spluttered.

"Em, careful, ladies present," coughed Dick as he saw Nanette approaching, " but I do understand what you mean. No doubt he'll honour us with his presence next week, provided there are no pressing prayer meetings needing his presence. Still he has a point. Wouldn't it be splendid if we did beat them next week?"

"No doubt about it." Toms added "After all, with Liddell on the team we're bound to have God on our side!"

Dick put his arm around Nanette and they all laughed as they made their way to the presentations.

The athletics were now more or less completed and the next day the team would be returning to Britain. That evening they were all to gather together for their final party before going their separate ways. Dick insisted on including Nanette in the proceedings, as this was to be their last evening as well. The others raised no objections, especially when she agreed to bring half a dozen of her friends!

The evening went well, but was tinged with sadness. It had been a very special week for everyone. There had been triumphs and disappointments, new friendships forged and a comradeship unlikely to be experienced again. For everyone there were enough memories to last them a lifetime. Now they had to return to reality.

Next morning they had to vacate their rooms early to make way for the American swimming team. The swimming events were to take place in Tourelles during the following week. By the time the British team were assembled, awaiting departure, the American swimmers had already arrived.

One tall and extremely handsome member of their team seemed to stand out from the rest and certainly impressed the ladies. He was called Johnny Weissmuller. Dick read later that he won three gold medals for the United States that year, but he won far more acclaim many years later when Dick was surprised to see his face again, but this time swinging amongst the trees as Hollywood's most famous Tarzan!

Chapter 17

As the boat left France Dick could just make out Nanette's hair as she waved. She had been crying as they said their goodbyes, and Dick had a lump in his throat as he watched his final sight of her disappear.

They had promised to write to each other but Dick was not sure whether that would really be a good idea. A clean break might be best.

Dick took full advantage of the rest provided by the sea trip home. The Olympics may be over but there were still races to be run. He knew that he would not be able to rest for at least another week. He would not arrive back in West Hartlepool until Tuesday evening. One day unpacking, then to Darlington on Thursday for the Northumberland and Durham Championships, back on the train on Friday, to join the team again for the Empire Games on Saturday. Finally returning home for a further Championship event in Durham, on the following Wednesday.

"No peace for the wicked!" Dick finished explaining to Guy why he wouldn't be spending the week in London with the rest of the team.

"You must be a sucker for punishment Dick, these last three weeks have been gruelling enough without all that extra travelling. Are these Northern races really that important?" Guy asked seriously.

"To me they are." Dick replied. "I won my first Northumberland and Durham title just after my nineteenth birthday and I've retained that ever since, as well as adding a few Yorkshire titles to my collection. You bet your life they are important! I intend to keep winning them every year until I need a wheelchair to keep up! A little thing like competing in the Olympics and the Empire Games won't stop me anyway."

"Well good luck to you, I'd never have the stamina." Guy laughed, "but what are you going to do once Sam has you running all over the place as a London Poly Harrier as well?"

"Just enjoy it." Dick replied, relaxing back with his pipe firmly clenched between his teeth. "I'll enjoy every minute!"

Dick didn't join in many of the festivities on the return trip and spent most of the trip dozing on the sun deck.

The Press were out in force as the ship docked. Their athletics team had taken three gold, eleven silver and eight bronze medals in that week and the public wanted to know how their heroes felt. Abrahams, Liddell and Lowe were the centre of attention. Dick and the rest, after a team photograph, managed to slip away. Dick had a train to catch. The Olympics were over but the excitement had not stopped!

As the train pulled into West Hartlepool station Dick was surprised to find a crowd of people waiting to congratulate him.

Mrs Johnson and Martha were first to reach him. Harry was close behind and helped with the bags. Most of the West Hartlepool Harriers were there and everyone was firing questions at once. Dick felt himself being lifted up on to some boxes and everyone went quiet.

"Oh dear," started Dick, "I didn't expect to have to make a speech. Thank you all for your support and good wishes. I have been very privileged to represent, not just my Country, but also the North East of England and particularly West Hartlepool. At least some of those stiff-necked Southerners now know where West Hartlepool is and I have no intentions of letting them forget it." Dick held up his medal. "This may not be gold, but it is only the first. I intend to bring home a gold from the Empire Games on Saturday. Then, who knows, with the wonderful support that I receive from you all, perhaps it will be an Olympic gold in 1928. Thank you, thank you all very much."

Dick felt very near to tears as a huge cheer went up from the crowd.

"I didn't know so many people cared," he said to Harry.

"Oh you are a real celebrity now." Mrs Johnson bustled forward. The ladies at my tea circle have a photograph of you, acting as part of the Prince's Guard of Honour. I said I would persuade you to come and talk to us about it, once you get time."

"We saw you on the Newsreel on the Picture House." Betty chipped in. "I was there with my new young man, George, and I almost swooned when I realised that my own brother was on the screen. I've told all my friends about you."

"I bet you have!" Dick whispered to Harry quietly. "Who is this young man then Betty?" He asked. "He is the son of that auctioneer in York Road. A very respectable family. He would be considered a very good catch. I must introduce you to him." Betty ran off to chatter to one of her friends.

"Is he slow witted, blind or just desperate?" Dick asked Harry.

"Actually he's a nice chap." Harry replied seriously. "Unfortunately he's too nice and dear old Elizabeth has him wrapped around her little finger. He'll never escape now!"

Dick had hoped for a relaxing evening, sitting quietly in the Johnsons' parlour. Possibly explaining to Mrs Johnson about Nanette. It was not to be. In true Johnson style the table was laden with food and, it seemed to Dick, the whole town had been invited to welcome him home. Dick wasn't ungrateful, and, as usual the party turned into a sing-song that carried into the early hours.

As Dick closed the curtains before retiring, he noticed the sun was just starting to rise. Pinks and golds painted even the dull chimneys with a beautiful hue that reminded him of Paris and Nanette. There was no denying that he was missing her. How long would it take for that large empty pain in his heart to heal? Thank goodness he was going to be busy for the next few weeks. Perhaps the emptiness he felt when he thought of her would not hurt so much by the time his life returned to normal.

Dick slept late next morning. The kettle was singing on the hob and the kitchen was already full of the delicious smell of fresh baked bread when he came down to breakfast, or rather lunch.

Mrs Johnson had already unpacked his bags and his washing was blowing on the line.

"I've sponged down your Olympic Uniform and your evening suit." Mrs Johnson assured him. "They will be nicely pressed by this evening."

"Mrs Johnson, you really are too kind." Dick gave her a peck on the cheek. "I've brought you some real French perfume and some lace handkerchiefs. I do hope you like them." Dick produced a parcel from behind his back.

Mrs Johnson went quite pink. "Oh but you shouldn't have. I'm not your Mam. She quickly opened the parcel. Dick could see that she was delighted but also embarrassed. She rapidly pushed them into a draw and hurried to pour some tea.

"Me with French perfume, whatever next?" She giggled. "There is a note for you on the mantle, hurry and read it, it's from your father!"

"I think I'll leave it then. I'm much too happy at present. I'll wait until I'm feeling depressed and then I can turn myself suicidal with it." Dick replied.

"Now don't be like that. I thought you and your father sort of made up just before you left." Mrs Johnson scolded.

"I suppose you're right". Dick sighed, reaching for the envelope.

The note was quite brief. It offered sincere congratulations on Dick's success in the games and invited Dick to call round at his office at his earliest convenience. Dick couldn't help but smile at the formal tone of the phrases. He handed it to Mrs. Johnson.

"He probably wants to make the peace love," she said, putting the letter to one side whilst she heaped a plate with thick rashers of bacon, two eggs and a heap of mushrooms. "Here, have a snack now. We're having stew and dumps for dinner this evening. This should keep you going until then." She cut two great slices of steaming fresh bread and heaped them with butter.

"When you've eaten this, take yourself a walk along and see him, best to get it over with."

"You're probably right, but I think I might wait until I get back from London next week. I wanted to write a letter this afternoon and I promised the lads I would be at the Harriers meeting tonight. I will go though, I promise." He winked as he started tucking into the overloaded plate. "I thought the French bread was delicious but you could give them lessons Mrs J." He added, changing the subject before she could insist.

"Now who could you possibly be wanting to write a letter to that is so important?" Mrs Johnson asked. She didn't miss a thing. It wasn't long before Dick had told her everything about Nanette.

"I did think that it might be better not to write. After all there's not much chance of a future for us is there?" He sighed at the end of his tale, pushing his now empty plate to one side.

"Who knows love? You should never say die 'til you're dead, you know." Mrs Johnson patted his shoulder as she removed his plate and replaced it with a steaming cup of tea and a plate full of hot buttered scones. "Keep in touch with the lass, it can't do any harm can it?" Suddenly Mrs Johnson gasped. "Ee, I'm sorry lad another letter came for you yesterday. I put it on the sideboard so I wouldn't forget it, then with all the excitement yesterday, and with your Dad's letter arriving today, it went right out of my head." She scurried into the parlour, returning with the official looking brown envelope.

The letter was from the Amateur Athletic Association and enclosed his ticket for admission to the Empire games on Saturday, together with instructions that full Olympic Uniform must be worn.

"It's just as I expected," Dick informed Mrs Johnson, as she watched inquisitively. "Oh wait a minute though." Dick read the next paragraph out loud:

"On this occasion the Officials, Competitors and other guests will dine together at the Trocadero Restaurant, Piccadilly Circus, (Empire Suite of Rooms) when His Royal Highness, Prince Henry will be present- Dinner 7.15 for 7.30pm, prompt."

"Well I never," exclaimed Mrs Johnson, "you'll be on first name terms with the whole Royal family, if you keep on like this!"

Dick was thrilled. He had felt sure that the wining and dining was over, and that the Empire Games would be an anti-climax after Paris. Perhaps he had been wrong.

Wednesday flew by. Dick did write his letter and he found that it did help. He kept the letter chatty, explaining the journey home and the forthcoming games etc. He could not help but confess, in the final paragraph, that he was missing her and would always hold a place for her in his heart, but he would not have called it a love letter.

The rest of the day passed in a whirl. He ran with the lads that evening and, over a jug of stout later, made arrangements to travel to the Darlington Cycle and Harrier Club Sports the next day, with Harry, who was also running.

"It will be good to get back to racing with the old crowd." Dick confessed. "It is really exciting running in international competitions but it's so dog eat dog with those lads. It's great to be home Harry!"

"Well don't get too used to it. Most of the lads think this is only the start for you. Even Father thinks you need someone to manage your affairs now. Hasn't he seen you yet? He's been all fired up about how much advice and support he can give you. He's telling all his friends and associates that he is going to make sure that your athletics career is correctly managed in future!"

Dick almost choked on his pint. "He is doing what? Just who does he think he is? He gave me five pounds and thinks he owns me. It's not five minutes since he was telling me that athletics could only ever be a hobby, and that I needed a good career. I got his letter today but I'm damned if I'll go and see him if that is his style. Of all the cheek!"

Harry tried hard to pacify Dick "He is proud of you Dick. He wants to be your father again. He means well, honestly he does. I probably haven't put it very well. Why don't you just see him and listen to what he has to say? Please Dick, give him a chance!"

Dick was too content with the last few weeks to stay angry for long. Anyway, the last thing he wanted was to fall out with Harry.

"Okay, Harry. I'll give it some thought over the weekend. I can't see him before next weekend anyway, I haven't the time." He smiled at Harry. "It won't do him any harm to sweat for a while will it?".

The brothers set off for Darlington before lunch the next day. Mrs Johnson and Eva accompanied them and they were weighed down under the weight of the enormous picnic basket that Mrs Johnson had carefully packed that morning.

"Good Heavens, have you packed the kitchen sink in this?"

Puffed Harry as he tried to strap it onto the back of his car.

"Oh hang on a minute," shouted Mrs Johnson, pretending to alight from the back seat, "I've forgotten that". They all laughed as they set off. It was a very pleasant day. Dick was only entered in the 220 yards, in order to defend his title as Northumberland and Durham Champion over that distance. He would be defending his title over 100 yards and 440 yards in Durham on the following Wednesday.

He found that his fame had preceded him and he had to run from a back mark of five yards. Harry was entered in the same race and Dick thoroughly enjoyed the event. It was all so casual after the tension of Paris. The five yard penalty did make the race slightly tougher than he had expected but he retained his title by covering the distance in 22.3:5 seconds. Harry came in a respectable third. Dick was content in the knowledge that he had now held that title for four years. Even Liddell did not have that sort of claim to fame.

It was a very merry party that left the sports ground that evening. They laughed and sang all the way home. All the more content because they were full of Mrs Johnson's homemade elderberry wine and rich fruit cake!

Chapter 18

All too soon Dick found himself, once again, sharing West Hartlepool station with the pigeons. He was looking forward to the Empire Games but had to admit to himself that he was starting to feel tired of all the travelling. His whirlwind visit home had been a pleasant break but it had left him feeling decidedly homesick.

Dick was alone at the station, apart from the pigeons. It was still very early and most of the town hadn't woken up yet. Mrs Johnson, Jack and Harry had offered to see him off but he had sensed their relief when he declined their company.

"I'll only be gone a couple of days, it's not as if I'm going to sea or something." He had said, after Harry had suggested yet another group send off. "You two gentlemen have your ladies to consider, and Mrs Johnson is far too busy tending to her household chores in the morning. I'll be fine, but thanks for the thought."

As he looked at the huge clock ticking high above the platform Dick heard footsteps approaching behind. He turned to be confronted by the unexpected figure of his father.

"Good Heavens Father, what brought you from behind your newspaper at such an early hour?" Dick exclaimed.

"There's no need for profanity Richard. You are my son and I wish to support you in these auspicious times." Richard paused impressively. He removed a £5 note from his wallet. "I have no doubt that this will, again, become useful. When you return I would like to speak with you. I did send a note to the Johnsons' but that ridiculous woman has obviously not delivered it."

"Now wait one moment!" Dick said angrily. "Mrs Johnson is a kind and loving lady, both words you wouldn't understand, and for your information, I did get your note, I just did not have the time or, I must admit, the inclination to call immediately. I had intended to contact you next week, but if the purpose of the meeting is to slander my friends, forget it and forget your fiver too!" Dick roughly pushed the money back towards his father.

"Don't be too hasty Richard. I did not mean to insult your friends, although I do think you could choose more wisely." Richard hurried on as he saw that again he had said the wrong thing. "It is a business proposition that I have. I have been talking to your employer, Mr Boyd. Although he is keen to support your athletic career, he is afraid that you may be spending more and more time undertaking athletics events in future. He is quite naturally concerned and does not feel that he can continue to pay your remuneration when the work is not being done."

"I understood that that had been settled." Dick cut in furiously. "He is only paying me a retainer when I am away."

"Exactly!" Richard said enthusiastically. "I am willing to take you back as an insurance agent, on a basic salary, plus commission. You were always good at selling insurance and could probably make far more on a part-time basis, than you make full time as a bookkeeper. You must need the money with all this travelling." The train approached the station.

"It seems like a very generous offer," Dick acknowledged grudgingly, "but I must admit to being rather sceptical. We do not always see eye to eye and you are a business man. There has to be a catch." The train whistle blew. "I must go Father, but I will come and see you on my return."

"That was all I wanted to hear. There's no catch. I just want to support my son." His father said, pushing the £5 note back into his hand. He turned an walked swiftly away leaving Dick to stare after him.

"All aboard." The guard shouted and Dick hurriedly climbed up into the carriage, not quite sure if he was dreaming or not. This could answer his money problems. There was no denying that his current "career" was definitely an expensive business. "But where's the catch." He thought to himself. "My father is not a generous man, there has got to be a catch!"

As the train wound its way along the coast and then through the Cleveland hills and on towards York, Dick could not concentrate on his newspaper. He tried very hard to focus on the articles. The Pope was alarmed and upset by the current fashions. Dick smiled, had the Pope seen Nanette's night attire he wondered?

The Matrimonial Causes Act had finally been passed. Mother could now divorce father for adultery if she wished. Not that she ever would. She was completely under his control.

"Is that what it's all about?" Dick said out loud. An elderly gentleman looked over his glasses from across the carriage.

"I beg your pardon? Did you address me Sir?"

"Oh no. I do apologise." Dick blushed. "I'm afraid I was thinking out loud." The old gentleman smiled.

"Not to worry, I always talk to myself. Get more sensible answers that way, don't you?" He smiled and resumed his newspaper.

Dick had been surprised by the reception he had received on his return from Paris. He was almost a local hero. Is this what his father wished to be part of? Did he want to "take control"? It would certainly agree with what Harry had told him, that his father wished to "manage" his athletics career!

Well Dick would wait and see, but father was batting a sticky wicket if he thought he could manipulate him in the same way as he did with mother and the rest of the family.

Dick settled down to enjoy the journey, content in the almost certain knowledge that he had seen through father's intentions and would be ready for him.

Unfortunately Dick's contentment was short-lived. Not long after Doncaster the train seemed to slow down. It struggled on to Grantham but seemed to take far longer than usual. Dick looked at his pocket watch apprehensively.

"Oh dear I do hope we are not to be delayed," the Old Gentleman sighed. "My daughter is a worrier and she will be pacing the station if I am late. I am to holiday with my family in London. I thought that I might visit the Empire Exhibition and see the games tomorrow." He added.

"I'm also going to the games," Dick replied, "but I'm hoping to take part in them. If I arrive on time, of course."

Just at that moment a guard opened their carriage door.

"Apologies gentlemen, but I'm afraid we have a problem with the boiler." The guard explained. "I do have to ask you to leave the train now. We are hoping to fit you on to one arriving from

Edinburgh and bound for King's Cross. It is due in thirty minutes." He withdrew immediately and passed to the next carriage.

"What a nuisance. I do not like the sound of that." The old gentleman retorted. "They hope to fit us into the Edinburgh train indeed. Well I intend to see the Station Master about this." He pulled his bag from the rack and left the carriage hurriedly.

Dick followed almost immediately but the gentleman had already alighted from the train and was nowhere to be seen.

Dick had to admit to himself that he could have done without this delay. The next day was to be very hectic and he had hoped to spend a quiet evening with the rest of the team, discussing tactics and enjoying an relaxed dinner, before having a reasonably early night. At this rate he would be lucky to get to the hotel while dinner was still available. Oh why had he travelled all the way home for one race? 220 yards wasn't even his best distance! Pride. He knew that that was all it was. He had been determined to uphold his title and now he might even lose his place on the relay team, especially if the selectors think there is the slightest chance that he won't turn up.

The old gentleman suddenly appeared at his side again.

"I've made a formal complaint and I explained that you were needed at the games tomorrow." He laughed. "Please excuse an old goat for using any excuse but, thanks to you, we are now guaranteed a seat, even if it is in first class, and at no extra charge. It always pays to shout you know."

Dick thanked the gentleman and introduced himself. The gentleman was called Mr King and came from Middlesbrough.

"But I know of you Mr Ripley." He exclaimed. "I followed the reports of the Olympic games very carefully, but I am also a keen athletics follower in our own region. I have seen you run."

The conversation continued until the train arrived and, true to Mr King's word, the guard hurried forward and directed both Dick and himself to the first class carriages at the front of the train. The rest of the journey passed very pleasantly with Dick and George, as he insisted on being called, discussing the various races Dick had run, as well as the remarkable achievements of his team members and the other countries during the Olympics.

The train was only an hour late in arriving at King's Cross and Dick bid Mr King farewell. He was surprised to see Eric Liddell just a few yards ahead of him as he went in search of a cab.

"Eric!" Dick shouted. "I hadn't realised that you had travelled home. We must have arrived back on the same train."

Liddell seemed quite happy to see him.

"I had to go home. I was very honoured to be presented with a degree by Edinburgh University on Thursday." Liddell explained. "How did your race go. You had a title to defend I understand?"

"After the Olympics it was a piece of cake." Dick admitted.

A taxi cab drew up and the two decided to share. Dick was quite surprised to find that Liddell was quite easy to talk to when he was alone.

They did arrive at the hotel, in Wembley, in time for dinner and for the team discussion afterwards. Dick was somewhat perturbed to find himself shown as a reserve on page eleven of the programme prepared for the event, but Harry Barclay assured him that Mr Betts was not a runner and he had been intended as part of the team for some time.

"The problem was, Mr Ripley, that the programmes were printed some months ago. It was by no means certain, at that time, that you would even make the Games. We are aware of the problems travelling from the North."

"Oh and Mr Liddell does not have any problems travelling from Edinburgh?" Dick retorted angrily.

"That is hardly the same, Mr Ripley." Mr Barclay explained. "You are a relatively unknown runner, Mr Liddell had already established his reputation." Sam Mussabini stepped forward and guided Dick away politely.

"This is one of the problems I mentioned to you earlier Dick." He spoke quietly. "It is not so much how fast you are or how many races you win, but which athletics club or University you represent. You must join the London Polytechnic Harriers if you wish to further your career. We will discuss this later, but be assured that you are part of tomorrow's team, and it is not advisable to be rude or bad tempered with Mr Barclay."

Dick felt rather ashamed and immediately apologised to Mr

Barclay for his ill humour. He had to admit to himself, however, that he was rather resentful of the fact that he had to go along with, what could only be described as "The Old Boys Club", in order to ensure his future career in athletics.

Abrahams came to talk to him shortly afterwards.

"I heard a little of your conversation," he said to Dick quietly. "You are not alone you know. If you think being working class, from the North, is bad, you should try being Jewish for a while." Dick laughed, his good humour returning.

"It's no good Harold. I haven't got the nose." He punched Harold lightly on the shoulder and they returned to the main party. The rest of the evening passed very pleasantly, and the whole team agreed that an early night was essential. Tomorrow was to be a very busy day. The games were to commence at 2.30pm, with a parade of the teams, and after the races, everyone was looking forward to Prince Henry's invitation to the Trocadero Reataurant!

None of the team doubted that they would beat the American relay team this time and they were all in high spirits as they bid one another goodnight.

As Dick left the hotel bar to climb the staircase to his room, he could not help but notice a huge poster: "The British Empire Exhibition, Great Attraction. Bring the whole family to Wembley for the event of a lifetime. Admission 1/6d Child 9d. throughout July and August."

"The event of a lifetime." Dick thought. Was this to be the event of his lifetime or just one of the first of many?

"I'll just have to wait and see." He said quietly to himself as he ascended the stairs.

Chapter   19

Dick woke early, as usual, and had a short run before breakfast. He had not had a good night, but he was starting to get used to the pre-race nerves and was not therefore particularly worried by the lack of sleep. It was a beautiful morning and Dick did not push himself unduly as he paced around the nearby gardens. The fragrances of the many blossoms bombarding his nostrils, as he practised the controlled breathing that Sam had stressed as so important. Lavender was particularly strong and he smiled as he thought of Mrs Johnson and her lavender polish.

"No doubt she'll be hard at it by now," he thought, as he completed another circuit. He was not alone for long. Harold and Guy soon appeared.

"Grand day for slaughtering the Americans!" Guy shouted, as they passed.

After breakfast the team met for the customary training session with Sam. After all the lads had been through, in the Olympics, there seemed very little to say.

"With the efforts of Mr Liddell joining you today, I expect to see a new record at the very least!" Sam finished his debriefing. "After all, Mr Ripley managed to cover his 400 metres in Paris, in 48.8   seconds, I am sure Mr Liddell will equal that, if nothing else. That means that you gentleman, Mr Toms and Mr Butler, can just stroll round and still wipe the floor with them." He laughed. "Well lads, the honour of our Nation rests on your shoulders today. Just get out there and show them your heels!"

The team were in high spirits as they made for the changing rooms. Dick wished that Sam had not singled out his time though. In the Olympics he had given his heart and soul, he was not sure that he could do that again, especially while all eyes were on Eric Liddell. Suddenly he felt unwell.

"What's wrong Dick," Guy asked, "you've gone very pale?"

"Just nerves I think," Dick repied. "Suddenly this afternoon seems even more important than Paris. Everyone is so convinced we can beat the Americans. Let's face it, they are good. They set a new world record in Paris for Christ's sake!"

"Steady on Dick, we're good as well you know!" Guy threw a towel at him. "We've got an hour before the opening ceremony, let's take it easy for a while and calm down."

Once they were settled in the hotel gardens and Dick had his pipe blazing well, he soon calmed down again.

"Sorry Guy, I don't know what came over me." Dick smiled.

"Don't give it a thought," Guy looked concerned. "The last few weeks have been very stressful. We're all tired. At least those of us who stayed in London did get to relax a little. You are pushing too hard. Dashing about the country, defending titles. You need a break."

"I've just got the amateur sports in Durham next week and then I intend to get back to normal for a while." Dick reassured him. "Anyway I'm supposed to be well known for my stamina!"

Soon the whole team were once again assembled in full Olympic uniform, ready for the opening parade. Dick felt very proud to be British as they lined up. The parade was headed by the Pipe Band of the 1st Batt. Scots Guards. As they started forward with their pipes well primed and their colourful kilts swirling, Dick felt a lump in his throat. This was not a world event, as the Olympics, but this was even more important. This was the world's two great nations battling for supremacy, in a gentlemanly manner, on the athletics field.

Dick looked at the American team lined up ahead of them. Bowman, Scholz, Fitch, Paddock, and many more, all great athletes and here was he, Dick Ripley, an ordinary chap, from the North of England about to take them on. What's more, thanks to Mrs Johnson's care, Dick knew that he looked immaculate in his blue tunic, flannel trousers and straw hat. The Americans wore their running attire and did not look in the same league!

As they entered the ground the crowd went wild. Dick had never realised how much interest these games had created. He read later that there were 20,000 present for the opening ceremony and this increased to 30,000 once the games started. He had never experienced anything like this, not even in Paris. He felt his tension start to mount again. Thank goodness the races were to start immediately!

The 400 yard relay was first and Harold and the rest of the team took their places. America had drawn the inside position, which Harold was convinced gave them an advantage. He was to be proved right. Scholz quickly took the lead for the Americans in the first lap. Harold tried to make up the difference when he took the baton for the second stretch but he just could not get ahead and the Americans finally won in 37.5 seconds, beating the world record by 1½ seconds.

Dick was mortified. If Harold couldn't beat them what chance did he have!

He didn't have time to worry, they were next out. Toms was to take the first stretch, followed by Dick, then Guy and finally Liddell.

Toms made a good start and won the lead from Wilson in the first quarter mile. Dick grasped the baton firmly but saw the American, Robertson, come level. He had made a fatal mistake, he had glanced back. The few seconds he had taken to do that had lost him his edge. Robertson passed the baton to Stevenson a second before Dick passed to Guy.

Dick was distraught. He knew that he had committed one of Sam's deadly sins and, if they lost, he would never forgive himself. Guy failed to catch Stevenson and Fitch went away with a seven yards lead on Liddell. Dick could see by the determination in Liddell's face that he was not giving up.

"Come on Eric!" Dick heard himself screaming, as Liddell drew level with Fitch. The whole team were screaming their hearts out. Liddell started to take the lead and soon it was all over. Liddell had run brilliantly and had won for Britain, by three yards. Liddell's personal time had been 48 2.5 seconds.

The team time was 3 mins 18.2 seconds. Just 1/5sec. short of the world record and 1.5secs better than the British record.

The crowd were ecstatic. The stands were shaking with the the cheers. The press later reported that there was "such a roar of applause as Stamford Bridge has seldom heard."

Even Dick forgot his brief mistake, in the excitement. Liddell was beaming.

"Well I told you all I would make it up to you for my failure to run in the Olympics. Sorry we didn't make a new record chaps but I did my best. Perhaps if I had not had such a distance to make up I could have done it!" He looked across at Dick.

"Ignore that Dick," Guy whispered. "I didn't make it either remember. Who cares anyway. We still won."

"I thought I was starting to like that man." Dick replied "Guess I was just getting soft in my old age!"

Guy laughed as they made their way to the changing rooms. They were not running again and decided to change before watching the remaining events. Harold still had the long jump at 4.25pm, so he didn't join them.

Spirits were high as they finally left the sports to get changed for their appointment with Prince Henry that evening.

Mrs Johnson's efforts were evident again, Dick's evening suit was impeccable, and he felt like a real gentleman decked out in his satin lapels, cravat and cummerbund.

The evening went well but quickly became a blur as the champagne flowed. "I could get used to this life!" Dick admitted to Guy, as they sipped their vintage port, after yet another excellent meal. "It's a pity that life must return to normal next week."

"I don't think it will ever be normal again." Guy replied."Sam has been telling me of a match against the French Olympic team, which will be coming up shortly."

"I don't know anything about this," Dick replied. "Are you sure I will be selected? I didn't exactly shine today you know."

"Forget that Dick, we can all make mistakes, and in the circumstances I would have been tempted to glance back myself. I'm sure I heard your name mentioned, when the match was discussed last week. Why don't you ask Mr Barclay, he would know?"

"I might just do that," Dick replied."I might have to consider my father's offer, if this keeps up. I can hardly expect to keep my job open if I'm dashing about Europe. Oh I do hope you are right Guy."

"So much for that rest you were going to have after the

Durham race then?" Guy laughed.

"Rest? Who needs it? I've got my whole life to rest." Dick replied.

"Well Mr Barclay is over there, get on with it," Guy urged.

Guy had been right. Life was not to return back to "normal" again for Dick during the next few months.

Later that summer both Dick and Guy ran against the French Olympic 400m runners, Teneveaux and Galtier. Dick beat both of these gentlemen and Guy took fourth place in the same race. Dick joined the London Polytechnic Harriers, as Sam had advised, and in between championships, he spent as much time as he could in London and the Home Counties training.

On the Wednesday after the Empire games, Dick retained his Northumberland and Durham Championship title at Durham: "In fine weather and before a poor attendance," as the local paper reported. Again he had to run from a back mark of 5 yards but easily retained his title in the 440yards and also took the 100 yards flat, just for good measure.

Just a week later, on the 31st July, Dick came second in the English Athletic Championships, beaten only by his team mate, Toms. The idea of taking a rest and returning to normal was quickly forgotten.

Chapter 20

Dick had given some thought to his conversation with his father and was determined to face him as soon as possible. As he had admitted to Guy, he would require help if he was to become British Champion. He arrived home on Monday evening, after the Empire Games, and decided to strike while the iron was hot. Having dropped his bags with Mrs Johnson, he went straight to his father's club.

"I'm not beating around the bush Father," Dick came straight to the point. "You offered me my job back and I am happy to accept. I will work hard, when I am able and want no charity. Harry seemed to think that you wished to organise my career. Well you can forget that. I am grateful for the help you have given me recently, but it will not give you the right to control any part of my life. Is that understood?"

"Richard, I would not dream of interfering," his father insisted. "Here shake on it." He proffered his hand. "Come and meet my friends, they are very interested in your progress."

Dick had to admit that he enjoyed the interest shown in his recent races and the gentlemen he met seemed very knowledgeable about his career so far. They were also delighted to hear of his forthcoming events and were particularly interested in how he rated his chances against the future opposition.

A chance remark that he overheard did worry him though.

"Looks like we're onto a definite winner here Richard," one gentleman remarked. "We should be a great deal richer by Christmas!"

"Father what did that gentleman mean, we should be richer by Christmas?" Dick asked.

"Oh just a friendly wager between gentlemen Richard," his father replied. "Nothing to concern yourself with."

"I do hope you are not involved in betting Father." Dick was beginning to feel uncomfortable. "You know it is strictly prohibited by the Amateur Athletics Association, not to mention highly illegal. I couldn't be a party to anything like that. I would never be allowed to run again." Dick was horrified.

"Don't be silly Richard." His father reassured him.

"Gentlemen have had small "unofficial" wagers on sporting events, amongst themselves, for centuries. Of course I would not do anything to harm your career. Trust me, please."

It was Autumn before Dick really returned to his work as an insurance agent. He quickly realised that without his father's support he would not have been able to continue and expand his career as he had. He was determined to work hard to repay him.

He found that his job had improved since his teens. He was no longer an office junior. Now he seemed constantly in demand and spent more and more time "on the road", selling and collecting. He loved visiting clients to discuss their insurance requirements and was more than happy to discuss his athletics career while doing so. Indeed, it became increasingly obvious that most of his customers were keen athletics followers.

"It's funny, I never realised just how many people follow athletics in this town, Harry," he remarked to his brother, as they were changing after a training session with the Harriers, one evening.

"Oh Dick, you really are not in the real world are you?"
Harry laughed. "You don't think it is just coincidence that all your customers are keen on athletics, do you? Father arranges it that way. Not only does he get an arrangement fee for sending you along personally, but he has increased sales. People buy policies from you just so they can say that you arranged it for them."

"That can't be right." Dick hesitated while buttoning his waistcoat. "I'm not that well known yet and people wouldn't pay extra for something like that. Please say it isn't true, I won't be able to look my customers in the face again."

"Don't be daft man." Harry chided "Father is a brilliant business man and he has made good use of an asset that he has in his company. It's not illegal or anything."

"Are you sure?" Dick was still worried. "It doesn't sound ethical to me."

It did continue to trouble Dick. There was no doubt that his father's help was indispensable at the moment, but Dick was beginning to realise that the gains were not all one sided. His father was milking his success for all he was worth, gambling, advertising. It all sounded highly suspect.

"I really don't know what to do about it." Dick confessed to Guy, next time they met.

"Well, can you manage without your father's help?" Guy asked.

"Of course not, I cleared my savings travelling about for the Olympics and Empire Games. I haven't got a private income like Harold and a lot of the other lads."

"Exactly!" Guy replied. "So if you want to continue, you just turn a blind eye and make sure that your nose is clean. It is out of your hands, you are not responsible for your father's actions. You are running for your country and pretty soon you will be the best. Any of the lads would bend the rules slightly to continue, if they had to. It is disgusting that ordinary lads like you aren't supported financially by the Amateur Athletics Association, but until they are, what choice do you have?"

"Well put like that I suppose you're right," Dick agreed. "Perhaps this new idea of Communism that seems to be raising it's head in the press these days, isn't such a bad one. Things would not need to be so under handed if everyone was equal."

"Well the theory is good but it doesn't seem to work in practice does it?" Guy commented. "All we read of is revolution and disruption. I think I prefer free speech and freedom of choice to the alternatives that Communism seems to offer."

The conversation quickly turned to politics and the forthcoming election. It seemed that the Conservatives were almost sure to win after the recent press story about a letter from Zinoview, urging British communists to cause revolution in Britain. The voters were becoming afraid of the threat of Communism and the Labour party seemed to encompass that threat.

Dick quickly forgot his worries in the lively discussion that followed and he later resolved not to concern himself about his father's affairs in future. After all, as Guy had said, it was all out of his hands!

Dick's athletics career went from strength to strength. He found himself representing his country all over Britain and abroad, but it was not until summer of 1925 that he found himself once more en route for Paris. He was to run against Jamois, Teneveax and Galtier, the top three French 400m men and Delvart, the holder of the French 500m record. He was now the undisputed English 400m/440yds runner.

The excitement that Dick felt was not due to the European Championship this time though. He was going to Paris again. Even though a year had past since his last visit he had never forgotten Nanette. They had not kept up a regular correspondence, but Nanette had replied to his first letter and they had exchanged a couple of short notes since. These had been friendly but not particularly affectionate. Still Dick couldn't help but hope that things would be just as they were once they met again. He had not warned her of his impending visit, though he knew that she did follow his career and may well be aware of his arrival. He dared to hope that she would meet his ferry when they docked.

He scanned the quayside as the ship docked but there was no sign of that incredible hair anywhere. The dock was bustling. People and bags everywhere. The race officials were there to welcome him and he was quickly directed to his cab, but he felt incredibly disappointed.

"Come on now Dick," Guy said cheerfully, "if you didn't let the lady know when to expect you, how could she be here? Be realistic. Anyway it's been a year now, anything might have happened. Find yourself another admirer, surely one is as good as another?" Dick couldn't help but laugh as he noticed a blue gollywog sticking out of Guy's bag. It had become a good luck symbol to Guy, ever since a certain young lady had pushed it into his hands, just before he won a very important heat.

"Well if that's true, how come Golly has come along again?" Dick remarked. Guy hurriedly pushed "Golly" out of sight and grinned sheepishly.

"Well you have a point and I do understand, but just because she wasn't at the dock doesn't mean that she won't be pleased to see you when you call."

Once Dick had settled into his hotel he quickly made excuses to leave the rest of the party and head for Nanette's apartment. He hesitated before knocking. There was no answer in response to the first knock and Dick wondered if she was out, but he could hear some noise inside. He knocked again.

"Comment?" Shouted a rough male voice from behind the door. Dick searched his limited French vocabulary to try to reply.

"Je chercher Nanette." he replied through the door. The door opened and a huge, rough looking man stood in front of him.

"I'm terribly sorry but I don't speak much French. I thought Mademoiselle Nanette lived here." Dick really did not know what to do next. He looked at the stairs and knew full well he could out run this man, if necessary, but where was Nanette?

"Je crois que vows avez tort. Ma femme s'appeler Madame Nanette," the man replied. Dick didn't entirely understand but the words "femme" and "madame" were plain enough.

"Pardon," Dick replied, raising his hat as he turned to leave. He was very confused. Why had Nanette not mentioned this marriage? It must have been sudden. Yet she had written and never mentioned this man. As Dick started along the street he saw Nanette coming towards him.

"Nanette!" He called. He was distressed when she turned and tried to run in the opposite direction. He easily caught her. "What is going on?" Dick spun her round and looked into her eyes. "There is an uncouth looking individual in your flat and I believe that he told me that he was your husband."

"Oh Dick, why did you have to come back? I didn't want you to learn the truth, things were perfect as they were." Nanette started to cry. "I am married. Jean is not a gentleman, but he does treat me quite well. I married him four years ago. I thought I loved him, until I met you last year. Jean was away, looking for work in Calais. I know I should not have let our affair happen, but I just could not help myself and it was so wonderful."

"But you replied to my letters. Why couldn't you have ignored them, or told me the truth?" Dick felt as though his world had exploded. "Why Nanette? You could have ended it so easily."

"I didn't think you would ever return to Paris. Oh I read of your success, but I never dreamt that you would become European Champion. Why did you have to be so good?" Nanette pushed him away and ran towards home.

Dick was numb. He did not know what he felt. Holding her closely for those few moments had brought all the memories flooding back. The wonderful summer they had had, the incredible passion, the excitement, the tenderness, all destroyed in one short moment. Worse still, not only had he been deceived, but what about this poor Jean? Dick didn't know the man but, by her own admission, he treated her well, cared for her, and was even away looking for work when Dick had come along and taken his wife. How could she?

Dick wandered the streets of Paris aimlessly. The sun was going down as he approached the Cathedral of Notre Dame. Even in his despair, he couldn't help but be struck again by the incredible beauty of the sunset, touching the Cathedral with a golden glow. As he had found on so many previous occasions, the splendour of the moment brought a much needed feeling of peace. He entered the Cathedral, and for a moment, relived the magnificence of the day, when he had been part of the Guard of Honour for The Prince of Wales. He sat for a while and gathered his thoughts.

His feelings for Nanette were a year old. True they had fired up quickly on sight of her, but he had survived for twelve months. Now he must move on. He was at the height of his athletics career and had no time for women anyway. If he was honest with himself, Nanette had been a convenient excuse for not getting involved with other ladies and there had been plenty who had tried. He didn't need an excuse. He had a full-time commitment to athletics and a part-time commitment to insurance. There was no time for anything else. He smiled as he left the Cathedral. Yes that was another ghost from the past laid to rest. He would win in Paris and go on with the rest of his life. Women who needed them!

Chapter   21

Dick not only won all his events in Paris but he ran the fastest time in Europe over the 400 metre distance. He had still not beaten Liddell's world record, but he was working on it.

Despite his success he did not rest on his laurels, but returned to Britain to win the Northern Counties 440 yards title for the 5th successive year. There was no stopping him.

"Well Harry, your brother is certainly beating all records now." Jack remarked as they met in the bar after a "West" Harriers meeting. "The weather was dreadful when he took that last Northern Counties Title. Yet even on a soggy track he managed 51 seconds. The "Northern Daily Mail" reported that it was the fastest time, over the distance, since 1887."

"Yes but I think Dick is more concerned by the fact that he's now won five years running. No-one has ever won more than three of these championships consecutively, you know," Harry replied. "Where is Dick anyway? I thought he was right behind us?"

Jack laughed. "Dick is never behind anyone anymore. You know him, he just wanted a few more laps. I can't believe his stamina. Do you know, mother is having a few back problems at the moment and can't manage her garden? Anyway I went round the other night to give a hand, only to find it all done. Dick arrived home from Paris, dropped his bags and turned the whole garden over before tea!"

"I didn't realise Dick even knew how to dig a garden over," Harry replied, "although I do remembering him helping Martha when we were children."

"Apparently he's becoming quite knowledgeable about gardening now. Mother tells me he's always interested in what she's planting, how she's pruning and what composts she's using." Jack replied.

"Well I never. My brother never fails to amaze me!" Harry laughed.

"And how do I manage to do that little brother?" Dick

clapped Harry on the back. They had not noticed him arrive.

"We were just discussing your new gardening skills." Jack replied. "Mother was telling me that you do all the hard work for her now Dick. I am very grateful."

"There's no need to be. I love it. There is something so special about watching things grow. I feel at peace when I'm in the garden. I forget all about running, father's devious schemes and the world's problems. I can totally relax." Dick's voice took on an almost reverent tone. "If the time ever comes when I can't run anymore, I think I'd like to become a gardener full-time."

"Don't be stupid Dick!" Harry retorted. "There's no money in gardening. It's the labouring types who do that sort of menial work!"

"Well, our Harry, I never had you pegged as a snob," Dick chided. "I'm afraid that I think you've lost it if you think all that matters in life is money. Can't you see? That's what happened to Father. Money became his God. Mother and us, we were just things he had to have to sit right in society. Money is the thing he really loves. Oh yes he's very successful, but do you think he's really found happiness? Does he ever stop to smell a rose or watch the changing colours in a sunset? I doubt it!"

"It's a fine sentiment Dick," Harry replied, "but you don't really live in the real world yet. You have no responsibilities. No wife and family. You will see things differently once you fall in love and settle down. Then money is very necessary. You will want to give your loved ones the best you can manage. Not a life of hard graft in some scruffy street house, trying to eek out an existence on a gardener's pittance."

"Well lads, how about we agree to differ, and change the subject?" Jack could see Dick's face darkening and did not want to see a full scale argument develop. "I hear you are off to Dublin to defend your title shortly Dick?"

The next race was always a sure way of distracting Dick and the conversation quickly turned again to sport, not just Dick's races, but also Harry's football. He now played on a regular basis for Hartlepool Old Boys. He was not one of the star players but could hold his own.

Dick enjoyed a successful trip to Ireland. During his trip, he found another love which was to remain with him for the rest of his life, but not a woman this time. He found that nothing could revive you, after a hard-fought race, better than the rich, dark smoothness of a cool glass of Guinness!

It had been a very successful, but very hectic year and Dick was starting to feel tired. He had not explained to Harry that the life he was leading, although exciting, was basically a lonely one. Endless trains, endless hotel rooms. The success was worth it, he was sure of that, but sometimes he just longed for Mrs Johnson's garden, a glass of beer and a pipe full of tobacco!

Although it was already early evening as Dick's train puffed into York Station, it was still quite light. Changing the clocks to British Summer Time had become a permanent fixture that summer, thanks to the Summer Time Act. Dick appreciated the extra hour of daylight when he had such a long journey. He alighted from the train and made his way to the notice board to check his next platform. He did not have far to go and settled on a rather uncomfortable bench to wait for his train.

A very smartly-dressed young lady approached him.

"Please excuse me, but am I on the correct platform for the Darlington train? I am trying to get to Hartlepool and I find all these platforms very confusing." She had a beautiful smile.

"Funnily enough, I am bound for Hartlepool." Dick smiled back, moving along to make room on the bench. "Perhaps we could become travelling companions, train journeys are so tedious alone?"

"Well that is very kind of you, but I really could not presume to inflict myself upon you like that." She seemed suddenly rather embarrassed. "Please accept my apologies for approaching you. I really did not mean to be so forward. I am just not used to travelling alone." She turned and hurried to the other end of the platform.

Dick shrugged and went to a nearby barrow-boy to buy a paper for the rest of his journey. The train was on time, which was very unusual. He was just settling his bags on the rack above his seat when the door to his compartment opened and the smart young lady started struggling through with her suitcase.

"Allow me," said Dick, removing the case from her hands and quickly swinging it on to the rack next to his own.

"Well we meet again. Allow me to introduce myself." He held out his hand. "I am Richard Ripley, but my friends call me Dick, and, despite your worst fears, I do not bite." The young lady laughed.

"You must think me an absolute idiot," She smiled. "Your name is familiar to me though. Are you a writer perhaps?" She was clutching a copy of "She", by Rider Haggard. "I'm very keen on literature, I'm a teacher. That's why I have been to York. I went to attend some lectures on Rider Haggard. It was organised as a sort of memorial, following his death in May."

"Oh I have read "King Solomon's Mines" but I would never aspire to writing such things." Dick laughed. "No, I'm an athlete. As you live in Hartlepool you may have read of some of my achievements in the Northern Daily Mail?"

"I'm afraid I do not follow sport with any enthusiasm, but my father is very keen on athletics. No doubt that is where I have heard your name. Do you mind if I share your journey after all?" Dick realised that they were still stood looking at each other. He quickly moved to allow her to be seated.

"I do apologise Miss, erm, I don't think I caught your name?" Dick could not take his eyes of her. There was none of the incredible beauty of Nanette but there was something about this lady that stirred his emotions. She had very dark, neatly styled hair and very dark brown eyes. Her eyes were her main feature. They were warm and friendly and reminded Dick of Lady, the dog he had loved so much. He laughed to himself. No doubt this lady would not take kindly to being compared to a dog, but then Lady was no ordinary dog!

"My name is Kathleen Newcombe. I am very pleased to meet you," She replied politely, bringing Dick's thoughts back to earth.

The journey passed very quickly after that. They soon found that they had a lot in common. Both loved literature and the cinema. Kathleen had even taken holidays in the Dales and loved walking. She helped her father in their garden and adored roses and dogs! By the end of the journey they felt that they had known each other forever and as Kathleen loved dogs, Dick even told her of Lady.

"She had wonderful eyes," he concluded, "dark brown and incredibly warm, just like yours, in fact." Kathleen blushed. "Well, it appears that we have arrived. I don't remember a journey ever being so short." She started to struggle with her bag again.

"Here I'll do that!" Dick reached up and brushed against her arm. He felt as though an electric shock had passed through him. He lifted the bag outside and returned for his own. They stood facing each other on the platform.

"It really has been a pleasure," Kathleen breathed. "I hope we will meet again sometime?"

"The Picture House...   ." Dick stuttered, "I mean could I accompany you to a film at The Picture House. I'm afraid I don't know what is showing but it doesn't matter, they are all good anyway aren't they?" He realised that he was starting to babble and looked at his feet. Kathleen laughed.

"I'd be delighted to accompany you. Perhaps you would care to call tomorrow evening and introduce yourself to my father first. I'm afraid he is terribly old fashioned." She quickly scribbled her address on a sheet of paper, taken from her purse, and then turned to leave. A porter had come forward for her bag.

"See you tomorrow, don't forget!" She called back.

Dick arrived at Kathleen's home shortly after six the following evening. Mrs Johnson had fussed about, making sure that he was suitably attired. Dick had drawn the line at digging out his full Olympic uniform but had happily worn the blazer, with some neatly pressed grey flannel trousers.

Mr Newcombe answered the door. "Mr Ripley this is an honour," he said. "Kathleen has told me the circumstances of your meeting and I would be delighted if you would call on her whenever you wish."

Dick took to him instantly. He had been visualizing a rather stern, overbearing man, something like his own father, instead the little bald-headed man before him seemed totally the opposite.

"Don't keep the young man at the door." A woman's voice called from inside. "Which film are you planning to see?" The same lady asked as Dick entered. This little rounded woman was obviously Kathleen's mother. She had her eyes, shaded by thick spectacles but they were still the same underneath.

"Well it appears that "The Ten Commandments" is showing at The Empire and "The Hunchback of Notre Dame" is on at The Picture House. Both sound quite good and I understand that Lon Chaney is outstanding as the Hunchback. That could be a little scary though. If Kathleen prefers there is a Buster Keaton comedy on The Gaumont. I think it is called "The Navigator". I've never seen any Buster Keaton films myself, but my brother assures me that they are very funny."

"Well you've certainly done your homework anyway, young man!" Kathleen's father smiled. "She's just powdering her nose and won't be long. Please sit down." Dick felt rather awkward as Mr Newcombe kept looking at him. "What's it like to run with Mr Liddell?" He suddenly asked.

Dick didn't have time to reply as Kathleen finally arrived in the room and apologised for keeping Dick waiting.

They did see the Buster Keaton film that evening and all the others during the course of the next few weeks. Autumn had arrived and the race meetings had finished for that year. Dick was, just for once, happy to relax and enjoy life a little. He still made monthly trips to London to train with the Polytechnic Harriers and did his regular morning and evening training sessions, but there was still plenty of time for Kathleen.

As she had admitted, she was not really interested in sport and, although she accepted Dick's monthly excursions, she found all talk of championships and training rather boring.

At first Dick enjoyed the novelty of their courtship. They took long walks, visited friends, had bicycle rides and enjoyed the cinema. They had their quiet moments as well but Kathleen made it very clear that, whilst holding hands and an occasional kiss was acceptable, there could be nothing more until there was ring on her finger. Dick wasn't ready for that. He liked Kathleen a lot. Sometimes he even thought that he loved her, but something was missing.

The troubles started in the Spring, when the race season once again got under way. With Dick's reputation now well established he was expected to represent the Amateur Athletics Association in all the representative matches, as he had done in 1925. This meant that he was away from home a great deal and working very hard, selling insurance, when he was home.

He saw less and less of Kathleen and began to dread their meetings.

"Oh nice of you to turn up!" Kathleen snapped tartily when Dick arrived at her door one evening.

"Kathleen I only arrived home yesterday." Dick tried to explain.

"Well I heard you were with your cronies in the Royal last night. The lads and the drink must come first with you." She snapped.

"I need to unwind after an international event and, when I've won, I enjoy talking about it. What's wrong with that?" Dick demanded. "After all, you won't even let me mention my running!"

"It's about time you grew up and settled down," Kathleen retorted. "You are just messing me about. There's plenty of nice young men would have married me long before this. If I wasn't loyal to you I could have lots of admirers. Ronnie Hendry is always asking me out."

"Well damn well go out with Ronnie Hendry then!" Dick snapped. He turned on his heels and marched away without a backward glance.

Dick did regret loosing his temper, but he was not yet ready to give up his racing for anyone. He was only two years away from the next Olympics and there could be no doubt in his mind that he would have the gold this time, and for more than one event, if things followed the present course.

The Bronze Medal & Dick. 1924.

149

*Top : Dick (left in picture) as part of the
Guard of Honour to
HRH the Prince of Wales in Paris 1924.
Bottom : The Empire Games Team :
L-R Liddell, Butler, Toms & Ripley*

*Dick's
Olympic Games
Lapel Badge
1924*

*Souvenir Programme
from the
U.S.A. v British Empire
Games*

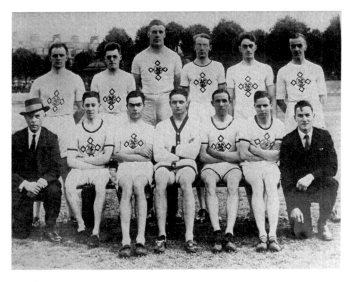

The 'Great Britain Athletic Team ... 1924 Olympic Games

*Dick in his youth (top)
and later in retirement (bottom)
with some of his trophies.*

Chapter 22

By the summer of 1926 Dick had won 44 first prizes in open competition and he held 17 individual titles. He had won the Northern Counties 440 yards for the sixth time and had never failed to count in any of the Amateur Athletics Association events that he had been chosen to represent, but the pace was taking it's toll..

Dick had been upset at loosing Kathleen and missed her friendship. It had been special. True, he still had Harry, Jack and the other lads but his life did not seem complete. As with Nanette, his running helped heal the wound, but this time it did not seem to completely fill the gap.

Kathleen did try to make the peace but Dick knew that it would not work. Within six months of their final argument, he heard that she was engaged to Ronnie Hendry and, although he genuinely wished her well, he had to admit to a few pangs of jealousy.

"You seem so content, Harry," Dick sighed as he watched Harry smile into the cradle of his new born son. The baby was sleeping and Dick had been invited to tea, to meet his new nephew. "You have a steady job, a lovely wife and a beautiful son. I sometimes wonder if I'm missing something important, dashing about the country, in search of more races to run and trophies to win."

"Well there can be no doubt in my mind that I wouldn't swap you lives right now," Harry agreed. "However I might not agree with you at 3am in the morning, when this little fellow is testing his lungs." He laughed. "Don't worry Dick, you'll find someone one day and I've no doubt that, if you find the right lass, she'll support your athletics career as well. Kathleen wasn't the one Dick."

"How on earth am I meant to find the right one dashing about the country though?" Dick sighed.

"Well you met Kathleen, and Nanette, while you were on your travels. If it is meant to be, it will be. Come and have a beer and cheer up. Lots of lads would give their eyeteeth for your life!"

Things didn't improve though. The Johnsons had asked Dick to a family gathering, but Mrs Johnson would not explain. Dick was rather worried about her, she was not getting any younger and her back problems and arthritis were getting worse.

After a lovely dinner, cooked by Daphne, Jack asked Dick if he would come into his study for port and cigars. Nothing unusual in this, Jack had always continued the tradition of withdrawing to allow the ladies to clear away the meal etc.

"It's mother, Dick," he started. "I don't know how to put this but she can't manage to keep up her house any longer. I know you have helped her a lot, what with taking over her garden and helping with heavy work. The thing is, you're not usually home much these days and she is lonely and spends much of her time here, with Daphne and myself. She only goes home when she knows you are coming back. Anyway Daphne is expecting a baby and would like mother's support. We have asked her to move in with us Dick, and the only thing stopping her doing so is you."

"I really hadn't realised," Dick cut in. "Of course I will look for alternative accommodation immediately." He actually felt like crying. Mrs Johnson had always been there for him. She was like a mother to him. More than a mother, a friend. He knew that what Jack was saying was true. He had no right to stand in her way, and the house was too much for her now, but what would he do? Most of his life lately was spent in unfriendly hotel rooms. Was he to live in an unfriendly boarding house when he came home as well? Jack was speaking again but Dick's mind was in a frenzy and he only caught the end.

". .said that they would be pleased to have you at home." Jack paused.

"Sorry Jack, I really didn't catch what you said. I am very fond of your mother and I agree that she should have an easier life. Oh and congratulations about the baby by the way. I'm just a bit thunderstruck. I had always thought of Mrs J being there for me. Very selfish, I realise that, but it just never occurred to me that things would have to change." Dick stammered on, taking a good pull at his port. Jack topped up his glass.

"Mother is very fond of you, as well Dick, and would not hear of this, until Harry told us of your father's determination to have you living at home again. He would have spoken to you by now, but I asked him to let me talk to you first. Your mother and Martha are very excited about the idea, especially now that Betty is to be married and Gertrude is taking a teaching post away from home."

"I don't know about any of this." Dick was horrified. "How can I live under the same roof as my father again. I still love mother and always had a soft spot for Martha but my father is a different kettle of fish!"

"You work with him every day Dick, he supports you." Jack said quietly. "I thought you needed his help?"

"I do!" Dick retorted, quite angrily, "but that does not mean that I want to live with the man as well!"

"He's older Dick, and proud of you. You have grown up now as well. There shouldn't be a problem. That house is huge anyway, you probably won't even have to see him." Jack continued to reason calmly, but he knew that Dick would not be persuaded. He would have to be allowed to make up his own mind. The last thing Jack wanted was to fall out with Dick over this.

"Anyway I am sure that you'll find somewhere easily, if you prefer not to return home. Let's rejoin the ladies." Jack rose from his seat and Dick followed grudgingly.

Dick excused himself fairly quickly that evening. He said that he had to leave for London again early the next morning and wished to take a walk before retiring.

"Oh but I thought you weren't leaving until tea-time tomorrow," Mrs Johnson cried. "I haven't finished ironing your kit yet!"

"Thank you but I am quite capable of looking after that myself. Please don't distress yourself!" Dick snapped, as he left the room.

It was raining quite hard as Dick joined the street, but he decided to walk for a while to cool down. He knew he had been unreasonable and rude, but he felt as though his world had fallen apart again. What was the matter with him? Jack was right, Mother and Martha would look after him well, and Father was a lot more reasonable these days. Would it be that difficult? Perhaps he should just go home.

His feet took him towards Hutton Avenue and he turned into the garden gate. He stood for a while, in front of the door, willing himself to knock. He was just about to give up and walk away when the door opened and Martha flew out. She threw her arms around him.

"Come in Master Dick!" Martha started pulling him through the door. "I saw you from the parlour window. What are you doing getting all wet like that? You'll be getting that malady thing again." Martha continued to fuss, removing Dick's hat and unbuttoning his coat, just as she had done when he was a little boy. For a moment he felt as though he had really come home.

Dick had always resisted visiting the family home and the few visits he had made were during the daylight. He was therefore very surprised by the intensity of the light in the entrance hall. It was very brightly lit and Dick realised that there were no gas lamps or candles. Many of the hotels he had stopped in had this new electric lighting installed but very few houses in Hartlepool had this yet.

"Father must be doing very well to have electricity installed." He commented to himself, rather than Martha. "I rather like it." The twinkling crystal chandeliers, coupled with Martha's warm welcome, lifted his spirits. Perhaps it would be not be so bad to come home after all. He could not deny that he enjoyed luxury, and being pampered, as much as the next man.

"Who is it Martha?" His father's voice came from the study at the end of the hall.

It's me Father," Dick replied. "I would like to ask your help, if you have a moment."

Richard came out of the room and shook Dick's hand. "Nice to see you son. What is the problem, perhaps I can guess?" He guided Dick into his study. "Sit down son." Dick settled into the impressive leather armchair next to his father's desk. "So your friends have finally let you down, and you need accommodation?"

"It's hardly like that!" Dick could feel his temper rising and he rose to his feet again. Why did his father always have that effect on him? "For your information Mrs Johnson is unwell and needs care herself. It was Jack who suggested that I contact you. Apparently Harry told him that you were keen to have me back home, with both Betty and Gerty flying the nest. If he's wrong, don't put yourself out, I'd rather sleep in the gutter than beg you for anymore favours!" Dick turned on his heels and started to leave. Then, suddenly, and for no apparent reason, he remembered Uncle John and the cottage in the Dales. He turned back.

"Oh, but come to think of it, I am, or should be, a man of property myself. What happened to the cottage that Uncle John left for me in the Dales? You could release that to me. I always hoped to move there one day, but I must be practical. I can sell it and buy somewhere locally."

"I think that you are forgetting that John never made a Will." Richard corrected him sharply. "That property passed to your grandfather and then to me. You cannot sell it, because it is not yours to sell! However come and sit down again and we'll discuss the matter, there's certainly no need for tempers."

Dick returned to his chair. Winifred had come out when she heard the voices but decided that it was best not to interfere. After all, as Richard had told her, on so many occasions, Dick was inclined to be hot-headed. It was best to leave this to Richard. She did hope that Dick would decide to come home though.

"I will put my cards on the table." Richard offered Dick a cigar. "This house did not come cheaply and the electric lighting, that I had installed, cost far more than I anticipated. No-one was using the property in Swaledale at the time, so I sold it."

"What!" Dick rose to his feet again.

"Please hear me out," Richard said quietly. "You are my eldest child and my next of kin. One day this house and everything I own will be yours. The money from that cottage has been invested into this property. You haven't lost it. Come home, enjoy the house that the cottage partly financed."

"Hang on just one minute," Dick was not happy. "I

understood that you changed your Will after I left home. I get nothing and you have broken your word to John. Oh Father, I knew you were a swine but how could you? John trusted you."

"Let me explain Richard. It's true that I did change my Will but I can change it back again. I will go to the Solicitors tomorrow. Come with me. Please Richard, you have to see my point of view. You had left home and wanted nothing more to do with me. As far as I was concerned, my obligations to you were over and I had a cottage that I did not want. I know it was wrong and I have tried to make amends since. Give me the chance to put things right. I know John would turn in his grave if he thought I had fallen down on his dying wish. I don't often admit to my mistakes but let me put this right."

Dick was too tired to argue. Anyway it did mean that he could come home without loosing face. They shook hands and Dick agreed to bring his stuff round the next day, before he caught the over night sleeper to London. Winifred and Martha were called and informed.

"We'll give you Harry's old room at the front. It's South facing so you can enjoy sun." Martha couldn't keep the delight out of her voice. Both women rushed off to prepare his room, giggling like school girls.

Dick left as soon as he could to return to the Johnson's. He had some serious apologising to do!

Chapter 23

The journey to London seemed long and difficult this time. Travel throughout the last four months had been arduous. There had been the General Strike in May, when Dick hadn't been able to get to London at all. Then, after that, all the transport workers had been too busy protesting in London to run trains regularly. Still Dick couldn't blame them. The ordinary workers had little enough to live on, without the Royal Commissioners' proposal to cut wages and abolish the minimum wage. The miners were still on strike, four months down the line and Dick didn't know how they were surviving. Everyone else had returned to work after nine days!

Now the trains were persistently running slow or not running at all. Lack of coal or co-operation, Dick wasn't sure exactly what was causing it, but he had started to dread the journeys.

As luck would have it he arrived at Kings Cross only two hours late. It was getting towards the end of that year's athletics season and, although he was racing for the Poly this time, it was not an important event. He won the race easily and was soon in a cab making the return journey to the Station. He was surprised to find a long queue of vehicles, as they approached Piccadilly Circus.

"What seems to be the trouble?" Dick asked the driver.

"Oh it's them new-fangled traffic lights," the driver retorted. "They were put up a couple of weeks back and we've never had so many problems getting through Piccadilly."

"What on earth are traffic lights?" Dick asked, somewhat puzzled. Why would anyone put up lights to cause traffic problems, he wondered?

"They're supposed to stop traffic being held up and give

people from the side roads a chance." The driver replied. "They might be quite good if they ever worked proper, but they're always breaking down."

"Whatever next?" Dick sighed and sat back to wait, hoping it was not the start of another difficult journey. He felt rather unwell, as though he had a chill. He hoped he could get home quickly, in case he had taken a fever of some sort.

Dick's luck was out. His train was cancelled and he had to spend four hours in a draughty waiting room, before the next one.That, in turn, did not go by a direct route to York and he had to divert to Doncaster and change trains, then York, then Darlington. Even that close to home he had still more windy platforms to wait on. Thornaby didn't even have a waiting room.

By the time he arrived there it was pouring down and he was feeling decidedly ill. He had managed to telephone home and warn them of his late arrival. He was actually relieved and pleased to see his mother and Martha at the station, when he finally arrived.

"Good Lord Master Dick," Martha said, rushing forward, "I told you last week that you'd be sick, getting wet. Now look at you. You're burning up."

Martha and his mother got him home and insisted on putting him straight to bed, after a hot bath. Martha had four stone water bottles and a bed warmer in the bed, when he pulled back the blankets. He couldn't help but laugh.

"Good Heavens Martha, there's no room for me." He said as she bustled forward to remove the bed warmer.

"Well happen it'll sweat the fever out of you." She said hurrying out with the warmer. A nice warm fire was glowing in the hearth and Mother arrived a few minutes later with some homemade broth. Dick didn't feel like eating but did his best, as he knew both these wonderful women would be upset if he didn't eat.

"That's right," his mother said, "feed a cold and starve a fever. We'll soon have you up and running again!"

Dick smiled, his mother obviously didn't realise that she had just made a joke. "Running" was the last thing he felt like right now!

"It's good to be home Mother." Dick said as he felt himself

falling asleep.

"He's been overdoing it I think Martha," Winifred sighed "Still we can keep an eye on him now can't we?"

Dick knew he must have slept for a long time. He had many strange dreams, of being lifted into a wagon and of people talking in whispers near him. He even imagined that he was back in the hospital of his childhood, with Sarah, the nurse, mopping his brow again. He opened his eyes and was shocked to find that it was not a dream, but it was not Sarah either.

"Ah Mr Ripley," the immaculate vision looking down at him said. "You are back with us. I thought you were starting to wake, at last. You've been drifting in and out of consciousness for several days now. Do you remember anything?" She asked in a beautifully soft, soothing voice.

"No, but I have had a lot of dreams." Dick found that he could only whisper. His voice was hoarse and his throat was sore. "Where am I? What has happened?" He asked as she helped him take sips of water.

"Not too much now. You had an attack of malaria, a bad one. We really were not sure that you would pull through, but your mother told us that you were a fighter, with incredible stamina. I knew that anyway, I've seen you run on numerous occasions. No one could give their heart and soul to running, as you do, and then be beaten by an eight year old mosquito bite." She laughed.

"Now you must rest. I will get the doctor to have a look at you now you are awake." She turned to leave.

"First, please tell me your name and where I am." Dick pleaded.

"You are in the General Hospital. This used to be the Workhouse, but the infirmary became more and more in demand and the Workhouse lost its popularity, so we admit a lot of men now. It's easier for your family to visit here, than St Hilda's, I would think." She pushed a stand of hair away under her head-dress. Dick couldn't help but notice that it was auburn, not red like Nanette, but a rich deep colour, like polished mahogany, touched by the glow of a cosy fire on a cold winter's evening.

"Oh my name is Sister Swales, by the way, and I run this

ward, so you had better behave and get better. I will not have people saying that I lost West Hartlepool's best young athlete." She smiled and she turned to leave.

"Sister Swales seems very formal," Dick croaked. "Don't you have a christian name?"

"It's Cecilia, and don't you dare call me Ces or Cissy, I hate it!" Her almond eyes flashed a warning.

"I wouldn't dare." Dick smiled as he sank back into his pillows and drifted back to sleep, this time to dream much more exciting dreams!

Dick made good progress, but was in hospital for another two weeks. He had no urgent desire to leave. Cecilia was an interesting woman, very widely read and with an interest in athletics that Dick had not known in a woman since his friend Freda, in his childhood.

During her working hours Cecilia was very busy and had little time to talk, but she quickly developed a habit of spending half an hour chattering, after the end of her shift. By the end of the two weeks they knew almost everything about each other. Cecilia lived in the nurses' hostel. She came from one of the colliery villages and, at the moment, was supporting her family through the strike. Her father and brothers were miners. She had been fortunate in that she had completed her nursing training before money had become tight for the family. As she enjoyed nursing, she quickly learnt the skills required and obtained promotion to Ward Sister within a couple of years of completing her training. Her ambition was to be Matron one day.

"Don't you want to marry and raise a family though?" Dick asked. He was rather surprised to find a lady who seemed to want to work, rather than run her own home.

"Oh, if I meet the right gentleman, perhaps I will think about it someday." She replied. "To be honest I have never really bothered with gentlemen callers. I have been very busy with my studies. I did walk out with one of my brother's friends for a short while, but he considered my career as a waste of time. He actually resented the time that I spent with my books. Then again, he wasn't a very good reader himself. I think my desire to learn frightened him a little. What about you, do you not have a steady lady friend?"

Dick found himself telling her all about Nanette and Kathleen. "Like you, I really haven't had that much time for a steady relationship and Kathleen definitely resented the amount of time that I spent running and travelling to races."

"Well she should have travelled with you. Silly girl!" Cecilia rose to leave. "Well Dick, the doctor says you may leave tomorrow. I will miss our little chats, I must admit. I feel like I have known you all my life. I do wish you the very best with your career and hope that you will attend to your health better in future." She held out her hand.

"It's no good," Dick grasped her hand. "I can't just let you disappear out of my life like that. You have become a very dear friend, in the last two weeks. Please can we meet sometime?"

Cecilia laughed. "I thought you would never ask!" Dick and Cecilia became almost inseparable from that day forward. Cecilia not only attended his races, but even held the stop-watch during training. She was not athletic herself but devoured the sports reports in the newspapers almost as avidly as Dick did. Dick, in turn, encouraged her studies, often testing her from her books before her examinations.

Although the relationship started on a friendly basis, it quickly developed into a warm and passionate affair. Dick found that he never tired of Cecilia's company and actually missed her dreadfully when they were apart, even for a few hours.

By Christmas of 1926 they had already met each other's families and Father even approved of this beautiful and intelligent lady.

"Don't let her get away Richard," he whispered after dinner one evening. "Get a ring on her finger before someone else does."

Dick laughed but it did start him thinking. He had not known Cecilia as long as Kathleen, but already they were far more united in spirit, and body for that matter. He had thought that he had loved Nanette, now he realised that it was probably no more than boyish lust. What Cecilia and he shared, was not just a passion, it was a uniting of two souls. Neither of them were particularly experienced, but that didn't matter. In fact it meant that they could explore and learn together. Yes Dick was sure this was love. There was no doubt in his mind. He felt a glow when Cecilia walked into the room, an excitement when they touched and a warm contentment when they were together.

"Do you think people would think that I was rushing things if I proposed on Christmas Day?" Dick asked Harry, a week before Christmas.

"Don't be daft man, you've been walking out for nearly four months now. Everyone can see in your faces that you are in love." Harry laughed. "Anyway who cares what anyone else thinks, how do you feel?"

"There is no doubt in my mind Harry. I love her, I'd even give up athletics for her!" Dick declared.

"Good heavens, you have got it bad." Harry laughed. "Get on with it then. It might be nice if you asked her father first though. Those brothers of hers are well over six foot. I wouldn't like to get on the wrong side of them!"

Dick asked both Mother and Mrs Johnson's advice about the ring and set off to see Mr Swales one evening, after he had left Cecilia at the hospital.

The family lived in a terrace of small, two storey, miners cottages. The small living room cum kitchen was very cosy with its black range and fire roaring up the chimney. Mrs Swales was baking bread and fussing with the preparations for the Christmas dinner. Mr Swales was puffing on his pipe and warming his toes, staring into the flames, when Dick arrived. The family did not stand on ceremony and he had been told the first time that he had called, that he must let himself in.

"Come in lad and sit yer self down." Mr Swales greeted him. He didn't rise and Dick took the seat opposite. He felt uncomfortable.

"Hmm," He started. "Mr Swales, Sir, I would like to ask your daughter to marry me and I would like your permission to do so. My prospects are good, I have a good, steady job, as an insurance agent, and I come from a good family."

"Oh shut up lad and have a beer," her dad said. "If you want to marry our Ces, good luck to yer. She has a temper in her mind. It's that red hair of hers, but she's a good lass at heart."

The rest of the evening went very well and Dick was rather the worse for wear when he left. The miners were back to work now and Mr Swales was only too happy to celebrate!

Dick was only allowed to leave on condition that he would come to share their dinner on Christmas Day. He readily accepted. He knew that Mother was planning a big family dinner, but that was to be in the evening. Hopefully Cecilia would agree to attend that as well, then both families would be happy.

It turned into the best Christmas Dick had ever known. The Swales were in high spirits. He waited until dinner was over. Mr Swales had proposed a number of toasts and then Dick rose. Firstly he thanked the ladies for a wonderful dinner, then he turned to Cecilia.

"I haven't given you my main present yet," he started. He removed the small parcel from his pocket and took her hand.

"Sister Swales," he started formally, "would you please consent to become Sister Ripley instead?"

"Are you asking me to marry you?" Cecilia teased, bemused by the way he had put the question.

"Of course you daft thing," her mother chided. "Put the lad out of his misery, and be quick about it!"

Cecilia threw her arms around Dick's neck. "Oh yes, it will be wonderful." She opened the parcel quickly. Inside was a beautiful ruby, surrounded by tiny diamonds. It twinkled and caught the fire light. "It's beautiful Dick, but why a ruby?"

"I thought it would compliment your hair. Martha didn't approve," he continued. "She came up with some old wives' tale about rubies meaning blood and bad luck, but I thought it would suit you. I can change it if you don't like it." Dick felt crestfallen.

"Don't be daft, it's beautiful." Cecilia said, putting it on her finger, "and it fits too. Oh you are clever, how did you get the size?"

"I cheated!" Dick grinned, relieved. "Do you remember when we were out with Daphne and Jack, and Daphne got you to try her ring on?" Cecilia nodded. "Well her ring fit you, so she came to the jewellers with me, and tried yours on. I hope you don't mind?"

"Of course I don't. It was very thoughtful of you. I love

rubies and Martha can keep her superstitions to herself!"

The conversation turned to weddings. Dick hoped that Cecilia didn't want a long engagement.

"The athletics season usually starts in April," he explained. "It would be nice if we could marry before that, then, we could have a honeymoon somewhere. The Dales perhaps?"

Before long it was all agreed. the wedding would be in March. Dick could not wait to get home to break the news to his family. The rest of the day was an excited whirl of congratulations and celebrations. Boxing Day continued in the same vein, when they broke the news to the Johnsons. The day turned into one of the Johnsons' famous parties and they were dancing well into the night. Dick had never performed the "Black Bottom" or the "Charleston" with so much enthusiasm!

"Oh Dick, this has been the best Christmas ever!" Cecilia puffed happily, collapsing onto the sofa, after a particularly wild bout of dancing.

"This is just the start," Dick promised. He reached for her hand and kissed it. "Life for us will be laughter and happiness from now on, I insist."

Chapter 24

It was a spring wedding in every sense. Daffodils were tossing their golden heads all over the grounds of the tiny village church. Birds were excitedly dashing about, gathering grasses and tiny pieces of wool for their nests. The air smelled sweet and the sun was smiling. As Dick made his way to the church door he felt that his heart would burst. Everything was so perfect.

Cecilia arrived in a horse-driven chaise. She hadn't wanted an automobile. "They are so smelly and noisy," she had explained. "I want our wedding to be normal and homely. I don't want to be fashionable."

Dick could not help but smile as he saw her approaching him at the alter. She looked an absolute picture in her cream lace three quarter length dress, that could not be denied, but it was the very height of fashion. Certainly not at all homely or ordinary! The bouquet though, that was absolutely beautiful. It was a melee of spring flowers, tied with a huge cream satin bow.

Dick moved to her side, as his sister Gertrude moved forward to take the bouquet. As the only unmarried sister on either side, she had the role of chief bridesmaid. Two of Cecilia's young nurses were also in attendance. Harry was, of course, best man.

The day continued as perfectly as it had started. After the ceremony the whole party returned to Cecilia's family home for the wedding breakfast. Fortunately, according to the male members of the party, the house was far too small and everyone had to retire to the local hostelry to continue the celebrations.

It was well into the afternoon when Dick took his new bride to one side.

"Well Mrs Ripley, you are even more beautiful than the spring flowers that you held so nervously this morning. I have loved today and I wish it could never end." He kissed her gently. "However we must be sensible. The roads in the dales are not good. I think we should sneak away soon. After all it is a long way to Swaledale and it is still dark by seven o'clock?"

Dick had arranged to stay in Debra cottage again. He could not wait to show Cecilia his favourite mountains.

"Dad's car is quite fast, if we leave now we might just catch the sunset on the mountains. It would be just a perfect end to a perfect day." Cecilia laughed. She already understood Dick's love of sunsets. They had watched many from the Fish Sands and the end of the Heugh. She had loved those peaceful and contented moments, but Dick had insisted that they could not compare with the splendours to be seen in the Dales.

Although they did make good time they had not reached Reeth before the sun vanished behind the fast gathering clouds. Dick seemed troubled by this.

"I do hope it is not a bad omen for us," he sighed. "I did so want the day to be perfect right to the very end."

"Don't be silly!" Cecilia laughed. "It has been perfect. We can't always have everything we want you know."

Debra cottage was just as Dick had remembered it. It was rather cold when they arrived but someone had laid the fire, and it did not take long to have the flames roaring up the chimney. They snuggled together on the hearth rug, a huge raggy mat that smelt of peat and heather.

"This is just perfect," Cecilia sighed contentedly. "Life is going to be good Dick. I just know it."

The honeymoon only lasted a week but it was the happiest week of Dick's life. The two shared all the pathways of Dick's youth. During the evenings he told her some of the tales he remembered from his hours in front of the fire with Uncle John. They climbed up Great Shunner Fell, crawled into Swinnergill Kirk, wandered amongst the deserted miners cottages built at the Old Gang lead mines and felt the despair that those same miners must have felt at Surrender Bridge. Cecilia particularly understood the plight of the miners, vividly remembering the recent hard times her own family had felt during the 1926 strike.

On their last evening they stood in the outline of Maiden Castle. The wind was blowing softly and the sun was just starting to set. The silver and gold rays of the setting sun crept across the valley and the whole dale was bathed in an unearthly glow. The wind caught in the heather and grasses. It was as though the valley and mountains were whispering to them. Dick shivered.

"It's like Heathcliff and Cathy in Wuthering Heights." Cecilia whispered. "Do you think that we will roam these moors when we are gone Dick?"

"Don't talk like that!" Dick replied quietly, "we are young, we will walk these moors hundreds of times before we die."

"Well, promise me that if I die first you will have me cremated and you will scatter my ashes up here." Cecilia had taken his hands and was staring intently into his face. Dick felt his skin prickle, as though someone had just walked over his grave.

"Please don't talk like that," he pleaded. "It must be all those stories I have been telling you, they are making you morbid. Anyway," he said more lightly, "we're not going to die, we're going to live for ever." He laughed and pulled away, taking hold of her hand. "Come on, we must get down into the valley before it gets dark. Bet you can't catch me." He ran off with Cecilia laughing behind. The spell had been broken but Dick would never forget that moment.

Later that night, as they were on the verge of sleep, Cecilia suddenly turned her face to Dick.

"You must promise me that one day we will be together forever on those moors." Her eyes held his. "Please Dick. I don't know why but it is important."

"Alright, if it's the only way you will let me get some sleep, I'll promise." He laughed, no longer afraid of the whispering mountains.

"Who said anything about sleep anyway?" Cecilia smiled, as she reached for him longingly.

Next morning saw the return to normality. Cecilia had moved in with Dick at his father's house, until they could find decent accommodation of their own. Winifred had insisted that they should stay there at least until the athletics season was over.   "You will be very lonely, with Dick gadding all over the place," she had insisted.

"Oh, but when I can get leave I intend to travel with him." Cecilia had reminded her.

"Never mind that dear, you don't want to be trailing all over the country. You may want to start a family or something." Winifred had a glint in her eye.

"Well there is no doubt that I love children," Cecilia reassured her, "but there is no hurry."

That had been a month before the wedding. A week after, on their return from the Dales, Cecilia was already feeling tired and sickly. Being a nurse she knew the signs all too well. As both Dick and she had agreed that they would both love a family, they had agreed not to be too concerned about birth control. They had certainly not given it any consideration since Christmas. Now Cecilia was certain that things had moved on a great deal quicker than she had expected.

Dick had left for London, two days after they had returned from the Dales. He had to recommence training with the Poly and was to represent the Amateur Athletics Association in an Easter event. Cecilia could not accompany him as she had to return to work. She therefore decided not to reveal her secret until it was definite. Dick was away for ten days and on his return was so excited that she did not have chance to get a word in edgeways!

"I've already been told that I am certain for selection for next year's Olympics." He burst out excitedly, as soon as he alighted from the train. "They are treating me as they did Mr Liddell. No, better than Liddell! The Committee were always a little wary of Liddell's scruples, they know I won't give them trouble." Dick picked Cecilia up and swung her round laughing.

"How do you fancy a trip to Amsterdam next year?" He stopped suddenly realising that Cecilia had turned very pale.

"That could be a problem," she replied smiling. "Dick I may not be able to accompany you at all."

"What is the matter," Dick demanded, "are you ill? I refuse to allow you to be ill, you are too important." He held her hand tightly.

"No silly," she laughed, "not ill exactly, more pregnant really."

"Pregnant?" Dick asked, the true implication not sinking in immediately. "How? When?" He stuttered. His face lit up as he realised what she was saying. "Are you telling me that I am going to be a Dad? That is marvellous. What an incredibly clever woman you are." He kissed her excitedly. Cecilia pulled away and reminded him that they were still in the station, and gathering quite an audience.

"People are watching," she scolded. "Anyway I didn't do this alone you know, you did your part."

The baby was due in October, by Cecilia's reckoning. Their first decision was to find a home of their own. Winifred tried to persuade them that they would be better staying in Hutton Avenue.

"There's lots of room and Cecilia would have all the help she would need from Martha and myself," she explained. "You will need to be away a lot Dick, especially when you start your Olympic training. Cecilia would never be alone with us here."

"Really Mrs Ripley, I do appreciate your offer," Cecilia replied kindly but firmly, "but I would like to start my family in my own home. You will be very welcome to come and help when the baby is due though. In fact I would really love it if you would." She added quickly .

With Harry's help the couple soon found a lovely little home at No.9 Coleridge Avenue. It was only a two bedroomed terrace house, but it was in a nice neighbourhood, just near St Aiden's church, and the rent was very reasonable. Cecilia had to leave her employment as soon as her pregnancy became evident, so funds were fairly tight. It didn't matter. Their life was perfect. Dick was at the top of his career, Cecilia was blooming and now they had their own home. Soon they would be a proper family!

They were sitting on some packing cases in the yard, one evening, enjoying the last of the sun's rays. Dick was enjoying his pipe as usual. Twilight was heightening the colours all around and casting long shadows. The yard was hardly big enough to sit in and was a little difficult to get used to, after the gardens Dick had grown to love. Dick already had it full of tubs and pots. There were showers of colour in every corner. Vivid red geraniums, deep blue lobelia, white allysum and purple pertunias sprouted in profusion. Dick was not talking of this yard though. His thoughts were already moving towards their next house, which he insisted, would have a huge garden.

"Just wait until I'm rich and famous," he dreamed. "The garden will be divided into separate areas," he continued. "The vegetable patch over in that corner" Dick pointed with his pipe, as though it was all laid out in front of them. "We will have an apple tree with a tyre swing for the lads..."

"Hang on!" Cecilia laughed, "won't the tree be too small for a swing and what if this baby is a girl?"

"It doesn't matter," Dick continued, blowing smoke rings into the gathering dusk. "I will put a swing on the shed door then, and our daughter will enjoy it just as much!" He beamed as he continued and turned to face Cecilia. "But who cares if we never get that house with a garden, I can always rent an allotment or something and let's be honest, things can't get much better than this. Some days I feel frightened though. No-one is entitled to have this much happiness in one life time. I keep looking for the catch." He kissed her hand tenderly.

"Don't be silly Dick, everyone is entitled to happiness. You listen to Martha's stupid superstitions too often!" Cecilia suddenly shivered. "It's becoming cold, let's go in," she said, rising with difficulty.

Chapter 25

Richard Nicholson Ripley Junior made his loud appearance in October, as Dick and Cecilia had anticipated. The rest of the world accepted that he was approximately two months early, and everyone was far to polite to query the fact that a seven month baby could be 8lb 2oz at birth.

Cecilia handled the birth well. Dick found it a very traumatic experience. As soon as the pains started he was shooed out of the way, while the ladies and the doctor took over. Harry and Jack took him to the Blacksmith's Arms and tried to reassure him.

"There have been no problems with her pregnancy Dick. Cecilia is healthy and sensible. You really must not worry." Jack chided as he put the frothing pint glass in front of him.

"I just feel that I should be there," Dick explained. "It's my baby as well. I should help."

"Don't be ridiculous Dick!" Harry laughed. "You would only get in the way. Us men are best right out of the way at a time like this."

"What if something goes wrong though?" Dick fretted, "I should be there." The other two laughed and continued to ply Dick with alcohol, until he forgot how worried he was. When they returned him home, two hours later, he was very much the worse for wear, but everything was over. Cecilia was asleep, so Winifred and Martha merely bundled Dick into the spare room and left him to sleep it off.

Dick woke next morning to the sounds of a baby crying. Without stopping to think he ran into their bedroom, afraid that there was a problem.

"Come in Daddy," Cecilia smiled."You look terrible. I think you must have had a harder night than I did yesterday." Dick laughed, relieved that both his wife and his new son were fine.

"Is he all there?" He asked.

"Well if he takes after his father he will leave a lot to be desired." Winifred teased as she entered the room. "He had ten fingers, ten toes etc. if that's what you mean. We won't know whether he has all his wits about him for a year or two yet though. They don't come walking and talking you know!"

Dick loved his new son, but had been brought up in a strict Victorian household where fathers did not get involved with the care and maintenance of babies. He did help a little with the sleepless nights though and delighted in telling his baby son stories in the early hours of the morning. It didn't matter that young Richard could not understand. It was their time together.

Cecilia was an excellent mother and, with the help of Martha, coped very well with the extra responsibilities.

Winter passed quickly into Spring and athletics again demanded Dick's attention. Cecilia insisted that he should continue with his career and he did not take much persuasion, especially as this was the year of his second chance to win a gold in Amsterdam.

As he once more sat in the train to London, this time to compete in the heats to determine the Olympic team selection, he was filled with mixed feelings. His athletics were still his main driving force, but now he had responsibilities and it had been hard to leave Cecilia and young Dick. He knew they would be well cared for by Mother and Martha, but he felt a great emptiness as he travelled alone.

Cecilia had been very business-like that morning. His case had been packed on the previous evening, and a cab arranged. They had both agreed that Dick would not be accompanied to the station at so early an hour.

As he kissed his wife and son goodbye, Dick found a lump in his throat and he knew that tears were not far behind. He tried to be strong.

"Now young man," he whispered to baby Dick, who was sucking merrily on his thumb, "you be the man of the house until I get back, and take care of your Mummy."

"Get away with you," Cecilia had said, whilst pretending she had something in her eye, "we'll be just fine. You just go and win those races for us. We want to see you on the Picture House news again!"

Dick had hurried into the cab. As he turned to wave he saw that Cecilia was crying quite openly now.

"Good luck!" She shouted as the cab turned the corner.

Dick coughed as he felt tears prickling his eyes again. This was the big chance, the culmination of all his efforts over the years, he had to go, he knew that. He settled into the train and turned to his newspaper to try and collect his thoughts. He read that the public could now make transatlantic phone calls, London to New York, and a three minute call costs seventy five dollars.

"How come I can never get a call through from the office to Father at home then?"

"Pardon?" A gentleman queried. Dick hadn't even realised that he was muttering to himself.

"I do apologise," Dick said, lifting his trilby. "I was musing over this newspaper article about transatlantic telephone calls. I would have though it more beneficial to ensure that our local service was efficient before expanding across the seas."

The gentleman nodded in agreement and soon a lively conversation ensued which helped, not only to pass the journey, but also to lift Dick's dejected spirits.

On arrival at Stamford Bridge Dick knew that, once he got on with the task at hand, he would have little time to miss his family. He was sad that neither Abrahams nor Butler were to be involved with the forthcoming Olympics but, even more of a blow, was the selection of team trainer. Sam had retired and a man that looked more like he would fit on a parade ground than at an athletics match confronted him at his hotel.

"Now Ripley, I hear that you are our best hope for the 400 metres," the coach began. "Well things are changing. Methods of training are improving all the time and I am confident that under my tutorage you will easily take the gold."

"I intend to do my best," Dick replied, quite taken aback by

175

the man's brusque manner, "but the Americans are always a challenge. I don't intend to under-estimate the opposition."

"Best is not good enough and I have coached in America. They know nothing that I can't teach you. All you need to do is push harder." Dick tried to comment but the coach continued, "I have looked at the films of your earlier races and think that you have more in you than you are giving at present, I intend to see that you give your all!"

Dick started to protest: "No-one can ever say that I don't put my heart and soul into my training. My wife and son hardly see me because I am always running."

"Ah, divided loyalties then. Men should be married to athletics if they are serious, no room for sentiment in competitive sports!" The coach snapped. "Be ready to start in five minutes."

Dick was tired after the journey and had hoped to do a couple of gentle warm up sprints before getting down to the real training. Oh well, this man was supposed to be the best, so he would just have to go along with his ideas, he supposed.

Immediately on arrival at the sports ground Dick found himself hurled into a punishing exercise routine. He considered himself exceptionally fit but found this extremely tiring.

"I don't intend to continue with this much longer." He stood firm as the coach demanded a ridiculous number of press-ups. "Press-ups are hardly going to strengthen my legs."

"If you don't approve of my methods Mr Ripley, you can withdraw from the team at any time," the coach retorted, "but I do agree that this is only the first day and some rest may be required. Just let's do a dash to finish and we will continue tomorrow." Dick didn't mind a quick 220 yard dash and felt quite exhilarated at the end, but the coach's face was not as he had expected.

"Twenty-five seconds Mr Ripley. That was absolute rubbish." he coach snarled. "Do you know that Scholz only took 21.6 seconds or that distance in the Paris Olympics? Times have improved since then! That will never do!"

"For your information, Scholz was running 200 metres, not 220 yards and under Olympic conditions, over his chosen distance. I am a stamina runner, I do my best over 440 yards and right now

I'm training, after a long day travelling, so if you don't like it you know where you can shove it!" Dick snatched his towel from the ground and stormed off to the changing rooms. He could hear the coach shouting behind him but he did not look back.

Dick could hear someone running up to him and a familiar voice shouted:

"That told him good and proper Dick. It's time someone did. The man is power crazy." Dick turned to find Douglas Lowe grinning all over his face. Dick laughed, his bad humour instantly dispersed. He hadn't seen Douglas since the last Olympics.

"Dougie, it's wonderful to see you. I didn't know you were here. I was beginning to think that none of the old team had survived!" Dick rung Dougie's hand enthusiastically. "Abrahams is a high flying business man now and Liddell is converting the whole of the Chinese nation single-handedly. I was starting to feel like a grandad amongst all these young newcomers."

"Oh, I'm still around," Douglas agreed, "but, thankfully, I arrived too late for tonight's training session. I was just in time to see your magnificent exit." They both laughed.

"Well that could be me out of the running," Dick said seriously.

"Oh, I doubt it. You are England's best at the moment, after me, of course, and he knows it. Didn't you hear his grovelling little parting remark?" Dick shook his head.

"I was too angry to listen," he admitted. "My temper will be the death of me one day. What did he say?"

"That's all right Mr. Ripley," Douglas mimicked, wheedling. "We can try again tomorrow, when you are not so tired."

The next day was not much better. Dick was always an early riser and was already in his kit, ready for his morning sprint before breakfast, when there was a knock at the door. Dick was surprised. It was only 6.30am. A bell-boy bowed politely.

"Excuse me Sir, your coach has instructed that you are to rise and report for training before breakfast. He requests your attention by 7am." The boy bowed again and stood politely.

"Does he indeed?" As Dick gave the boy a tip he could feel his temper rising again. Who the hell did this man think he was anyway?!

Dick reported, as requested, and was surprised to find half the team already undergoing an assortment of warming up exercises. Dick stood for a while but the coach just ignored him. After a few minutes he shrugged and started a slow trot around the circuit, the way he always did.

"Mr. Ripley," the coach cried, "what do you think you are doing?"

"I'm warming up in my usual manner." Dick shouted whilst carrying on with his trot.

"Do you think you could make an effort to be part of the team and honour the rest of us with your presence over here please?" The coach shouted back sarcastically. Dick turned and ran full pelt towards the coach. He couldn't help it. A blind rage had hold of him now and all he could think was that this man had gone too far.   Douglas arrived, ambling across the field, smoking his pipe.

"Morning Dick." Douglas stepped in front of him and whispered, "calm down man, he's not worth it." Dick came to a halt but found himself still breathless with rage.

"I can't handle this Dougie. The man is deliberately winding me up. Why? I don't even know him for goodness sake." Dick said through clenched teeth.

The coach had turned away and was attending to another team member. Dick and Douglas joined the others and were soon involved in a more realistic workout.

The day did not improve. After breakfast they were involved in a punishing cross country run. Dick and Douglas quite enjoyed the outing. Both were used to beach training and were not perturbed by the muddy conditions. However many of the younger team members were feeling the strain by lunch. The coach had now become known as "The Sarge" and kept at them constantly with his belittling comments and criticisms.

After lunch they were to take part in some "friendly" races to get them prepared for the following day's Olympic heats. Dick knew as soon as the first race started that things were not going well. Everyone was tense and a young lad, named Charles, was almost in tears, after falling behind in his hurdle race and earning himself a particularly bad barrage of abuse from "The Sarge".

"I must win this next sprint." Dick heard Charles telling a friend. "If I don't I think I should just give up." Dick knew that the lad was a very promising sprinter and thought it was dreadful that his confidence was being destroyed by such a loud mouthed bully.

"Listen lad," he said reassuringly, "it's just his way. Take no notice."

"What do you know?" The lad replied rudely. "You are already established, running for the Poly, medals coming out of your ears. You don't know what it's like. It wouldn't hurt to let me win this next race. It won't affect your chances."

"It doesn't work like that," Dick tried to explain. "We all have to do our best, even in training sprints. Whether I beat you or not doesn't affect anything. I think you have missed the point if you think that getting me to throw even a training race, just so you can please the coach, will solve anything."

"Well thanks for nothing mister high and mighty, I'll beat you anyway, just you wait and see." The lad stormed off and started preparing his starting block.

It was only a 220 yard sprint and Dick easily won, with Douglas a close second. Charles came in third and had a face like thunder.

"What is the matter with that lad?" Dick asked Douglas when they were discussing the day, in the hotel lounge later.

"It seems to be a sign of the times unfortunately," Douglas replied. "People must achieve at all costs. I actually think there were signs of it in Paris in 1924. Do you remember the disgraceful scenes that the press reported in the boxing and fencing matches?"

"I think I did read about it after we had come home. Wasn't Harold quoted as saying something about the fiery contests being un-sportsman like or something?" Dick replied.

"That's right." Douglas agreed. "It didn't affect us but there were squabbles all over the place. People seem to think they have a right to win, even if they are not up to standard, and idiots like that coach just fire them up all the more. I don't know where they found him."

"Charles will be one hell of a good athlete if he just applies himself," Dick took a sip of his rum, "but he needs a more understanding coach I think. The lad isn't going to get anywhere if he thinks that letting him win now and again will do any good though," he continued. Douglas nodded in agreement.

The heats for Olympic selection were to take place next day and Dick felt on top form. As he lined up for the 440 yards he felt as confident as he had ever been. He had the inside lane with Charles next to him. He smiled at the lad but did not even receive an acknowledgement. Dick planned to take the race steadily and took off at an easy pace. As he approached the bend he noticed that Charles was running very close by. What he was not prepared for was the sudden foot that lashed out at him on the bend. He tried to avoid the trip, but only succeeded in twisting his ankle. A searing pain shot through his leg and he crumpled into a heap on the side of the track. His ankle and knee were both throbbing but he tried to rise to continue, only to find that his foot would not take his weight.

The coach ran across. He insisted that he sat down and felt his ankle and knee carefully. Dick was in a daze. What had happened? Why couldn't he get up and carry on? He kept trying to rise but the coach held him down.

"Careful Dick," he said quietly. "I think you may have broken something. Please lie still." The coach's face showed genuine concern and Dick remembered later that he did feel that the man really was worried.

Dick was carried off to hospital as quickly as possible. The ankle and knee were very swollen and blue by the time he reached the ward, and he feared the worst.

"I'm finished Douglas!" Dick said when his friend visited him later. Tears forced their way down his cheeks. "Even if I run again, there's no way I can qualify for these Olympics now. All those years of practice. What for? Oh why? I don't even know what happened."

"I'm afraid Charles deliberately tripped you. It was obvious and he was disqualified," Douglas explained. "He's been sent home in disgrace, but I know that's no consolation to you." Douglas looked down at his hands. He did not know what to say. Here was a

180

man at the top of his career, certain as anyone could be of a gold in the next Olympics, all taken away by a spoilt brat with a lust for glory. What could you say?

Dick found out the next day that he had not broken anything but he had torn a ligament.

"With rest and care you should recover completely." The doctor tried to reassure him.

"What about the Olympics though?" Dick asked hopefully.

"I'm sorry Mr. Ripley," the doctor explained, "these things take weeks, even months in some cases. There is no way that you will be able to run again this year. Even when the ankle if fully healed you will have to be very careful about over-straining the ligament again. Training will have to be taken very steadily to start with."

"I will run again then?" Dick searched the doctor's face with his eyes.

"Oh yes, I would think so, but.." The doctor looked away.

"But what?" Dick asked angrily.

"Your championship days may be over. You must face that."

The doctor continued. "It is not certain, of course. Most people make full recoveries from this sort of injury, but there are those who are not so lucky. Who knows, this time next year you may be once again representing England as though nothing had ever happened?" The doctor turned away.

Dick felt numb. Why? All his life had been geared to this year. Liddell had deprived him of glory in 24, but he had lived with that, accepting that his career had only just begun. Now he had been at his peak and it was all taken away in one quick fall. He knew that by 1932 he would be too old. Even if he did regain his speed, new talent, with better training methods, would out strip him by then. Dick turned his face to his pillow and wept until sleep obliterated his pain.

Chapter 26

The weather matched Dick's mood as he made his journey home. As the train wound it's way northwards, Dick watched the heavy rain forming grey gulley's along the side of the track. The windows had steamed up and he had rubbed a small area clear, so that he could stare out, lost in his grey thoughts.

He had spoken to Cecilia on the phone and she had been very optimistic.

"I have cared for a lot of torn tendons and ligaments. Everyone that I have come across has fully healed." She had said cheerfully. Dick had been less than kind in his response.

"What difference does it make. I can't run in the Olympics now. My life is over. Don't you understand?" He had retorted angrily.

Cecilia had continued to chat merrily, despite Dick's persistent bad mood and cutting comments. He knew he had not been fair to take it out on her. She really was a wonderful woman.

"I'll make it up to you Cecilia," Dick whispered to himself, "but first I need to find myself again." He watched the darkening clouds and thought he saw a flash of lightening over a distant field, briefly throwing light on an otherwise gloomy scene.

Coming home was the best tonic Dick could have. Cecilia and Baby Dick were at the station to meet him. Baby Dick smiled, or perhaps he had wind, Dick didn't care. Either way the look of welcome in his wife's eyes and the smile on his son's face cut through the gloom of his thoughts, like his own personal bolt of lightening. He knew then that his life was not over, but only just starting.

With Cecilia's care, Dick was soon fully mobile again and able to return to his father's office. His father bought one of the new radical Morris Minor cars in the September and allowed Dick to have the use of his Vauxhall D-Type Tourer. This opened up a whole new world for Dick and his family. Weekends meant rides into the country and frequent trips to the beach. Young Dick was almost a year old and the fine Autumn weekends usually found the proud parents picnicking on the top of Roseberry Topping, or Captain Cooks Monument, whilst young Dick crawled or toddled in the grass with their new dog Lass.

Dick quickly realised that he had been missing a great deal, spending most of his spare time training. He did not turn his back on athletics altogether though. By the Spring of 1929 he was fully fit again and started entering a few local events. His speed was not a problem but he was increasingly dogged by stomach problems, particularly during the week before a race.

"It's just not worth it." Dick told Cecilia one day in June. "I am due to run in Darlington next week and I am already feeling sickly. Is it nerves or what?"

"Who knows Darling?" Cecilia replied. "It certainly seems that way. The doctor can't find anything the matter with you."

Dick did run that week and ran a splendid race, winning by a clear lead. He did not feel the old exhilaration though. It was later that evening, whilst talking to Harry and Jack, in the Blacksmith's Arms, that Dick made his announcement.

"I'm giving up competitive athletics." He had just been to the bar and handed pints to his friends. Harry almost choked.

"But why? Your leg is better and you are almost as fast as you were." He couldn't keep the surprise from his voice.

"My heart isn't in it anymore. I love being with my family," he continued, "and I've just managed to get one of those allotments up near the Burn Valley. I won't be giving up running altogether. Ever since West Hartlepool Harriers disbanded last year, the secretary of the Burn Road Harriers has been asking me to join them and act as trainer to the new, young lads that are joining. I think I would be good at that." He took a pull at his pint. "If there's one thing my short experience of The Sarge taught me, it is how not to handle young, inexperienced runners. I'll be able to keep fit with them and give them the benefit of my experience."

"Well you seem to have thought it all out." Jack smiled.

183

Here's to you Dick." He said raising his glass in salute. "You seem to have decided what you want from life at long last."

Dick made the formal announcement of his retirement to the athletics world, through a reporter friend, who wrote under the name of "Mercury" for the "Evening World". The report ran on Wednesday 24th July 1929 and read:

"Most important news of the past few days from the arenas of district sport is the announcement made exclusively in the "Evening World" of the retirement of Dick Ripley.

It is a fact that no athlete in the area during the post-war period was more attractive and none produced the brilliant form that this West Hartlepool man revealed in races from 100 yards upwards.

There was a period I believe, when he was running better than four yards worse than "evens" over a hundred yards, and I would remind the reader that in 1922 he won district championships at 100, 220, 440 and 880 yards, a record which I doubt will ever be beaten...

Ripley's passing from our tracks will be regretted, for he was deeply earnest and invariably gave of his best..."

Dick did feel some regret at reading the report, but the transient shadows quickly lifted when his little boy stumbled across his paper shouting "Tell me a 'tory Daddy". The paper was quickly cast aside as Dick lifted the little boy on to his knee,

He kissed his forehead gently and began a tale of flying horses and runners with wings on their feet, bringing messages of presents and parties for all, from Cecilia, the Queen of Fairyland.

"I bet she didn't have to make the tea," laughed Cecilia as she came in from the kitchen, carrying cups of tea. She glanced at the paper lying cast aside on the floor.

"Are you alright?" She asked, noticing the article that Dick had been reading. He reached for her hand.

"Never better," he replied.

Dick had ended his athletics career and started his career as a full time husband and father. He knew, without a shadow of a doubt, that this was where he wanted to be!

Chapter   27

Life was good in West Hartlepool in 1929. The town was prosperous and things were looking good for the ordinary working man. The Labour Government had returned to power in May and had cut the working day in the mines from eight hours down to seven and a half. Excellent news for Cecilia's family. Harry and the building trade in general were also benefiting from the re-started slum clearance programme. Dick found that sales of insurance had never been better.

Things were not so good in the world in general though. Unemployment had spread in America and Prohibition had created a bootleg liquor industry that was not only destroying law and order but was having an effect on the nation's economy. February the 14th had seen the St Valentine's Day Massacre, when Al Capone's gang of bootleggers had murdered seven members of "Bugs" Moran's rival gang, in an attempt to gain control of this illegal liquor traffic.

Dick listened to the reports of unrest in America on the wireless and did not give it a second thought. Even when the "Daily Express" reported the Wall Street crashes on 29th October he did not think that such events could affect his life that much. After all, that was another country, thousands of miles away, and he wasn't rich enough to invest in stocks and shares.

Other articles seemed much more important, like the discovery of a new wonder drug called penicillin, or John Logie Baird's experimental broadcasts with something called television.

"Whatever next?" Dick remarked to Cecilia one evening as they were seated by the fire. Dick reading his paper and Cecilia knitting a new pullover for young Dick.

"What Dear?" She asked.

"It appears that this Logie Baird man actually transmitted colour pictures a couple of month's back. The newspaper seems to think that we won't have to leave our houses to see Greta Garbo one day." He knocked his pipe out into the fireplace "They will just transmit pictures from a studio somewhere, into our homes."

"That seems a bit far-fetched to me," Cecilia said. "They must have been interviewing that writer again. What do they call him? You know who I mean."

"H. G. Wells," Dick replied, "but I don't think this is science fiction. Things are moving so fast these days. There are more cars than horses on the roads now, and most people have a wireless, or at least a gramophone. Lots of houses even have electric lights..."

"Anyway talking of Greta Garbo," Cecilia interrupted. "When are you taking me to see "A Woman of Affairs"? It's on at the Palladium you know?" Dick laughed. They really did have a good life he thought.

Dick's life fell into a contented routine. When he was not selling insurance, he divided his time between tending his allotment, enjoying his family and training new athletes at the Burn Road Harriers. He even found time to enjoy his Guinness with the lads, every Friday night.

"I don't know how I ever found the time for all that dashing about, attending race meetings." He confided to Harry, one evening. They were seated in a side room of their favourite meeting place, the Atheneum Club.

"Don't you miss all the excitement though?" Harry asked.

"Oh I still get lots of excitement," Dick replied. "I get excited when my son draws me a picture, and when my wife wants an early night." He winked. "Not to mention the pride I feel when Dick helps me plant seeds in the allotment. You should see the look on his face when we plant them one weekend and there are tiny shoots peeping through the next." Dick took a puff at his pipe. "Better still is the pride I feel when they grow into carrots or broccoli, and we take them home and present them to Mammy for dinner. You would think the lad was giving her a box of diamonds." He laughed and reached for his pint. He looked over the rim of the glass into Harry's bemused face. "Oh I know you think I have lost my wits, but I think that this is what it's all about Harry." He put down his pint and tried to explain. "There can be no denying that this does not compare with the pride that I felt when I was included in the Prince's Guard of Honour, but that is not real, it's like part of one of the fairy stories that I tell Dick. Being loved and happy, now that's real."

Dick's happiness increased on the 9th November 1931 when their second son, Stephen, was born. Young Dick was now four and full of life. Cecilia needed time with the baby, so Dick found himself taking his eldest son out more and more. He was fascinated by him and found him to be remarkably good company.

"Daddy can you hear that pretty bird singing to us?" Young Dick was sitting on an old bench, in the allotment, swinging his legs. It was Spring and Dick had started his double digging in preparation for planting his potatoes. "Why is he so happy?"

"Oh he is a Daddy Blackbird and he has probably got himself a new nest of babies." Dick replied laughing. The bird swooped down and grabbed a worm that Dick had uncovered. "Or he's just happy that we are giving him an easy dinner."

Young Dick quickly learnt to recognise all the garden birds and was very careful to say "good morning" or "goodbye" to each of them as they arrived or left the garden. His special favourite was a robin who became so tame, or cheeky, that he would sit right next to the spade and snatch the worms before Dick had even finished turning the sod.

When the two weren't at the allotment, they could be seen walking along the country lanes, especially in the early evening. They would watch badgers emerging from their sets as the dusk fell, listen to the hoot of the old barn owl or watch the swifts dash their merry dance around the skies in their frantic, noisy search for midges.

These were special times to Dick. Sometimes the tired little lad would insist on riding on his Dad's shoulders, as they returned from their rambles, but Dick never tired. He would often gallop and Dick would shout "faster horsey, faster," as they made their way home through the gathering dusk.

With the increased family, Cecilia and Dick found that their home seemed to be shrinking in size. It was after one of the evening rambles that Dick came in to find the room in chaos and Cecilia crying.

"Whatever has happened?" He asked, lowering Dick gently to the floor.

"Oh I'm so angry with myself." Cecilia dabbed at her eyes with an embroidered handkerchief. "Don't worry, it was just a silly accident." She smiled as Dick took her in his arms."I was getting out the tin bath, intending to fill it for Dick, and I tripped over Stephen's blanket. It was still on the floor from when I changed him earlier," she explained. "The trouble is, my skirt then caught the chair arm and it started to fall. I grabbed for it and knocked the clock Mother gave us, off the mantel. I think it's broken." She started to cry again.

"There's just no room to move." Dick said trying to comfort her. He picked up the clock. It didn't look damaged. "I'm sure it will repair. We must get somewhere bigger to live. I have a good income now. I will have a word with Harry. Come on cheer up."

Dick didn't waste any time before he asked Harry to keep his ears open for something bigger.

"It would be nice if we could have a proper bathroom and it must have a garden this time, as well," Dick explained, during another one of their Friday night gatherings. "The lads need somewhere for a swing and a sandpit. Not to mention a nice lawn for Cecilia to sit on in the summer. The yard just doesn't fit the bill somehow."

I wish my garden was half as colourful as your yard," Jack cut in. "You do seem to have green fingers Dick, everything you plant thrives. Everything I plant shrivels. I just don't understand it."

"It's all in the compost," Dick laughed, "and it does help if you water things occasionally as well, you know!"

"Well if ever you are out of a job," Jack continued, "just give me a ring, I could get you a gardening job easily."

"I'll remember that but I can't see it happening," Dick replied. "I would love to be a gardener but I don't think it would pay enough to bring up a family."

"Or rent a big house with a garden and a bathroom!" Harry

interrupted. "I did try to tell you that once, if you remember, but you were living in a dream world then and thought you would live on fresh air." Dick laughed as he remembered their conversation several years before.

"Well, you were right," Dick replied. "It would be wonderful to do a job you loved everyday, but you do need money to raise a family properly. Having said that, money should be a means to an end, not an end to the means. Father would have me working every evening and weekends. He can't understand that I'd rather spend time with my family and my friends, than building up a large bank account and only having time for "business associates" with the same avaricious tendencies. I don't think he will ever learn."

Dick sighed. "He missed an awful lot, always working when we were small. All the money in the world could not replace watching my children grow." Harry and Jack nodded in agreement.

"Fancy a game of dominos?" Jack changed the subject.

It didn't take Harry long to find the perfect house for Dick, and at a rent that he could easily afford, only eight shillings a week. It was in Welldeck Gardens.

It was a splendid three bed-roomed terrace house, with a neat little garden to the rear. Situated in a very pleasant part of West Hartlepool, within easy walking distance of Harry and his father's homes. It was not as grand as their houses, but it did have a bathroom and an inside toilet. It was not fitted with electricity but it did have gas for lighting and cooking, and coal fires in every room.

Dick made sure that the lads soon had their swing and sandpit, but vegetables were kept to the allotment. Instead the garden had a pocket-handkerchief lawn, edged with a glory of colour. Blue delphiniums, pink and white phlox, golden loose-stife and fronds of delicate golden rod danced everywhere. Climbing roses were trained up the walls and filled the air with their fragrance on the mild summer evenings.

Dick and Cecilia loved nothing more than sitting on the bench, watching the sun go down, after the children were asleep, or watching Stephen try to crawl after Dick, as he and Lass careered around the lawn in the afternoons.

"No need to trip over the tin bath anymore." Dick laughed, as they watched the children. "We'll save up a little and have electricity installed," he continued, "then, who knows, we might be able to get one of those electric heaters fitted in the water tank, like Father has just got. Perhaps we could get our own car, instead of borrowing father's all the time."

"Don't get carried away Dick," Cecilia laughed. "You always said that you wouldn't want to be like your father. Life is wonderful as it is. Let's not spoil it by reaching for the moon. Look how lucky we are." She laughed as she pointed to the children, copying the dog as she dug holes in the sandpit.

"You're right as always," Dick squeezed Cecilia's hand. "We have riches far more precious than cars and electricity.

Dick's world was perfect but, unfortunately, not everyone lived in a prosperous area, with a rising standard of living. By 1933 unemployment had reached over 13 million in America and three million in Britain. 1931 had seen a collapse in trade and Hartlepool's ship building industry had suffered badly, leading to increased unemployment in the town.

Nationally a coalition government had been formed between the Conservatives and Liberals, and many unwelcome measures had been introduced, including reduced wages for Government employees and teachers, and a reduction in unemployment benefit. Hunger marches by the unemployed became common and for thousands of people it was a time of great hardship and personal suffering.

Dick still did not feel any cause for concern. Less people needed insurance, but many still had small policies for their health care, if nothing else. His income did start to take a cut, but then, at the same time prices were falling, and his allotment was providing a great deal of their fruit and vegetables, so he was not unduly worried.

Consequently, when Cecilia broached the idea of increasing the family, Dick did not hesitate to agree.

"I love our sons very dearly," Cecilia explained, "but it would be nice to have another lady in the house."

"Well, at least we'd still out-number you," Dick laughed.

So it was that in 1935 they decided to add another member to their family. Patrick was born on 10th January 1936. Dick was not disappointed that he was not a daughter though.

"Well Harry," he said to his brother, a week after Patrick was born, "what with your lads and mine, we could start our own football team shortly, if we keep this up!"

"I don't think that we will be having any more," Harry replied. "Eva seemed to take a long time to recover from Ian's birth. There's none of us getting any younger you know."

"Rubbish," replied Dick."You are only as young as you feel and these little lads of ours certainly keep you fit. I don't feel any different to when I was twenty. Look at the old King, still going strong and seventy years old."

"He's not doing that well from what I read," Jack replied. Prince Edward is at his side in Sandringham. Apparently he is very ill."

"Oh I am sorry to hear that," Dick replied. "He's a wonderful old man. I suspect that Edward is a bit of a lad. He certainly had an eye for the ladies. Still that doesn't make him a bad monarch, I don't suppose."

Patrick was christened in June. It was a grand affair.

Tables were laid in the garden and were laden with the best pies and pastries the ladies could produce.

"Now lass, what a wonderful spread!" Cecilia's Father rubbed his hands with glee. "It seems almost a sin to tuck into such a fine table when there are those in our family that can't even manage a decent crust these days."

"Surely things aren't that bad Father?" Cecilia had heard of the unemployment problems but had never really realised that it had touched her own family.

"Oh yes lass. Your cousins up in Jarrow lost their jobs two year back, when Palmers' shipyard closed. Some of 'em got took on in the mines, but times are hard up there, there's no doubt."

"I heard tell that a lot of the folk in Jarrow are planning to March to London to protest," one of her brothers cut in. "They have been trying to get the government to open a new steel works, so the lads '11 have work but there's nothing doing so far."

"Lots of people are thinking of backing the new BUF at the next election," her father continued, "because Oswald Mosley reckons he can solve all the problems. I reckon he'll just cause more myself. That fellow, Hitler, has taken over in Germany and he's a Fascist. He's power mad. I reckon he's trouble and we don't want none o' that in this country. You mark my words!"

"Alright Dad," Cecilia laughed. "Lets not get too serious with all this talk of politics, it is meant to be a christening you know!" She looked round and saw Dick on his hands and knees making sand pies with the children. "Dick, how about a few songs?" She shouted. Dick stood up and dusted off his hands. He never refused a chance to run his fingers over the piano keys, and pretty soon his deep baritone voice was giving an enthusiastic rendering of Noel Cowards "Mad Dogs and Englishman" and "Don't put your Daughter on the Stage, Mrs Worthington". Everyone gathered round the piano and before long the whole party had forgotten about hunger marches and Hitler, singing their hearts out to the latest musical hits.

The music carried on well into the evening, until families drifted away and Cecilia put the boys to bed.

Finally after all was cleared away, Dick and Cecilia, once more sat enjoying a perfect evening. The dusk was gathering and Cecilia snuggled into Dick.

"Another perfect day," she sighed. "My brothers were saying that Hitler is a power crazy lunatic, that will not stop until he rules the world." She looked into Dick's eyes. "Tell me that can't happen Dick. I would hate it, if there was another war."

"No," Dick reassured her, "they learnt a lot in the last war. So many people died so horribly." He paused. The thoughts of Uncle John's death came flooding over him, and he shivered. "No, the government wouldn't be stupid enough to let that happen again. Let's go in, it's getting late and you have worked very hard today." He kissed her forehead. "Thank you for being you!".

Chapter   28

War was declared between Britain and Germany on the 3rd September 1939, after Germany invaded Poland. Dick was exempt from conscription because of his medical history, but he was determined to "do his bit".

Nothing changed much, at the start. Rationing was introduced in January 1940 and Dick found that it was even more important to keep his allotment thriving. Young Dick was now 12 years old, and was as excited as his father had been, at the start of the First World War. The two Dick's were not just father and son, they were friends. Many hours were spent digging and planting the allotment together. They had worked up quite a sweat one summer Saturday afternoon, and were resting, with a mug of tea, on the old bench.

"Oh I do hope the war doesn't end before I'm old enough to join." Dick was saying enthusiastically.

"It's not a boy's club, with social days out you know," Dick chided. "People are dying. I was about your age during the last war. We thought the submarines and zeppelins were wonderful. They weren't, they were just death machines."

"Oh I know all that," young Dick replied, his enthusiasm unabated, "but you have told me so often of your travels around the world. I just want to see it all for myself."

"Well there's nothing to stop you, when you're old enough, but you don't need to do it with a war on!" Dick playfully punched his shoulder. "I couldn't bear the thought of anything happening to you." He was suddenly very serious. "I don't think those men who were lifted off the beach at Dunkirk a few weeks ago would share your enthusiasm for sea travel," Dick continued. "They are very lucky to be alive. Don't be too quick to grow up, please Dick."

When the two returned home at tea time Dick found Cecilia sitting at the kitchen table, with her head in her hands.

"Whatever is the matter," Dick asked, "where are the boys?"

"They have gone to your mother's for tea. I have had a dreadful headache all day and thought a lie down would help. Unfortunately it seemed to make matters worse." She started to rise and staggered for a moment. Dick rushed forward to catch her. "I seem to be a little dizzy." She smiled weakly.

"Dick go and get the doctor," Dick ordered. "Let's get you back to bed." He put his arm firmly around Cecilia's waist and started leading her to the stairs.

"Don't be silly," she pushed him away. "I'm just a little tired. I will make the tea, if you or Dick will go and collect the boys."

Young Dick was hovering. "Do we still need a doctor?" He was not sure what was expected.

"No, just go and collect your brothers please," his mother replied.

"Well, if you are sure." Dick was not convinced, but Cecilia was a nurse, and did know best.

Cecilia did seem to be fine over the next few days. In fact she was quite excited by the end of the week.

"I have been asked to return to the hospital, as assistant Matron," she greeted Dick excitedly, when he returned from work one evening. "Martha and your mother have agreed to care for Patrick, while Stephen and John are at school. He will be starting school himself, after Christmas anyway." She hurried on. "Oh Dick, please say I can. It's only five hours a day, and some shift work. I'll still be here for you and the children, evenings and weekends." She took a deep breath then continued enthusiastically, "they are so short of qualified nurses with the war and everything."

Dick couldn't help but laugh. "Of course you can, if you really want to. Are you sure it won't be too much for you though? You were almost ill with fatigue, last week."

Oh, that was just silly women's things. I'm as fit as a fiddle!" Cecilia's eyes pleaded.

"Well go on then. I'm earning next to nothing these days. No insurance policies cover war, so no-one is buying. I'll do everything

I can to help with the children and the house."

Cecilia threw her arms around him. "Just watch the lads for me while I go and tell Sister George that I accept." She grabbed her coat and ran out of the house. Dick laughed as he watched her scurrying down the street.

"How could anyone get so excited about working?" He mused to himself, then set about preparing the vegetables for the tea.

Cecilia's employment came at a very fortuitous time, as, by the beginning of 1941, his own job had diminished so drastically that his father had to let him go.

Dick had seen gardening as his way of "Digging for England", and was already converting flower gardens to vegetable patches, all over Hartlepool. However, following frequent sorties by the German Luftwaffe, the Fire Guard was formed in West Hartlepool in 1941 and Dick was one of the first to volunteer.

With bombing raids, rationing and the black out, when Dick and Cecilia were not out "doing their bit", they spent most of their evenings at home, listening to the radio. The favourite programme of the week was Tommy Handley's ITMA (It's That Man Again). Everything had to stop between 8.30 and 9pm on Thursdays while they tuned in to listen to such outlandish characters as Mrs Mopp, the cleaner, with her catch-phrase "Can I do you now Sir?"

It was just after one such programme when Cecilia had gone to make a pot of tea. Dick was knocking out his pipe when he heard a crash from the kitchen. He ran through to find Cecilia sprawled on the floor. He helped her up.

"Whatever happened?" He asked, very concerned.

"I slipped, what do you think?" Cecilia snapped. "Go away and don't fuss." She pushed him away roughly.

Dick was concerned, it was not like Cecilia to be so sharp and he was worried that the demands of home and hospital, may be taking it's toll.

Over the next few weeks he tried to keep a discrete eye on her. He noticed that she took longer to rise in the mornings and seemed to take a lot of aspirin. Many things were dropped and broken. Ornaments and dishes began disappearing. More and more often he heard her shouting at the children for nothing and he found that it was easier not to try and talk to her.

Then one night, after he had been out half the night, fighting a blaze at one of the local factories, he returned to find Cecilia in a heap at the bottom of the stairs. Dick sent his eldest son for the doctor and carried his wife to bed. He noticed that she had become pale and had lost a lot of weight. She opened her eyes and smiled at him.

"What happened?" She asked. "I remember thinking of checking on the children and then I don't remember anything else."

"You must have past out," Dick took hold of her hand. "What is happening Darling? You don't talk to me anymore. You are shouting at the boys and dropping things all over the place. If the nursing is too much, you must give it up. We can manage and you are too precious to loose."

" I have been feeling unwell lately, but you have enough on your plate, what with the gardening and the service with the Fire Guard at night." She burst into tears. "It's the headaches that are the worst. I wake up with them.

Just then Dick burst in with the doctor following. The two Dick's left the doctor to complete his examination and Winifred and Martha also arrived.

"Dick called past on his way for the doctor, and told us the problem," Winifred explained. "How is she my dear?"

"I don't know, the doctor is still here," Dick replied.

The doctor came down and explained that he thought that Cecilia could be anaemic.

"She is very pale and all her symptoms are classic." He took a bottle of dark medicine from his bag. "Give her this three time a day and make sure that she rests. She must have plenty of liver and broccoli," he continued.

"Well the broccoli is not a problem but liver is not easy to come by." Dick replied despairingly.

"Don't worry Dear," Winifred reassured him. "I know a friendly butcher." She tapped the side of her nose and winked.

Winifred and Martha took turns to care for Dick's family, while Cecilia rested. Although still shaky she was soon back on her feet and insisting on carrying on as normal. Dick still felt that something was not right. Cecilia was not herself. Her character appeared to be changing. Some days she was so angry that Dick took the lads out walking through the dark streets to avoid her venom. Other days she was her old loving self.

Dick did his best to care for her and the boys, whilst carrying on his gardening and being on call for the Fire Watch. Once more his determination and stamina helped him, but things came to a head when he returned home one tea time to find Patrick in tears.

"Whatever is the matter?" Dick asked Cecilia.

"He's been playing with those Nazis," Cecilia replied haughtily. "I will not have him playing with that kind."

"Who were you playing with Patrick?" Dick put his arm round the sobbing little boy. "Hush now." He wiped his eyes with his handkerchief.

"That's right, encourage him, take his side against me." Cecilia snapped.

Dick stood up and tried to reason with her. "The lad is only six. He doesn't even know what a Nazi is. No-one is against you. We all love you very much." He was disturbed by her wild eyes and realised that he had to handle this carefully.

"Go on son," he turned to Patrick. "It'll be alright, go and play in the garden." Patrick ran off, looking like a frightened rabbit, who had just been released from a snare.

"Come and sit down Cecilia," Dick said gently. "We must talk."

" Talk," Cecilia uttered irritably, "What is there to talk about? Have they brainwashed you as well?" She demanded.

"Has who brainwashed me?" Dick asked gently.

"It's those Carters down the street," Cecilia looked around herself, as though expecting someone to leap out at any second. "The Wrays are in it too." Dick knew both families well. They were kind and pleasant people, who definitely were not Nazi sympathisers!

"Come on Cecilia," Dick said quietly. "They are friends."

"They're watching us and listening to us." She stared at the wall adjoining the Wrays."They will be listening right now." She sprang up and started beating the wall with her fists. "Leave us alone! Oh leave us alone!" She screamed, slumping into a heap at the base of the wall.

Stephen came in from the garden "What's up Dad?" He saw his mother crying in the corner. "You haven't hit her have you? I know she has been strange lately, but it's the headaches and dizziness. She's told me it will pass."

"No, I would never hit your mother son. I love her more than anything." Dick went and helped Cecilia to her feet. "Please go and get your grandmother and ask her to bring the doctor," Dick said quietly, leading Cecilia back to the sofa.

"This has got to be more than anaemia."

Chapter 29

Thanks to Cecilia's connections with the hospital, she was quickly admitted for tests, despite the overcrowding caused by the recent spate of bombings.

"I am not going to tell your wife, Mr Ripley, and I leave it to you, what you tell your children, but I am afraid that the X-rays have revealed a massive tumour on her brain." The doctor paused as he watched the colour drain from Dick's face. "I'm sorry, but things will get worse and we do not have the facilities to care for her here. I would advise a private nurse."

"I don't have the money, I'll care for her myself," replied Dick in a determined voice. His mind was in a turmoil. Cecilia could not die, he needed her, the boys needed her.

"Oh my God," he cried, holding his head in his hands. "What am I going to do?" He looked up at the doctor "How long has she got left? Is she in much pain? What can I do to help her?" He pleaded like a drowning man reaching for a floating log, just beyond reach.

The doctor rose and patted him on his shoulder. "I really can't say how long she will fight on. We can administer morphine to help with her pain. For now, just try to live life as normally as possible, for her sake and for your children. She will have days when she is quite herself, just try to enjoy those, while you have them."

Dick tried to follow the doctors advice. Martha and Mother helped, and Young Dick was a tower of strength. Dick automatically confided in him. When he got home from school, he got the tea on and saw to his brothers, when necessary. Cecilia did have good days and insisted that Dick still fulfil his Fire Guard duties. They just lived through the bad days, one at a time.

One dark and dismal evening, Dick was on watch with a lady officer, called Wendy Storey. Wendy had lost her husband when HMS Hood was sunk in the previous May and she was left with two little girls to support. Dick had found himself confiding in her during the long cold watch.

"There isn't anything I can say to reassure you," she said honestly. "When I found out that Brian was gone, something inside me died, but you have to go on for the children." She laid her hand on his arm. "I didn't have to watch him die though. I think that will be very hard." She gave a half-smile in the dim light.

"Think of me as a friend Dick, if you need a shoulder, just ask."

"Thanks Wendy. Everyone is so kind, but no-one can help really," Dick sighed. "I suppose lots of people are loosing their loved ones during this vile war. I'm not alone, but somehow I can't feel for them right now. I just feel so wrapped up in my own pain." The siren sounded.

"The Steelworks has been bombed. All hands to the deck!" Someone shouted.

The night was dark and wet but, as they set off in their makeshift fire engines, they could see the glow of the flames above the Steelworks, leaping high into the night.

"Good God," breathed Wendy. "We'll never get that under control." Firemen from all over, volunteers and regulars, fought the blaze for several hours. At last, filthy and worn out they felt that they were winning. In the distance the air raid sirens screamed through the night. Dick heard the drone of aeroplanes approaching from the sea.

"Please God, let them be ours," he prayed silently. Wendy was suddenly beside him.

"We have to take cover Dick, it's Firebomb Fritz again, look at them coming, there's hundreds of them." She pulled his sleeve urgently. Dick could see the Swastikas clearly now. He was still holding the hose towards a dwindling flame.

"Come on," Wendy screamed. "Forget the fire, they'll just start it again anyway." Suddenly there was a a series of sharp cracks and the whole area around them seemed to erupt as small missiles hit the ground. It was machine gun bullets.

"My God they are shooting at us!" Dick screamed as he dropped the hose and threw himself under a half demolished roof. Wendy had hit the floor under the same roof just seconds before. She was shaking from head to foot and Dick wasn't much better!

"Th..th.. that was close," she stammered. Her teeth started chattering with cold and shock. Dick put his arms around her.

"I think we are safe now," he reassured her. "They seem to have flown over, no doubt heading inland." Neither of them dared to move. They huddled together for what seemed like hours, but was probably no more than twenty minutes.

"Dick, Wendy, are you okay?" Someone was shouting. Dick looked down at Wendy's face and brushed some of the soot from her cheeks with his thumbs. He bent towards her and almost kissed her but checked himself. He stood up abruptly and helped her to her feet, clearing his throat with embarrassment. She smiled.

"Don't worry Dick, it was just the tension." she laughed

"Pity it wasn't another time, another place, I almost enjoyed having your arms round me there." She punched his arm. "Don't look so serious, I'm only teasing you."

As things became more difficult at home, Dick found himself looking forward to his fire watches with Wendy, more and more. She listened and allowed him to pour his heart out. He could not do that at home. There he tried to be as normal as possible, not only for the children, but also for Cecilia.

It was hard restricting Cecilia's pain killers and sleeping tablets. He felt like dying when she cried with pain. Slowly she deteriorated until she could no longer leave her bed and her good days were becoming more and more infrequent.

It wasn't just at home either, she would somehow manage to telephone the Fire Station, screaming that the Nazis were coming to murder her and the children, begging Dick to save them. Often resulting in him having to return home, only minutes after he had arrived. The Leading Fireman was very understanding, but would only take so much. Again Wendy proved to be a true friend, often covering for Dick, while he dashed home to sedate his tortured wife.

Cecilia lingered on and so did the war. People became used to the wail of the air raid sirens, the drone of the enemy aircraft overhead, the rationing, the blackout, the taped up windows and the Anderson shelters. Dick could not get used to Cecilia's suffering!

It was late one night when Cecilia woke Dick.

"I must talk to you, now, while my mind is clear," she explained. Dick looked at her poor worn face. Once so serene, it was now so clearly twisted by endless pain and suffering. He knew that she had, more or less, lost the sight in one eye. The growth was pushing through, like some creature from a horror film. It was already visible in the corner of her, once beautiful, eyes.

Pity filled Dick's heart. He wished that it was some horror film, at least he could drive it out with holy water or something. There was no way of fighting the evil monster that was consuming his precious wife. How she must be suffering, well aware, in her lucid moments of what was consuming her.

"I have worked in hospitals long enough to know what is the matter with me, and also to know that there is no hope." She started, breathing heavily from the effort of her speech.

"There is always hope..." Dick began but she silenced him by placing her emaciated finger against his lips.

"No. Let me speak, please Dick, you must help me." The tear started to run down her cheeks.

"I cannot go on, my babies are being torn apart, watching me die and I know that I am a burden to you." Dick started to protest but again she silenced him. "Each time you deliver my medication, you take it away. I know that you mean well, taking it out of my reach, but if you love me, you must give me all the tablets. I want to finish this Dick, for all of us. Please, please let me have the bottles of tablets. Do it now, while I have the strength to fulfil my plan!"

Dick did not know what to do. Here was his wonderful Cecilia talking of taking her own life and asking him to help her.

"My Darling," he started, "you are asking too much. I would be guilty of murder." He felt the tears wet on his cheeks. He wanted to help, but it was so wrong.

"Listen, you and the boys deserve to start living again. I could go on for months. Think of them, not me or you. They tiptoe around, terrified of disturbing me. Then I have rages. I know I do, I have seen it in patients before, and it is not pleasant, especially for children." She caught her breath, her energy almost exhausted. "Please Dick. Remember that night in the Dales, when we promised to be together forever, wandering the Moors like Heathcliffe and Cathy?" Dick nodded, weeping openly now. "Well now is the time for me to go and start making ready for our eternity. I want you to be happy, live a long life, marry again, even have that daughter that we never managed. Then at the end of your life, I will be waiting on Harkerside Moor and we will be together forever." She gasped. "Quickly now, go and get the tablets and help me take them."

Dick staggered from the room. He knew that the tablets were in the cupboard in the bathroom, but could he do it? How many would she need to kill her? What if he didn't give her enough? He grasped the bottles tightly, holding them to his forehead.

"Lord help me," he whispered as he ran back to the bedroom and fed the tablets to her. She swallowed them greedily.

"Count them," she instructed, "I must take enough."

Soon she was satisfied that she had a fatal dose and laid back on the pillow. Gently she drifted to sleep and her face held a look of peace that Dick had not seen for some months. He straightened the bedclothes, kissed her forehead gently and went downstairs to wait. He wasn't sure what he was waiting for exactly.

He stared into space until dawn started creeping through the curtains. He went out into the garden and was greeted by the most incredible sunrise. Fingers of silver were reaching across the sky, as though stretching to collect Cecilia's soul. Birds were starting their dawn chorus but to Dick it sounded as though the angels were singing hymns of welcome. The air was fresh with dew and seemed to revive Dick from his daze.

He turned back into the house. He knew that he must soon go upstairs and see if his evil work had been successful, but he could not face it.

"Oh God, what have I done?" He whispered. He sat at the table and wept. He wept for Cecilia, for their poor, motherless boys and for himself. "Why? Life was so good, why us?" He thumped the table in despair.

Through the kitchen wall he could hear that the Wray's were starting their day. They had switched the wireless on and the strains of Vera Lynn singing "We'll Meet Again" drifted into Dick's haunted mind. He took a deep breath. Cecilia had promised that they would "Meet Again". She had wanted him to get on with life, so he must. He dried his eyes and headed for the stairs.

Chapter 30

The funeral passed in a blur for Dick. He remembered everyone being there, the kind words, the flowers, the tea afterwards, prepared by Martha and Mother. Then everyone had left, Patrick was in bed, after crying himself to sleep. Stephen and Dick had gone to friends and, for the first time in a week, Dick was alone with his thoughts.

His mind was still not able to accept all that had happened, particularly the fact that Cecilia had ended her own life, and worse still, he had helped her!

Her ashes were in pride of place on top of his Steinway. He would need to take them to the Dales, but that was impossible with petrol rationing and blackouts.

"Sorry Cecilia," he whispered. "I will get you there one day, I promise." There was a knock on the door and a young girl from down the road came in.

"Are you there Mr Ripley?" She called.

"Yes, come in Doris." Dick replied, trying hard to pull himself together.

"Old Mrs Ripley asked me to come and sit Patrick for you," Doris explained. "She said you would be needing help now and I'm needing money, so I can stay on at school. I can babysit, clean, cook, and do the shopping if you like." Doris hurried on, becoming nervous. "Mrs Ripley said you should go back on watch tonight, it'd do you good, so I should come after tea and stay until the lads got home. You won't get anyone older. All the older lasses go into the munitions factories now, none of them want domestic work."

Dick smiled. "I'm very grateful to you Doris, and of course you must babysit but I don't have much money." Dick reached in his pocket. "Will a tanner do?"

Returning to the Fire Station had been the last thing on Dick's mind, but he realised that his mother had done this with the best of intentions. Besides it would be nice to explain how he felt to Wendy. He hadn't been able to talk to anyone about the night of Cecilia's death and he needed for someone to tell him that he had done the right thing.

"Don't be silly Dick," Wendy quickly reassured him. "You didn't murder her, she took her own life. It was a very brave thing to do. The poor woman had had enough. If Lass had been suffering like that you would not have hesitated to take her to the vets." She laid her hand on his arm. "Cecilia must have been a remarkable person. You must not blame yourself."

Cecilia had left a very large void in Dick's life. An emptiness that even the boys could not fill. As the weeks passed he found himself looking more and more towards his shifts, so that Wendy and he could be together. He hated leaving her to go home to his empty bed.

Cecilia had only been dead a few months when Dick decided to invite her to tea and she jumped at the chance. Mother was not so impressed by the news.

"Whatever are you thinking of, Richard!" His Mother exploded. "Poor Cecilia is not cold yet, you haven't even scattered her ashes, and you are wanting to bring some common fire woman into her home. You have pulled some stunts in your time but this takes the biscuit." She sat down suddenly, fanning her face with her handkerchief. "I can't imagine what your father will say!"

"Father!" Dick shouted. "Don't you quote "father" to me. I haven't been having an affair with Wendy, while Cecilia was alive, as Father has done to you so often." Dick took out his pipe to calm himself down. "I need company. Cecilia made me promise to get on with my life and that's just what I'm doing." He could feel the anger rising like bile in his throat "Oh to hell with you, you and Father are both hypocrites! You care more about what people think than how they feel. I'm alive Mother. I need to give my son's a happy and normal life as quickly as possible and I will do it, whatever you and Father think." He left the house slamming the door after him.

He regretted his outburst almost as soon as the cold air hit his face, but he was damned if he would go back and apologise.

Every word he said was true anyway.

Wendy arrived for tea as arranged. Dick had told her of his mother's objections. "We will just have to pacify her somehow." Wendy had said thoughtfully. "You mustn't fall out with your family Dick."

Dick had laughed scornfully. "I've managed without them before and I have no doubt that I can manage without them again."

"Oh but they are wealthy and have lots of influential friends." Wendy insisted. "When Brian died my biggest problem was how to make ends meet. If I had had rich parents my life would have been a lot easier. I wouldn't upset them if I were you, they could be useful! Perhaps we could just keep our meetings secret."

Dick thought she was joking and started to laugh, but he quickly realised that she meant every word as she continued.

"What you should do is, play on your circumstances a bit. Get their sympathies and then see if you can take them for a couple of hundred quid. Then when you have got as much as you can out of them, bring me out into the open and fall out with them, so you don't have to pay the money back!" Wendy's face was alive with excitement. She hurried on. "You could even get them to buy you a car or a house. Tell them you want to get the lads out more, or you need more space. Anything. You have the perfect opportunity Dick, use it!"

Dick could not believe his ears. "Are you seriously suggesting that I use the death of my wife as a tool to swindle my parents into giving me a better life-style?" Wendy gave a little nervous laugh. She realised from the look on Dick's face that he was not convinced and that now was not the time to push it. "Only joking," she said with a shrug. "Come and give me a kiss and stop looking so serious."

Dick was not sure what to think. He did not want to spoil the evening or fall out. He needed Wendy's company and she had been so supportive. Perhaps he was just over-reacting to a silly joke. Yes, that was it. He gathered her into his arms.

Whether it was in defiance of his family, or a real need for Wendy's company, a relationship quickly developed between the two. For a while after that evening Dick was a little wary of Wendy. Was she just a little too fond of spending his money? Did she make too much of the silver and trophies that he had displayed on the sideboard and in the cabinet? There was no doubt that she enjoyed a good time and had even suggested that he should sell some of his memorabilia from his running days.

"What is the point of all this silver, Dick?" She had asked one day. "It takes so long to clean and you could get a good price for it. I know a bloke that would snap your hand off for it."

"It is far more important than money," Dick had replied. "Each piece has a memory of my running days. I had that cabinet especially built to show it all off anyway. What would I do with an empty cabinet?" He picked up a huge silver trophy. "This was part of several trophies that I won as English Champion. I could never replace that."

"I just thought that you could buy so many nice things off the black market, if you sold that lot. It seems such a shame to be penny-pinching and putting up with all this rationing when you have all this stuff cluttering the place up," she continued.

"Well I don't think of it as clutter," Dick replied angrily, "and I would not want anything to do with the black market, thank you." He could not believe what she was suggesting. "To be honest it is nothing to do with you anyway."

There had been other similar occasions and, although Dick did start to wonder if there was another side to Wendy, somehow she always managed to convince him that she wasn't serious. She only had to reach out and touch him for any doubts he had to be dispersed.

Consequently Wendy and her daughters moved in with Dick and his family, just a few weeks before Christmas 1943. It was Christmas Eve when Dick first had doubts about the relationship. It was his habit to divide any money that he earned into different jugs on the kitchen dresser. One for the rent, one for other bills, one for housekeeping and one for fun and extras. The last jug had become empty as Dick wanted to have a good Christmas and hadn't spared the expense! He decided to pay the rent early to ensure that there were no debts outstanding over Christmas and the New Year. (He was a little superstitious about carrying debts into the New Year.) He was shocked to find that both his rent and his other expenses jugs were empty. When he had questioned Wendy her reply had worried him.

"Well it's Christmas isn't it. I wanted that new dress I saw in Blackett's and the girls needed new frocks for their school parties. You don't expect me to be an unpaid housekeeper do you?"

"I've already bought you a new outfit for Christmas," Dick replied patiently. "How am I going to pay the bills?"

Wendy minced up to Dick and put her arms around his neck.

"Don't be an old meanie, you want me to look nice don't you." She kissed him passionately. "It's Christmas, forget the bills!"

Young Dick, who had just turned sixteen, also made it clear that he did not approve. It was a fine winter's day and father and son had taken a walk to the allotment to feed their chickens, a recent addition. Dick had been very quiet all the way.

"What's the matter Lad?" Dick asked his son, with genuine concern. The lad had been through a lot and Dick knew he had had to grow up too quickly over the last twelve months.

"Pop," Dick had taken to adopting everything American, like most other kids, since the GI's had started making their presence felt in the previous year. "We've always been able to talk to each other, haven't we?"

"Oh I do hope so son, what's the matter?" Dick could see the worry in Dick's face.

"Do we really have to have this awful women and her unruly kids living with us? There's no privacy. I've lost my room to those girls and Stephen and Patrick think you don't care about them anymore. You always take that woman's side against us!"

Dick's face was becoming redder, as his words rushed on. "I don't think you've thought of us at all since Mam died, you're so bound up in getting yourself into bed with this ...this.."

"Just watch what you say son." Dick tried to keep calm. "Wendy is trying to help us get ourselves back on our feet. There will be frictions to start with. Her little girls, Allison and Vera, have had a hard time too you know. They lost their father and had to get on with it. There's a war on, thousands are loosing their loved ones, we just have to make the best of it. Wendy was finding it hard to manage and, to be honest, I can't really afford Doris, so for us all to live together seemed sensible."

"Doris came a lot cheaper than Wendy. Yeh, there's a war on but this has nothing to do with being sensible," Dick snarled. "Anyway, you won't have to feed me any longer. I have signed up for the Merchant Navy and I leave on Saturday. Thank God I did, God help Stephen and Patrick, that's all I can say!" He snatched up his coat and stormed out of the gardens.

Dick collapsed onto the bench. First he had lost his wife and now he felt like he had lost his eldest son. He had had such high hopes for Dick. He was doing so well at school. He knew he would have his National Service to do, at eighteen, but then he thought he would go to college. Dick could not help the tears. He had weathered his families disapproval of Wendy, but did his sons really hate her so much?

Dick tried to make the peace before Dick left. He insisted on taking him to the Station but, although Dick politely shook hands and promised to write, the warmth was not there.

"Look after yourself son. I do need you, you know?" Dick grabbed his son and hugged him, as he boarded the train.

Young Dick's words had burned deeply into Dick's mind. After that he made sure that he was there to tell Patrick his bedtime story or take him swimming, to support Stephen on the school football team and meet his friends when he brought them to tea. Wendy was not very pleased.

"I think I'm just here as a chief cook and bottle washer," she complained one night, six month's after Dick had gone to sea. "I must see to the boys, the boys need me," she mimicked. "I thought we were going to have some fun. Dancing down the Palace, seeing the new films on the cinema. "Gone With the Wind" has been out for ages and I haven't seen it yet." She continued to complain.

"I never mind you going out with your friends," Dick pointed out. "I look after your daughters as well as my sons so you can go dancing."

"Yes, well that's not all," she grumbled, "I never have any nice clothes and I have to use gravy browning on my legs because you can't get me any stockings."

"No-one can get hold of stockings Wendy, only the Yanks," Dick sighed.

"Your Dad could, but you had to go and fall out with him." Dick was getting angry now.

"I fell out with my family because of you!" He shouted. "I now have no family support and no eldest son because of you."

Wendy backed off, she had never seen Dick look so angry.

"I thought you were loaded," she said quietly. "You were famous until a few years ago. Just look at all this silver. Even without that, your grandfather built half the town and your brother is still building it. Your dad made a packet from insurance and other things..."

"What do you mean, other things?" Dick screamed.

"Well everyone knows that your Dad has connections in the right places. No-one is buying insurance now, but he's still driving fancy cars, when nobody else has petrol." She started picking her nails. "I'm only saying what everyone else says."

Dick pushed past her and left the house. Both Patrick and Stephen were at friends, so he was not worried. He had to clear his head. His feet took him to Harry's door. Harry had remained friends with him, but things had become difficult since his argument with mother. Dick knew that everyone had loved Cecilia and even Harry had not approved of his sudden affair with Wendy

"What's happened Dick?" Eva answered the door. "You look dreadful. Come in." She ushered him into the living room. Harry was in the living room, listening to "The Brain's Trust", Julian Huxley was answering some obscure scientific question as usual. It was one of Dick's favourite programmes too. Harry rose to switch it off.

"No leave it on," Dick insisted. "I don't want to disturb you. I was just passing and thought I'd see how you all were." Harry lead him to a seat.

"You don't just pass anymore Dick," Harry reasoned. "What is the matter, not Dick I hope." Dick looked up and smiled.

"Good Heavens no, I didn't think I looked that bad." He blew his nose. "Harry I need to apologise. I think I may have made a mistake." He explained about his conversation with Wendy.

"She seems to expect me to give her a high life and I just can't afford it." He blew his nose again. "Even if I could, that's not what I want anymore. I've done enough high living. I just want an ordinary life. Like I had with Cecilia." Tears started flowing down his cheeks.

"Wendy caught you when you were at a low ebb Dick." Harry patted him on the shoulder. "We tried to warn you, but she seemed to be the answer at the time. It happens so often these days."

Eva brought a cup of tea and some spam sandwiches.

"Here you are Dick, get this down you, you'll feel better," she said cheerfully. "Everyone has rows you know, even us. It'll probably turn out alright. At least you haven't married her!" She continued, "that would have caused problems."

Wendy had gone out when Dick returned later, and Doris was in charge. The boys were already in bed and Dick had an early night. He slept fitfully. Dreadful nightmares kept invading his troubled mind. Cecilia's face accusing him of her murder and Dick screaming at him that he had destroyed their family.
Dick rose early, his head and heart aching.

"Oh God, what have I done!" He whispered to Cecilia's ashes. "My Darling, can you ever forgive me?"

He had no idea what time Wendy had returned, but it must have been in the early hours, as he had not heard her arrive.

He decided not to disturb her, he couldn't bear to talk to her anyway. Instead he set off for one of the gardens that he maintained, in the hope of soothing his soul with some vigorous digging. He hadn't been working more than a few hours when Stephen came to find him.

"Why aren't you in school son?" Dick was surprised to see Stephen at the gate.

"She's gone Pop, just left us at breakfast." Dick started to gather his things. "It's okay Pop, no need to hurry. I got Patrick to school before I came for you. She taken lots of stuff though. A man came with a van." Dick started running for home, with Stephen hot on his heels.

Wendy had gone out of his life and with her, all the money from the dresser jugs, a silver cutlery set that Cecilia's family had bought, and a number of the trophies and prizes that Dick had won during his athletics days. Even his pocket watch had been taken from the dressing table. There was a note:

"I've only taken what you owe me, for all the slaving I've done over the last six month's. Don't try and find me, I'm leaving the town with a fella that appreciates me. He's a Yank and knows how to treat a lady."

The note wasn't signed and Dick was surprised that he felt nothing but relief.

Chapter 31

Peace came to Britain on 7th May 1945, shortly after Hitler committed suicide in Berlin.

For Dick peace was not so easily achieved. Once Wendy had gone, finding peace in the family was easy. They quickly accepted his apologies and he once more had the support of Martha and his mother. Finding peace within himself was the problem. Although it had been more than two years since Cecilia's death, the nightmares continued.

Dick Junior came home on leave in time for the VE celebrations and, Dick took the opportunity to finally "lay the ghost".

The night after Dick arrived home, they were sitting together in the garden, as they had done when Dick was a child.

"It's lovely here Pop, just as I remember it." Dick sighed as he sipped from the mug of tea his father had given him moments before. "Your tales of the Merchant Navy were all true Pop, I really love it. It's the best decision you ever forced me to make!" He grinned impishly.

"I have been meaning to talk to you about that," Dick cleared his throat and fingered his pipe nervously. "Firstly, I want to say sorry for bringing Wendy and her family into our home so soon after your mother died. I don't know what came over me. Desperation probably."

"She was not a lady Pop." Dick looked embarrassed. "I heard a lot about her, going out with men for what they could buy her. There was even talk of her caught with her fingers in the till in a shop she worked in before the war." He looked at his father sadly.

"I couldn't tell you Pop. I didn't think you would believe stories from a teenager and his mates. I'm really sorry that I didn't try to warn you." He gave a feeble smile. "The police had a file on her Pop. Do you remember Dave, my friend at school?" Dick nodded. "Well his old man was a copper and he told me to warn you. I just didn't have the guts."

"It's fine son," Dick smiled sadly. "I found out that out myself, when it was too late. How stupid was I?" He took out his pipe and started to fill it. "The women say that us men-folk keep our brains in our trousers, well I proved them right." He fell silent for a moment.

"Dick there's something more that I need to tell you. Something you are less likely to forgive me for." He looked his son straight in the eye. "Son, I killed your mother!" Dick looked confused.

"Don't be daft Pop, Mum died of brain cancer. Good grief it was obvious even to me!" Dick hurriedly told his son the whole story.

"I don't think I wanted to admit it, even to myself. I was tired of looking after her, and you lads. It was an easy way out." He was wringing his hands now, the pipe cast aside and forgotten. "Perhaps that was the hold that Wendy had over me. I had to talk to someone and she was in the right place at the right time. Somehow, her knowing made us closer."

"Pop, you didn't murder Mam." Dick laid his hand on his father's drooping shoulders. "She can't have had very much longer to drag on and you helped her out of the misery of those terrible last few days or weeks. I wondered why you never got the police onto that Wendy when she took so much of our stuff. Did you think she could accuse you of murder?" Dick laughed. "Good Heavens Pop, for an intelligent man, you can be stupid sometimes! We all knew Mam had taken too many tablets. I'm proud that you had the guts to help her. I don't know if I could have been that strong! You must forget about it. You did what Mum wanted and you saved us lads a lot of suffering as well. Forgive yourself, because, as far as I'm concerned, there's nothing to forgive."

Although "forgetting" was not quite that simple, Dick did

feel that he could allow himself to start living again, once he realised that his son no longer hated him. At the first opportunity the whole family made the trip to Swaledale, to scatter Cecilia's ashes as she had wanted. Dick would not leave the spot until the sunset kissed the Moor. As the gold and silver receded and the darkness started to descend, he finally said "Goodbye" to Cecilia.

With the end of the war, Dick's fire service had also ended. He knew that the odd gardening job would not be enough to keep him. He loved gardening though and could not face the idea of returning to office work, especially as his father had retired.

"Being cooped up inside all day will drive me round the bend." Dick confided to Jack, one evening at the Atheneum Club."Perhaps you could find me a place at your timber yard?"

"I can do better than that Dick," Jack replied smiling. "I have done very well from this war, although I hate to admit it. Timber was in constant need and I filled the need." He took a pull at his pint. "Anyway I've got myself a small estate now. You might know it. It's called "All Winds" and it's just behind the park."

"Yes I know it. It's a splendid house, set in it's own grounds," Dick replied.

"Well, I need a Head Gardener to sort out the grounds and keep them sorted, with a couple of lads, of course. What do you think?" He paused but already knew Dick's reply by the look on his face.

"Yes please!" Dick rung his hand enthusiastically. "I'll do a good job. It'll be like Paradise when I've finished. Just let me at it."

Dick soon settled to a normal life again. He had a succession of housekeepers. None stayed long but not because they weren't happy. Better money was available in the factories and shops.

It wasn't long after Dick Junior returned to sea that Dick's own father became ill. After a very short illness he died from thrombosis. The family were shocked, but not as shocked as Dick when the will was read. He was left nothing. His mother was left the house and an annuity, "For her lifetime". Harry received a legacy of £2000 and everything else was divided between his two sisters. The will was dated 1922.

"But this can't be right!" Dick rose from his seat as the solicitor finished reading. "Father wrote another will after that date.

He owed me for the cottage."

"He never got round to writing another will," Betty said sharply. "He told us he hadn't bothered, didn't he Gerty?" Gertrude nodded but without conviction. "He didn't sell the cottage either Dick," she added, looking very uncomfortable. "No and that's mine!" Betty added with a snarl.

"Mother this can't be right?" Dick's eyes pleaded. He had promised the boys their own automobile and lots of grand holidays. Now he was hearing that his cottage had never been sold. He could sell it and use the money from the sale. They had a right to that money. It would pay the lads through college. "I really don't know anything about it dear," his mother replied, still numb from her husband's sudden death. "Your father never discussed money with me."

"There has got to be a mistake. I'm the eldest son, but even without Father's estate, I am entitled to that cottage!" He turned to the solicitor. "You must know that he called your father to the office to make a new will. I was there when he arrived."

"Unfortunately Mr Ripley held onto his will himself." The solicitor replied apologetically. "We did not hold this at our office. If a will has gone missing, then presumably it is held by Mrs Ripley. I personally do not know of such a document and my own father died last year, so I can't ask him." Dick saw sympathy in his eyes, but sympathy did not pay bills. "There was no other will!" Betty stood up and faced Dick.

"You never did anything for Father. You were never there for him!" Betty spat the words at Dick scornfully. "You who have been so high and mighty, falling out with father one minute, then making up with him when it suited you. Why should he want to leave you anything?" She turned to her mother and sister. "Come Gertrude, bring Mother. No doubt Mr Bell will sort out the settlement of the estate as quickly as possible, to make sure that the people who deserve their legacies receive them without delay, in accordance with father's wishes." She picked up her handbag and swept from the room haughtily.

"I'm terribly sorry Mr Ripley." The solicitor held out his business card. "I really do not know of another will, but you could perhaps consider contesting this one and I would be more than happy to advise." Dick took the card and looked at Harry standing at the back.

"What do you think Harry, you haven't done very well out of this either? After all, Father was worth a small fortune."

"Oh I'm happy Dick," Harry admitted. "I'm pretty comfortable anyway and dead men's money never brought anyone happiness."

"But I was counting on that to give the lads a good future!" Dick's shoulders sagged. "Then there's the cottage. Uncle John promised that to me thirty years ago. It wasn't Father's to give away. Why did he hate me so much?"

"Fancy a pint?" Harry asked hopefully.

"No I bloody don't," Dick exploded. "Something has gone on here and I want to know what. I know Father made another will Harry. Bloody Betty doesn't even have a family and never had any intention of having one, but she does like to pretend to be the lady of the manor. I wouldn't mind betting that her and Gertrude had both those wills and managed to loose the last one!"

"Hey steady on Dick!" Harry tried to calm him down. "That's a dangerous accusation. You can't go around accusing your sisters of fraud. I never saw a second will and, as the solicitor says, you are the eldest son, you could contest the will."

"Oh yes, and what with?" Dick shouted, he was really angry now. "Court cases cost money and I don't happen to have much, in case you haven't noticed." Dick crammed his trilby on his head and stormed off down the street. He was seething and he did not know who to turn to. In his eyes even Harry was against him now.

Dick did not contest the will, but he did not want to remain part of that family either. It was only a few days later when he handed his notice in to Jack. He called at the front door of Jack's impressive Tudor-style mansion, but did not accept Jack's invitation to come in.

"I'll come straight to the point," Dick explained. "A man I used to know in my running days, owns the Wheatley Hotel, near Doncaster, and needs a gardener urgently." He hurried on. "I 'm accepted his offer." Dick had actually met Mr Bradbury at an athletics meeting a few weeks before but had not taken the job offer seriously. Now it seemed like the ideal way of getting away from his family.

"I'm really sorry to hear that Dick, would a pay rise help?" Jack started taking out his wallet.

"Don't insult me please Jack." Dick tried to explain. "You know what's gone on with the family, I need to get away."

"Well, it's your decision Dick," Jack looked his friend in the eye. "You know your father was a slippery character. There's a fair chance that he never did make another will. Do you really want to risk loosing your whole family over this?"

"Family, what family? As far as I'm concerned the boys are my only family now," Dick replied. "We don't need anyone else."

"Well think of the boys then. They love their grandmother and all their friends are here. You are taking them a hundred miles away. Is it fair on them?" Jack pleaded.

"They will be fine," Dick insisted. "Please don't make this hard Jack. I've made my decision. I rang Bradbury last night and I start next Monday. That gives me a few days to get packed up and the summer to sort new schools out for the lads."

"Well, I'm sorry to loose you." Jack threw up his hands in defeat. "Give me a call, if you ever want your old job back and best of luck Dick. You could use it."

"Luck," Dick smiled bitterly. "I've got plenty of that, it's just all bad these days that's all. See you around Jack. Look after Daphne and Mrs J for me." Dick shook his hand and then walked away without looking back.

Chapter 33

The summer of 1946 passed quickly, and Dick just as quickly came to regret his hasty decision. Stephen was fine, he always made friends easily and soon became a major player in the local rugby team. Patrick did not fair so well and missed his friends desperately. Dick understood. He was lonely too.

Living in the hotel created it's own problems. The three of them only had a two rooms and had to eat in the hotel kitchen. Patrick became bored quickly and Dick found that he was constantly getting into bother with the cook and other members of staff.

Dick was working in the rose garden one afternoon when one of the hotel guests came to sit on a bench for a smoke.

"Don't I know you?" The silver-haired gentleman asked. "I never forget a face and I definitely know yours."

"I doubt it," Dick replied politely. "I have recently moved here from Hartlepool, with my family."

"By Jove that's it. Ripley isn't it?" The old gentleman laughed. "I followed your athletic career vehemently. You had some real bad luck in the end. But, good gracious, whatever are you doing in this garden? Surely you have not fallen so low as to be a hotel gardener?"

"Oh I wouldn't say that at all," Dick argued smiling. "I garden from choice and I love it. I have to admit though, life is not exactly a bed of roses at the moment." He sighed and soon found himself emptying his soul to the man. Dick had never really confided in anyone, since Wendy left. It was as though the dam of pent up emotions had burst and words just poured out.

The gentleman, who Dick later found out, was known

throughout the area as "Old Eli", listened politely, nodding and encouraging when necessary.

" …….. and now Patrick is so unhappy and constantly in trouble. I really do not know what to do." Dick looked at his watch and was horrified to realise that he had been talking for over an hour.

"Good Heavens, is that the time?" Dick hurried to his feet. "I really am most dreadfully sorry for burdening you with my troubles. Whatever must you think of me? I must get on with my work, I'll be getting the sack!"

"Stuff and nonsense," Eli snorted. "I've thoroughly enjoyed the chin wag and I'm sure that you needed to get it all off your chest." He stood up and put his arm round Dick's shoulders in a fatherly manner.

"Now I have a proposition for you." Dick began to interrupt but Eli held up his hand to silence him. "I live in a rambling old place in Upton, called "The Garth". I live alone and neglect my garden dreadfully. I like my own company but don't always feel safe alone. If you and your sons would do me the honour of sharing my home, I would be delighted." Dick started to protest.

"Wait, hear me out," Eli insisted. "This is not a charitable proposition. In return I expect you to restore my garden to its former glory and I will require a small rent." He mentioned a very fair figure. Then continued, "as I said, I like my own company, so you will occupy the part of the house that I do not use and neither of us will trespass on the other's area. The garden will be common ground." Dick thanked him but asked if he could consult his sons and see the property first.

"But of course, young man." Eli clapped him on the back. "I would consider you very foolish if you didn't. We will iron out the fine details tomorrow when you bring your family across."

"Well thank you very much Mr er..." Dick said, shaking his hand enthusiastically.

"Call me Eli, everyone else does." The old man lifted his hat. "Until tomorrow then, shall we say 4pm?" Dick nodded. "Good, I look forward to seeing your family then. Good day to you."

The old man left with Dick staring at his back, he could not believe it, once again, just when he felt as though all hope was gone, something had turned up. Dick started humming to himself as he once more gave his attention to the roses.

The Garth was not perfect, but it was cheap and gave the family a home again. Old Eli had had part of the house altered to make life easier for himself, after his wife died. He lived in two comfortable rooms added at the back. He had his own small kitchen, complete with his pride and joy, a refrigerator. He even had a water tank with an electric heater installed in it. The rest of the accommodation was not so modern.

"I am sorry that the main kitchen is not fitted with these conveniences," Eli apologised, "but I couldn't face the place once the wife had gone. It was always her pride and joy." He sighed. "I had this built on the back so that I didn't have to feel the emptiness everyday." Dick nodded, he well understood that feeling. "You will use the main kitchen and the outside facilities." Eli continued "There is a tin bath in the coal house and a back boiler behind the fire, which will give you all the hot water you should need. The whole house has electric light, so as long as you don't enter my rooms or my bathroom, the rest of the house is yours. What do you say?"

"Rent of four shillings a week, including electric light and coal?" Dick confirmed.

"Yes but you must look after the place and do the garden as well." Eli reminded him. "You can eat anything you produce and you can sell the excess. I normally eat out, but will help myself when I need to. I don't mind if you redecorate your rooms," he added, "I know the distemper is peeling off here and there and it could do with sprucing up a bit." He held out his hand. "Well, do we have a deal?"

Dick looked at the boys. Patrick had already sized up the extensive garden and the old swing and see-saw in the orchard. He grasped Eli's hand firmly. "Definitely," he agreed enthusiastically.

"It'll be easier to get to school and rugby practice from here." Stephen added, as he too nodded in agreement.

The new home certainly gave the family a well needed boost. They quickly settled in. Patrick even helped to decorate his own room but seemed to get more distemper on himself than on the wall. The family were able to laugh again.

Although Dick was pleased to see the boys settled at last, he still had a problem. Eli's rent was very reasonable, even negligible, but the job at The Wheatley had not proved to be full time and the remuneration was far from adequate to meet the demands of two growing boys. Dick needed better prospects and quickly.

Dick set about making full use of the assets already at his disposal. Almost all his spare time was spent in preparing Eli's garden for spring vegetables and gathering the fruits that had not been harvested from the orchard. Amongst the few possessions that he moved from the hotel were several tomato plants, that he had grown for his own use. These had been grown in large pots and were heavy with fast ripening fruits.

There were very few shops in the village. Vans called once or twice a week with meat and vegetables, which did not always look particularly fresh. It didn't take Dick long to start selling the fruits to the neighbours. He also found a neglected vegetable garden which gave a huge crop of potatoes, which he also sold on.

Stephen and Patrick helped by collecting blackberries and raspberries from the hedgerows. Before long Mr. Ripley's fresh fruit and vegetables were in demand and, as word spread, he found that he could not meet the demand and the money started rolling in. Dick had noticed an old nissan hut in the centre of the village, used for storage during the war, but now left empty and neglected. No-one had much use for it and he soon managed to rent it for a few pence a week.

With the help of Stephen, and sometimes Patrick, he cleaned the place up and converted it to a small green-grocers shop. He knew he could not grow all his supplies but managed to negotiate a good deal from the man who supplied "The Wheatley". He knew his produce was first class.

The shop gave Dick a new lease of life. The boys seemed to be settling too. Patrick had plenty of friends in the village and both lads seemed happy with their new schools. Stephen moaned about the two buses he had to get to his grammar school but that seemed to be a small price to pay.

Dick was soon able to give up The Wheatley, working only for himself, but he found that he was still very lonely. Eli had been true to his word and kept very much his own company. The boys had their own friends and, Dick had to confess, he did not have much time to spend with them anyway.

The fact that the shop was so successful brought it's own problems. Dick spent most of his time either in the shop or in the garden, growing his produce. He had no time for cooking or cleaning. He had to resort to paying local women to help but they had their own families and were not very reliable.

The matter came to a head one evening, when he found Stephen eating a raw carrot at tea-time. "I know they are good for you son, but you need a bit more than that if you are going to become a rugby international," Dick laughed.

"Fine Pop," Stephen replied, "but I can't even find a loaf in the larder. You're always too busy with your precious shop or your garden to care whether we get fed or not." He threw the carrot at the sink. "It's lousy anyway." He turned for the door.

"Now just get back here and watch your language," Dick shouted. "We do not use language like that in this house." Dick felt his temper rising again.

"I don't understand." Dick forced himself to speak more calmly. He looked in the oven. It was empty and almost cold as the fire was nearly out.

"Mrs Kelly, from two doors down, promised she would come and put a stew in for us. I was going to make dumplings. I left the meat and veg in the larder. "Dick ran his fingers through his hair. "I told her I would pay her at the weekend." He raced to the larder, the meat and vegetables had gone.

"I'll go and see if she's taken it home to cook." He smiled at Stephen apologetically. "Perhaps the fire had got too low."

"But I have to go Pop, I'll be late for training," Stephen complained.

"Just hold on two minutes," Dick pleaded. "You can't train on an empty stomach."

Dick dashed out of the house. Mr Kelly opened the door in response to Dick's knock.

"Hello Dick, come in," he invited. "Mother has had to go to our Doreen's. There's been a bit of a crisis. She took yer stuff and said to tell yer she'll do t'stew tomorrer and bring it round."

"I do appreciate your problems Mr Kelly, but the lads are hungry now." Dick realised his rudeness. "I am sorry Mr Kelly, I do hope Doreen's problems are sorted quickly. I've no doubt we'll manage until tomorrow."

Dick thanked Mr Kelly and left. He did manage to find some bacon and eggs but realised that this temporary arrangement could not continue. Much as he distrusted live in housekeepers, he would have to find one and very soon.

Dick agreed his proposed action with Eli and put his advertisement in the Doncaster Chronicle, just after Christmas. He had tried cards in the newsagent's window first but had had no success.

Christmas had been very bleak. He had sent the boys to their grandmother in Hartlepool, but had stubbornly refused to accompany them. Eli had gone to friends for the day. There was nothing for it but to carry on with the decorating. He carried on well into the afternoon, determined not to have time to feel the emptiness. A rumbling stomach finally brought him to a halt.

There was no point in cooking when the boys weren't there, so he took a cheese sandwich and sat on the back step to eat it. The light was starting to fail on what had been a bright December day. A light covering of snow, hardened by a heavy frost, covered the ground. Everywhere felt silent and empty and the loneliness bit into Dick more badly than the frost ever could.

The sandwich seemed to turn to sawdust in his mouth and a tear started to form and hovered in the corner of his eye before escaping to roll into his mug of tea.

"Oh Cecilia, will I never stop missing you? What a mess I have made of things without you." He took a sip of the tea, it was almost cold. He could not hold it any longer, he wept. He wept for his lost wife, his motherless children, the family that he was no longer part of, the home that just did not exist anymore. Mostly he wept because he felt totally alone.

A blackbird landed very nearby, obviously hoping for the

discarded sandwich. Dick smiled through the tears and rubbed some of the bread into crumbs for the hungry bird.

"Are you alone too?" Dick asked, as he watched the bird hungrily devour the feast. The clouds parted and the last few rays of the setting sun kissed the frosty scene, colouring everything with a warm rosy glow. Dick dried his tears as the beauty of the winter garden started to thaw his frozen thoughts.

"Now this will not do Dick Ripley!" He said to himself out loud. "You must get on with your life." He threw the tea on to the path and gave the rest of the sandwich to the bird.

"Enjoy that young man," he told the bird with determination, "because I will not spend another Christmas like this. Next year it will be log fires, turkey and all the trimmings and there will be a woman in this house or my name is not Dick Ripley!"

Dick set his trilby firmly on his head, fired up his pipe, put his pail of distemper firmly away and set off for the Upton Arms.

As soon as the newspaper offices opened, he submitted his advertisement for a housekeeper. The first stage in his plan to create a proper home again was complete.

Chapter 33

Dick started to feel that his master plan was falling at the first hurdle. He had only one reply and that did not come until a week after New Year. He had almost given up hope.

The letter, when it came, was from a young lady, only 28 years old. She wrote that she was currently employed as an usherette in the Gaumont Picture House, in Doncaster. That position was only temporary and she was looking for a more permanent post. She signed herself Evelyn Elliott.

There was something of Dick's own desperation about the way the letter was written. It wasn't what the applicant said, it was just a feeling that Dick got whilst reading it.

"Well beggars can't be choosers," Dick said out loud. He placed the letter back into the envelope and looked at his pocket watch. "Just time to catch the next bus to Donny."

"What are you on about Pop?" Stephen looked up from his book.

Explaining his errand to Stephen and Patrick, Dick left immediately to catch the bus.

As Dick arrived at the cinema he noticed that the film was Bob Hope in "My Favourite Brunette".

"I do hope she will be," thought Dick to himself as he approached the doors.

The first film had already started and a group of usherettes were gathered in the foyer, enjoying a quick woodbine, before they were needed for the first interval.

"Excuse me," said Dick, raising his trilby, "would any of you young ladies happen to be Evelyn Elliott?" A rather round but pleasant looking girl giggled forward. "Hello Ducks, I'm Evelyn, but that's just me Sunday name, and I hate it, everyone as knows me calls me Mary. Who wants 't know like?" She had a pleasant smile, although Dick couldn't help but feel that she was rather rough round the edges. "You are only looking for a housekeeper," he remonstrated with himself, "not a movie star! She looks like a hardworking sort."

Dick lifted his hat again and introduced himself.

"I received your letter and, quite frankly, I am desperate to fill the position of housekeeper as quickly as possible." Dick noticed the other girls straining to listen and nudging each other. "Is there anywhere we can talk privately?"

"Oh Lord, I'm not dressed for any posh interview luv." Mary patted her hair and was obviously embarrassed, "and I'm working yer know." The girls behind her giggled and she shot them a threatening look.

"Look, there's a cafe on 't top floor of 't cinema, you wait there and I'll ask the manager if I can have 'alf an hour off after the next interval." Mary bustled off to see the manager, and Dick turned towards the stairs, well aware of the scrutiny of the remaining girls. He turned back and raised his hat again.

"Nice day ladies?" He waved politely.

"Hardly Ducks, there's a foot of bloody snow out there!" One shouted back sarcastically, nudging her friends and giggling.

"Good Heavens," thought Dick. "What am I letting myself in for?"

Mary was as good as her word and turned up at the cafe after half an hour. She apologised for the behaviour of her friends.

"Don't mind them," she tried to explain. "They don't mean no 'arm. They're just young, need a bit of growing up like." She smiled kindly. "Anyway, the manager says I can have 'alf an hour. He's a good sort really."

Dick noticed that her whole face lit up when she smiled, and her dark eyes sparkled. "There's some spirit in this girl," he thought. "She looks alive and, yes, almost attractive when she smiles." He chastised himself silently. "Good grief Dick, you must be getting desperate, you'll be fancying Martha next!"

The interview went well, although Dick would not have called it an interview, more a cosy chat. He was surprised to find this lass easy to talk to. His original feeling had been right, she was desparate to leave home. Like many girls of her time, she had been caught by the war. Determined to live every minute as the last, she had found herself pregnant and unmarried. The father had intended to marry her but was killed in a motor bike accident.

"They sent me off to his sisters in Lincoln, to have the bairn on the Q.T.," she explained. "They wanted me to leave her with them but I couldn't." She sighed. "Poor little mite were born early with all the hassle. She were no bigger than a bag o' sugar." Her eyes looked at him begging him to understand. "When she came out of t'incubator, I just had t' take her home."

"It must have been very hard for you," Dick sympathised.

"Ma, couldn't forgive me." She carried on quickly. "I live at home with Beth now. Dad is marvellous with her but Ma makes me life a misery. I've just got to get away." She placed her hand on his arm. "Look mister, I'm used to hard work. Ma's been dying o' summat most of me life and I'm the oldest, so it's been down to me to run the family, as well as working in the factory. With seven brothers and sisters, I know what running a house is all about! I'm not a bad lass really." A look of desperation swept across her face. "Just give me a chance, please!"

Dick knew what that feeling of desperation was like and felt an instant affinity with this girl. Anyway, he also fully understood what it felt like to suffer family disapproval, they had a lot in common.

"Right you've got the job," he said in a businesslike manner. "How quickly can you move in? I really need you to start immediately."

"I won't come without Beth mind," Mary stressed. "I wouldn't leave her for anything."

"That's not a problem," Dick reassured her, "though I am afraid that she will have to share your room. Still you can take my room, it's the biggest. The boys share a double room. I can have the small bedroom." He was almost thinking out loud. "It will be nice to have a little girl around the house. I'm sure the boys will love her."

It was all agreed. Dick said he would borrow a car and call to

229

Mary's home, in Rossington, the next day, to collect her, Beth and her things. He couldn't wait to get home to tell Patrick and Stephen. No more cold suppers and empty houses to come home too. "What do we need a housekeeper for anyway?" Patrick said churlishly. "I hate little kids, especially girls. How old did you say she is?"

"Mary is 28 and her daughter is nearly three," Dick explained patiently.

"It'll be like when Wendy and her brats took over," Patrick cried. "Don't do it Pop, we don't need anyone, we've managed, haven't we Stephen?"

"Well, I think it will be nice not to have so many chores to do and to have tea waiting when we come home from school." Stephen replied.

"This is a housekeeper, Pop isn't going to marry her or anything, are you Pop?" Stephen replied.

"Don't be silly, she is seventeen years younger than me, only eight years older than your brother, Dick." Dick put his arm around Patrick's shoulders reassuringly. "This will not be Wendy all over again. I promise you that. Stop worrying. Give the lass a chance. If there's any problems, I can sack her." He smiled. "Here's a ha'penny, pop down the newsagent and get yourself one of them sherbert dips you love so much." Patrick soon cheered up at the sight of the money and dashed out of the door without further comment.

Mary and Beth moved in next day. It was a dreadful day but Dick and Stephen had fires in every room to make the place cosy. Living in a colliery area meant that they were not so badly affected by the coal shortages and Dick had bought some huge logs to give an even more homely feel to the rooms.

The first few days went well, Mary quickly organising everything and producing the best Spotted Dick the family had ever tasted. Dick felt like he finally had a home again. Best of all, Dick had company. When the children were in bed, or out at friends, they would sit by the roaring fire and swap tales. A companionship quickly grew between them. They both needed someone and they had found each other. One night, Patrick was stopping at friends and Stephen was at a training session in Doncaster and would not be home until late.

"How about I ask Mrs Kelly to watch Beth for an hour," Dick suggested, "and we can have a walk down to the Upton Arms?"

"I would really like that," Mary replied, "but are you sure it's proper?"

Dick laughed. "To hell with proper, it will do us good and to pot with what people think!"

It was snowing hard as they struggled the few hundred yards to the public house. Mary stopped to scoop up snow and deftly knocked off Dick's hat, with a well aimed snowball. Dick was not sure how to act. It had been a long time since he had let his air down and behaved in a childish manner. Mary was laughing. Another snowball hurtled towards him. He ducked and ran for Mary scooping up a huge handful of snow.

"It's war then?" He shouted, dropping his snow on top of her hat. Mary turned and ran.

"You won't catch me like that again," she laughed, stopping at the entrance to the pub. She took off her spectacles to polish them on her handkerchief. Dick looked into her dark eyes and saw the mischief sparkling back at him. There was life and fun in this girl that he had never seen before. She did not care about convention. Life was for living and she knew it. Dick realised that he had been staring into her eyes and he laughed to hide his embarrassment.

"Just wait until we're on our way home!" He stamped the snow from his feet. He had not felt so young or carefree like this for years. The evening passed very pleasantly but after a couple of Guinness's Dick's mood started to become rather sombre. They were seated on a high backed settle, near the fire. The glow of the flames were reflecting in Mary's spectacles and her hair took on an almost auburn glow in the firelight. Dick reached out and took hold of her hand.

"We haven't known each other for a month yet," he explained, "but I already feel as if I have known you all my life and I already feel that you are more of a friend than a housekeeper."

Mary started to shuffle, he could see that she was worried,

but he hurried on.

"Please listen." He was embarrassed himself now, so he took his pipe out and knocked it out into the grate. "I made myself a promise this Christmas. I was determined to find a woman that would give me back my family." He started to fill his pipe. "No one will ever replace Cecilia but life must go on. You have made my house into a home again. The boys seem to like you and I am already fond of little Beth. I know there is a big age difference between us, but I am a very fit man and I am sure I could take good care of you." He paused, not sure where he was going with this.

"I'm not sure what yer trying to say." Mary was wringing her hands now and looking round the room as though looking for an escape route.

"Look we both needed someone in our lives for different reasons." Dick took a deep breath. "We've found each other and I, for one, have no intention of loosing you now I've found you. I'm not saying that I love you, but that may come with time. I'm just saying shall we...?" He looked away, feeling stupid and started to mumble an apology. Mary turned and looked straight into his eyes.

"Oh, yes please, lets," she said and threw her arms around his shoulders and kissed him firmly on the lips. The landlord came hurrying over.

"Now none of that type of behaviour in here young lady." He was obviously very annoyed. "Any more carry on like that and you will be asked to leave." He turned to Dick, "I'm surprised at you Mr. Ripley, I thought you were a gentleman." He picked up their empty glasses and walked away.

Dick thought Mary was going to burst into tears.

"We'd better leave," he whispered, picking up his hat.

"Perhaps we should talk about this tomorrow, when we have not been drinking. I did mean what I said though. I do think we should get married and as soon as possible." Mary smiled as tears started to run freely down her face. Dick ushered her out of the door, eager not to cause any further outburst from the landlord.

"Oh Dick, yer don't know how 'appy I am." Mary said as she ran into the snow. Dick stooped to gather some more snow and soon the sadness, caused by their embarrassment, was gone as the snowball fight resumed in earnest, not finishing until they fell into their own front door, frozen, soaking wet and very, very happy.

Chapter 34

March 1947 was not a happy month for most of Britain. The steelworks had closed through lack of coal. There were food shortages as a result of the hauliers strike and 15 towns were cut off by snow. By the middle of the month the thaw had started. That brought it's own problems, as the most severe floods ever recorded followed. People were faced with their worst problems since the end of the war, but not Mary and Dick. For them it was one of the best months of their lives.

The wedding was held at the end of March in Doncaster Registry Office. It was a very quiet affair. Mary's father was there to give her away. Dick instinctively liked his new father in law. He was a mountain of a man, with masses of red hair. Dick imagined him stepping straight from the pages of "Treasure Island", or leading a rough band of lowland marauders, kilt swirling, as he charged down the glen to reek revenge on some pure little English soldier. For all that he obviously loved Mary and Dick found him to be a soft spoken, gentle man.

Mary's mother was too ill to attend. Having only met the woman once, Dick was relieved that she would not be there to mar the day. She was a thin faced, hooked nosed individual, who would have graced the pages of "Macbeth" well. Indeed her acting talents would have suited that play as well, as they were remarkable. For at least 20 years she had had the whole family convinced of her ill health, and would continue to do so for the next 30, taking to her bed at every opportunity until she finally gave up the ghost in her ninety - sixth year, having seen off all her peers! Her temperament matched her face and Dick could only marvel that two such opposite people could ever have come to marry.

Harry managed to come to stand in as best man but, apart

from him and the boys, no-one else attended from Dick's family. Dick had realised that they would not approve of his new wife and was not surprised when Harry brought word that his mother did not intend to even meet her. They were sitting in the Upton Arms, the night before the wedding. Harry had only arrived an hour before and was only to stay until the following evening.

"I'm afraid she thinks that you have lost your wits all together," Harry explained. "She has actually suggested that you should send the boys to live with her, rather than have them brought up in such a household." Harry realised immediately that he had once again put his foot in it. Dick was furious.

"Who the hell does she think she is?" He stormed. "No-one will ever take my boys from me. At least they will live in a house where they can laugh without fear of being belted for it!"

He took a deep breath. "Still today is meant to be happy, I'm going to find my life again tomorrow. Mary is just what I need to put some fun back into my life. Just wait until you meet her, I just know you'll love her."

Harry breathed a sigh of relief as the conversation turned to Mary and their whirlwind romance. Harry had been concerned about the age difference but was pleased to see Dick happy again.

As the Registry Office was not far from the cinema, Mary suggested that they should have a wedding tea in the cinema restaurant.

"After all, that's where it all started," she had laughed. With food shortages and travel difficulties, it seemed as good a place as any. Harry left immediately after the meal, to catch his train, and Mary's father had to go home to see to her mother, who was again dying of something or other.

"It seems a shame just to go home after such a special day." Dick smiled at Mary. "Well Mrs Ripley, what do you think, should we take the lads to see the film? The Marx Brothers are on in "A Night in Casablanca"."

"Oh yes please Pop!" Stephen cut in.

"I don't know," Mary looked unsure, "Beth has been left with Mrs Kelly too long already today."

"Typical, Beth always has to come first." Patrick crossed his arms and turned away. Dick didn't want the day to end like this.

"Surely it won't matter just this once, the boys have been good today, they deserve a treat." He took some money from his wallet. "Here Stephen, run and buy the tickets," he said handing the money over. The boys ran off happily.

"So, although I'm married to you, the boys still come first do they?" Mary's eyes flashed in anger. "I'm Mrs Ripley in name only, I'm really just still the housekeeper!"

"Not at all," Dick said firmly, "but the boys are still important to me. You must understand that. They have not had much life since their mother died and I want them to accept you, not resent you." He took her hand. "I have not been a good father to those lads, I have not had the time. I have only a few years to make up to them for that. You and I have a lifetime together." He picked up his hat and stood up. "Come on now, let's go and enjoy the film, I love the Marx Brothers." Mary stood up and smiled.

"Of course, I'm just being silly, let's do that." She smiled but Dick felt a momentary doubt. He could not help but wonder if he had not gained a wife at the expense of his sons.

Even though there was some friction between Mary and the boys, Dick found family life everything he had hoped for. By the middle of April he had found a nice three bed-roomed, semi-detached house in Campsall, just a few miles down the road from Upton. "The Garth" had been fine as temporary accommodation but, now Dick had a family again, he wanted somewhere that he could call his own. The family moved into "Greenbanks", Bone Lane, just a few weeks before young Dick came home on leave. Dick was really excited.

The weather was picking up, and the spring crops were almost ready. Eli had agreed that Dick could still have the produce as he had no use of it. He was planning to sell up and move into a private home he had found outside Doncaster.

"I need a bit more attention these days," he explained to Dick, "and your decision to move has made me realise that I really don't need a place of this size anymore." Dick was sorry to leave the old man who had been so good to him, but he needed to get his own life back on track now, and depending on someone else's charity was not the way to do it.

The new house had a big garden but nowhere near as big as he needed for his ever expanding customers, so Dick rented a small, neglected market garden in Campsall. Mary agreed to run the shop when Dick was working in the gardens. Things were really looking up. Even the boys were happy. Stephen was closer to school and Patrick got on well with the village boys. Patrick still resented Beth's presence but Dick hoped he would accept her more as she grew.

Dick had to admit that he found problems with Beth himself sometimes. She was a strong willed child and very stubborn. Having found no difficulty in teaching the boys manners and good habits, he found Beth's determination not to be taught very frustrating and often found himself on the verge of loosing his temper with her. Mary spoilt her, which didn't help.

Dick was not too concerned. "Everyone has a few domestic problems," he thought one day as he took a mug of tea and sat in his gardens. Mary and he had had a heated argument on the previous evening. He couldn't even remember what it was about now, but Beth had been at the bottom of it. It had been great fun making up after though! He laughed gently to himself, remembering the warm feeling of her body pressed close to his, later that night. He smiled as he watched some blackbirds gathering straw for their nests and heard the wood pigeons cooing gently to each other.

"Life is pretty good again," Dick told the pigeons, "and Dick comes home tomorrow. What more could a man want?"

Young Dick's visit went very well. The two Dick's spent hours swapping sea tales and discussing everything from the economic situation, to the winner of the recent Grand National. Unfortunately his visit was all too short. The final night arrived and Mary suggested that the two should have a last drink at "The Old Bells", as Dick had to leave at first light the next morning.

"But you must come too?" Young Dick had insisted. "You're my new Mam now." Dick was so proud of his son. He had been afraid that he would not approve of his choice of wife, especially in view of the age difference. Dick had reassured him on his first night home.

"Look, Pop, you did what you could for my Mam. I know how hard it was for you when she died, and how difficult I was when you took up with Wendy. I hope I've grown up since then!" He laughed. "You just enjoy your life, that's what you used to tell me when I was small. What was it you used to say?" He scratched his head thinking. "Oh I remember now : This is not a rehearsal, we've only got one shot at life, so don't waste it worrying."

Throughout his visit Dick had treated Mary as though she was a real lady and Mary had loved it. Dick couldn't help but smile when he realised just how hard she had been trying to talk properly and do everything just right in his presence.

"Where did the posh accent come from then?" Dick chided when his son had left the room. "Well," said Mary, blushing, "'e's such a fine young gentleman, I don't want 'im thinking that 'is Dad has married a common lass wi' no manners." Dick couldn't help but laugh as he noticed that the attempts to talk properly had vanished.

"Ee Lass, a luvs thee!" He said, in his worst Yorkshire accent as he had gathered her into his arms.

Dick's departure was a sad affair.

"I won't be back for about twelve months, our next trip includes Australia." Dick sounded genuinely sad. "Perhaps I can get home for Christmas one of these years. I should imagine that Christmas dinner will be something special with Mary doing the cooking." He raised his hat to Mary. "You look after her Dad, and these strapping brothers of mine." He hugged everyone in turn, then boarded the train. Dick felt a strange shiver run down his spine, a feeling he had only felt once before, on the moors with Cecilia. He grabbed Dick's hand though the window.

"Take care son and be sure to come back to us." He felt a tear run down his cheek.

"Good Heavens Pop," Dick laughed, "I know Australia is the end of the world, but it is civilised nowadays you know." He shook his Dad's hand and raised his cap in salute, as the train moved off. Dick watched the train vanish with tears pouring down his face.

"It'll be alright ducks," Mary was taken aback by Dick's emotional reaction. "I know it will be a long time until you see him again, but he will be back, and for longer next time." She took

Dick's hand and started mopping his face with her handkerchief.

"Sorry love," Dick smiled through the tears. "I don't know what came over me." He smiled at the boys and little Beth, standing quietly by. "Who wants their breakfast in the railway cafe then? Last one to the door pays." He laughed as they all ran across the platform, scurrying to be first.

"You're right Dick," he thought to himself. "Life is for laughter, not tears."

Chapter 35

The summer of 1947 saw Dick a very happy man. his gardens were thriving and the shop was doing well, so well in fact that they had expanded and were now selling wet fish, as well as fruit and veg. Patrick was showing an aptitude for athletics and Dick was enjoying putting him through his paces. They even had an old Morris Minor. Not the car of Dick's dreams but it had opened a whole new world of days out.

One of the family's favourite outings was a trip to Doncaster Racecourse. Patrick was particularly fascinated by this. Dick and he poured over the form sheets and Dick just couldn't resist putting a few half-penny bets on. Mary didn't really approve.

"The only winner is the bookmaker," she chided.

"It's just a bit of fun Lass," Dick would reply. Indeed Dick and Patrick became so good at spotting the good prospects that they rarely lost on the day. Dick even became on good terms with some of the bookies and, on occasion, acted as a bookies runner. His aptitude for figures made it easy for him to quickly calculate the odds and, on those days, the few shillings that the bookies slipped him, more than paid for the whole day out,
including a few pints afterwards.

In summer the whole family took a caravan at Primrose Valley, near Filey. Dick had tried to persuade Mary to visit the Dales but she was not keen.

"There's nowt for miles up there," she protested. "I've always fancied the seaside." So of course Mary got her way. Dick didn't mind. The weather was good, the lads did their own thing and Mary and he even got to dance in the small ballroom on the site.

Dick was sat outside the caravan one evening, puffing on his pipe. Mary was busy putting a very tired Beth to bed. The sun was on the point of setting and all the colours around him had taken on a sharpness and clarity that only happens just before dusk. A deep pink glow started to paint the clouds and creep across the sky until the whole world seemed to be touched by the glory of the moment.

Dick felt Mary place her hand on his shoulders.

"This is what life's all about lass," he said, taking her hand in his. "A job I enjoy, with time to watch the sunsets or to feel the sun on my face. A hardworking, canny lass to love and care for me, a wonderful family and enough money for a few simple pleasures, without the worries that my father always seemed to have on his shoulders." Dick stood up and put his arms round her ample waist. "It has taken me 46 years to say this Mary, but right now I think I finally know that this is where I want to be." The tender kiss that followed put a perfect end to a perfect day.

Autumn quickly led into the start of winter. The lads were excited at the start of November as Dick had promised them their own bonfire and some fireworks.

"We'll have lots of bangers and jumping crackers," Dick had promised. "I'll make parkin and treacle toffee," Mary had added.

It was an exciting night and everyone enjoyed themselves and ate far too much. It was only a day later when Mary became concerned about Dick. He was very quiet all day and did not even bother with his pint at the "Old Bells".

"What's up duck?" She asked. "I bet yer caught a chill at the bonfire. Let's get to bed." She felt Dick's forehead.

"No, I'm not ill," Dick replied quietly. "Mary I can't get Dick out of my mind. I know it's silly but I just feel that he needs me. Oh what can I do?" He burst into tears. Mary was afraid, she had never seen Dick like this.

"Come on Pet," she said clutching him tightly to her.

"Dick's thousands of mile away, enjoying himself in Australia. Why would he need you?" She became business like as her own fear began to deepen. "Come on Dick, It'll just be a chill or something." She tried to push him towards the stairs. Dick smiled weakly.

"Yes, I expect you're right," Dick reassured her, suddenly

realising how much he was frightening her. "You go up, I'll bank up the fire and follow you up shortly."

"Well if yer sure." Mary left reluctantly.

Dick couldn't explain what he felt. Dick had been very much in his thoughts all evening. That was not unusual, he often missed the lad, but today he had had such an over powering feeling that he was in trouble. Dick went into the kitchen and made a cup of tea and sat at the table. He just felt that he had to wait.

"I'm here lad," he found himself thinking. "I'm with you and I won't leave you.

Several hours later Mary woke up to find that Dick had still not come to bed. It was very cold and she wrapped her dressing gown more tightly around herself as she came down to the kitchen. Dick was still sitting at the table, staring at the wall, the tea cold in front of him.

"Whatever are yer doing lad, yer'll freeze to death?" The fire was almost dead. Mary stirred it up with the poker and added more coal. "It's four o'clock in the morning, come 't bed" She pleaded.

Dick looked at her as though in a trance. "Go to bed Mary, I'll be up just now."

It was seven o'clock when Dick woke Mary the next morning. He looked worn but a look of peace was on his face.

"He's alright now Mary. I saw him a few moments ago." Mary was really worried now.

" How could yer see him?" She asked. She got out of bed and tried to get Dick to lie down. "Yer must have fallen asleep and had a dream." She covered Dick with a blanket. "You have a rest now. I'll call the doctor."

"No Mary, don't," Dick grasped her arm tightly. "I saw Dick, as clear as you are now. " He shuddered. "The trouble was I couldn't see his face properly, it was as though it was missing, but he told me that he was alright now. It was over. He had come to say goodbye Mary, I'm sure of it." Dick burst into tears and Mary sat beside him holding him until he fell asleep.

"Where's Pop?" Stephen asked as he made the toast, holding the bread over the fire with a toasting fork. "The fire was perfect for toast this morning, I thought it would make a change from porridge." He set the toast down. "What's the matter Mary, you look as though you've seen a ghost?"

"Oh nothing," Mary gave a small smile. "Yer Dad's a bit under the weather, he won't be getting up yet. He didn't sleep much last night." She started getting the butter and marmalade out. "By that toast smells good, hurry up." Stephen changed the subject and Mary tried to pretend nothing had happened.

When Dick woke up he wasn't really sure what had happened. He was inclined to agree with Mary that he had been a bit under the weather and had had a vivid dream. He expected that if anything had happened to Dick he would have had a letter or a telegram and, when a month passed with neither, he began to dismiss the whole thing as "a funny turn." He didn't talk about it again, not even to Mary.

Christmas was everything that he had promised himself that it would be, sat alone in Eli's garden the previous year. The whole family spent hours making paper chains and gathering holly and mistletoe to decorate the walls. Mary bought yards of ribbon and coloured beads to decorate the tree and Dick even managed to get some small clip-on candle holders and little coloured candles to fix to the branches. The pride and joy was an angel that Mary made for the top, using a small doll of Beth's and an old lace curtain.

It was the Sunday after Christmas when Dick's world shattered again. Stephen was sitting reading the "News of the World" shortly after breakfast. Dick was washing the pots.

"Good God Pop!" Stephen suddenly jumped up. "Read this, it can't be true, they would have told us. They've got it wrong." He threw the paper down as though it had burnt him and burst into tears.

"Steady on lad," Dick said quietly, drying his hands, "let me see." He felt as though an icy hand was reaching out and clutching his heart. He picked up the paper, still open at the page Stephen had been reading. "British Seaman murdered in Australia," he read. He sat down heavily. In his own heart he already knew what he was about to read, although he did not know how. The article was reporting the results of a Coroner's inquest held in Freemantle on 23rd December 1947, into the death of a young seaman, Richard

Nicholson Ripley.

The report went on to describe how Richard had left his ship, docked at the North Wharf, North Freemantle, early in the afternoon of the 7th November for a well earned shore leave. He was jumped by several men of Arabic nationality. Then he was dragged behind some packing cases and beaten up. One of the men had struck a blow to his face with a bottle. The report went on to quote the Coroner's findings:

"Death was from asphyxia caused by blood and sand blocking air passages on falling to the ground, as a result of the head injury." The report went on to say that Richard would not have died if he had not been hidden behind the packing cases. He had taken several hours to die and may have tried to call for help. He had finally drowned in his own blood, somewhere around nine o'clock in the evening. The men concerned had been apprehended and were held by the Freemantle authorities, pending trial. It appeared that they were part of an Arab crew that had been sailing with Richard. He had been their immediate superior.

Following trouble, laziness and insubordination throughout most of the trip, the young officer had suspended their shore leave. The men had subsequently jumped ship in the early hours, shortly after docking. They had then become very drunk on rum stolen from the ship's stores and laid in wait.

"Young Ripley appears to have put up a good fight," the report continued, "but overwhelmed by surprise and numbers, he had no chance. What a pity that no-one heard this promising young officer before it was too late."

"Oh my Lord, I heard you son," Dick cried, "but I was no use!" Tears started rolling down his face. "Not that I was ever much use to you!" He threw the paper down angrily. "Why?" He wailed, as bitterness and grief consumed him. He stumbled towards the door, knocking over a chair as he staggered out, trying to run from the truth. He felt as though he could not breath. It was raining heavily but he did not care. He fell to his knees on the sopping lawn.

"Why?" He shouted, shaking his fist at the sky. "First John, then Cecilia, now Dick. Must you take everyone away from me? What have I done?" Dick's shoulders drooped, his fury giving way solely to remorse.

"Poor Dick, what a way to die, alone and in pain. Was I there with you son? Oh please God, let him have felt that I was there with him, as surely as I heard him call." Dick whispered. He collapsed, curling up into a ball, and weeping himself into a state of exhaustion.

Stephen had shown Mary the paper and she had followed Dick outside. She did not disturb him until he broke down, she knew he needed to handle this in his own way. As long as she lived she would never be able to explain what happened to Dick in the early hours of the 7th November 1947, but in her own mind she was sure that he had been with his son, even though not physically, throughout those dreadful hours until he died. Young Dick had not died alone.

The months that followed passed in a haze for Dick. At first his wrath carried him through. Endless telephone calls to the shipping company, the Australian Consulate, the local Coroner. The company insisted that they had sent a telegram but Dick did not believe them. Dick's body had been released for burial on the 10th November and he had been laid to rest in the Anglican Cemetery in Freemantle. Dick would have liked to ship his body home, but it was too late. The shipping company had covered the costs and the whole ships' company had been at the funeral.

Finally after months of correspondence and frustration all Dick had left of his eldest son was a Death Certificate and a small photograph of a lonely grave, thousands of miles away. He sent a money order for £50, so that the grave would be properly cared for indefinitely. It was an awful lot of money, but it did nothing to alleviate Dick's intense mental anguish.

"I'll visit that grave one day Mary." Dick said when he finally received the photograph.

For months Dick lost interest in life. The gardens were neglected and his visits to the "Old Bells" became more and more frequent. Mary kept the family together and the shop running. She was happy to give Dick the time he needed, but was frightened by his black moods and drunken tempers.

245

Things came to a head one night in the summer. Stephen was discussing some homework with Patrick, when Dick came in from the pub. He over heard something Stephen said about "Huckleberry Finn". Mary couldn't even remember exactly what was said but before she could step in Stephen and his father were shrieking at each other. It finished badly.

"Typical!" Stephen was screaming. "You are never wrong are you? You weren't wrong when you took up with Wendy and drove Dick to joining the navy. Stop with the hypocrisy Pop. Grandma says you killed Dick, by driving him away, just as sure as if you'd held the bottle in your hand." He was a big lad now, well over six foot. He towered over Dick.

"Look at you, drunk and feeling sorry for yourself again," Stephen continued. "You don't give a damn about us and you didn't give a damn about Dick either. You're wearing his death like a medal. Well, in case you haven't noticed, you have two other sons. I shouldn't be helping Patrick with his homework, you should." He raised his fist but changed his mind.

"Get out," Dick screamed, "and don't ever come back!"

"It'll be a pleasure and don't worry, I won't." Stephen retorted and dashed from the room. Beth started to cry and Patrick ran after Stephen. Dick sat down. He suddenly felt very sober, very old and very tired.

"Dick, you can't let him go," Mary pleaded, "he's only seventeen."

"Dick was only sixteen when he left," Dick snarled.

"Yes and Dick is dead. Stephen isn't." Mary snapped back.

"Isn't it time to lay Dick to rest and get on with life now. You are destroying everything." Mary burst into tears and ran from the room.

Dick stared into the fire and felt the warmth on his face. He knew Mary was right but he did not know where to start. When the anger had finally left him and the sorrow had taken over, it was like a physical pain, crushing his will to live. When Cecilia had died he had managed to get on with life but this was far worse. Until now Dick had not realised just how deeply the depression had set in. It had swept over him like a tidal wave, washing everything else out of his mind. He realised now that he had just left everything to Mary, while he had allowed himself to slip into an ever increasing black hole of self pity. Was it too late? Had he destroyed everything? He needed to find himself again. Young Dick would not have approved of this.

"Life is for laughter not tears Dad." Dick could almost hear his son's voice. "Look after Mary and those strapping brothers of mine."

His eldest son had left with those instructions and Dick had let him down. Well not any longer. He stood up, reached for his pipe and his hat, and left the room to find what was left of his family and of his life.

Chapter 36

Dick's life did get back on course, with a major effort on his part and a great deal of support from Mary. Stephen did not return home, preferring the convenience of lodgings with a friend, but a sort of peace-treaty was agreed, and he was a regular visitor. Something was missing though, some spark had gone out of their life and Mary was concerned.

One beautiful late summer evening, when they were sitting in the garden enjoying an after dinner cup of tea, she decided to make her suggestion.

"Dick, I know we never talk about it, but I'm still worried." She started to ring her hands as she hurried on. "Things have not been the same since Dick died." She looked into his face but it showed nothing.

"What exactly are you getting at?" Dick took out his pipe.

" I don't know what you want. Stephen seems quite happy where he is and the garden is producing nicely again. What do you mean?"

"Well, I'm not talking about money and the kids," Mary tried to explain. "It's us." She sighed. "Well, not even us really, more everything." Dick was starting to look annoyed.

"What the hell are you prattling on about woman?" He seemed really angry now.

"This is what I mean," Mary hurried on, "I can't just talk anymore. We don't laugh or have a daft carry-on anymore. We just get on with everything, go to the "Old Bell's" once a week, go to work, go to bed. There's just no fun left." She looked down into her mug. She knew she hadn't found the right words but hoped that he understood. She plucked up her courage again and looked straight into his eyes.

"I don't think I matter anymore. There isn't even any excitement when we make love. In fact I wouldn't even call it making love, if the truth be known."

Dick did not look angry anymore. He understood what Mary meant. Something had died in him with Dick, but he did not know how to rekindle that spark.

"It's alright Mary, love." Dick reached out and took hold of her hand. "There's no need to look like a scared rabbit. I know what you are saying is true, but I don't know how to put it right."

"D'yer still love me then?" Mary slipping back into her Yorkshire accent, in her eagerness. She had taken such pains to try and "talk properly", as she put it, since she had married Dick.

"Of course I do you silly minx." Dick gathered her into his arms. "It's all been so difficult since Dick went. I've tried to get back to normal, but I still keep expecting a letter or something, saying he'll be in on the next train." He felt a tear forming in the corner of his eye. He pulled away and fumbled for his handkerchief. "Then something like this happens and I'm right back to square one." He sat down hard and looked at her with tear filled eyes.

"I don't want to be like this lass." He gave her a watery smile. "It's not what Dick would have wanted and it sure as hell is not what I want, but how do I stop it?"

"Well," said Mary hesitantly. "I have an idea but you may not like it."

"Go on." Dick leaned forward, eager for any suggestion that might help.

"Why don't we replace Dick?" Mary hurried on. "Well not replace exactly. That was a bad choice of words. Let's have a baby." She looked at him, not knowing what to expect. Dick thought for a while.

"I'm not sure that I am ready for being a father again just yet." Dick was not totally dismissing the idea. "I always rather fancied a little girl though." He realised that he was not being fair to Beth and quickly hurried on. "Not that Beth is not a lovely little girl, but she doesn't have my blood in her veins does she?"

Mary was not too happy with this line of thinking, she had thought that Dick had accepted Beth as his own. Still, now was not the time to take issue at this and Mary had enough about her to ignore the remark.

"Well there's no guarantee that our baby would be a girl, of course," she smiled, "but I think you would get evens from your friends on the racetrack, on the chances of a girl." Dick laughed. He was starting to like the idea. His best memories of Dick were their country walks, when Dick was a toddler, carrying him home on his shoulders at the end of their rambles. He smiled again. He jumped up and grasped Mary and gave her a hug.

"I think you have come up with the perfect solution." He kissed her excitedly. "Do you know that I have just had a wonderfully happy memory of Dick, as a child? That's what I need to do, remember the good things about his life. He loved life and everything about it." Dick started laughing. "We shared sunsets, watched badgers play, gathered wild flowers for his mother." Dick kissed Mary, with more feeling than he had for months.

"I can do it all again Mary, thanks to you." He smiled into her eyes. "Somehow, because of circumstances really, I was never a very good Dad to Stephen and Patrick. I wasn't really there for them. Beth is lovely but she is not the wild flower type."

Mary laughed. She couldn't help but agree. Beth was already a proper little madam, not the country ramble type at all.

"Right then." Mary moved away and gathered up the cups.

"That's settled then, we try for a baby as soon as possible." She started into the house and then looked back. "Dick would approve you know?"

Dick sat back down and watched the evening creeping across the garden, as he had done on so many occasions before. The sun was setting and the gold's turned to pink's and then deep red as the night advanced. It seemed like a lifetime had passed since he had gloried in such a sunset. They must have happened but he had not noticed. This one was not a disappointment.

"Yes, I'll have another chance," thought Dick, and as he gathered the chairs up to return them to the kitchen, he felt that life was beginning again.

Both Dick and Mary were disappointed in October, when Mary was not immediately pregnant.

"Well there's nothing wrong with either of us," Dick pointed out, "so it was just not meant to be this month." He laughed. "We'll just have to try harder!" Mary giggled. She had certainly got the old Dick back now.

Dick and Mary had the best Christmas ever. Mary had just been to the doctors and confirmed that their first "joint" child was on the way and would be born in August.

Josie was born on Tuesday, 23rd August 1949. She had shown a great reluctance to join the world and Mary had been admitted to Doncaster Royal Infirmary, because she was almost two weeks overdue.

"Just a precaution, Mr Ripley." The doctor had assured Dick. "Your wife is over 30 and has had an increase in her blood pressure. Better to be safe than sorry." Dick couldn't agree more. He was more excited about this baby than he had ever been with the others, and more worried as well. After all, he was 48 now, not much more time to try again.

As it turned out, everything went well and Mary had a "textbook" delivery. Stephen was in the hospital waiting room with his dad. Dick had had to sell the car to be able to afford the pram and other bits and pieces needed for the baby, and Stephen had given him a lift on his newly acquired motor bike. He was also lending moral support. The nurse came to tell them the news.

"You have a healthy baby girl, Mr Ripley. Congratulations." The nurse smiled at Stephen, "and she looks just like you. Your wife is resting now but you can come and see the little girl."

"I'm afraid you have got this wrong," Stephen stood up and shuffled uncomfortably. "Dad's the father, not me."

Dick laughed and clapped Stephen on the back. "It's the size of you lad, people think you're a lot older than you are." The nurse started to apologise. Dick held up his hand.

"Don't worry love." He laughed, nothing could spoil today. "It's always happening, after all, I am seventeen years older than my lady wife."

Josie was everything Dick had ever wanted and he

worshipped her from the first moment he saw her.

"She does have a look of Dick about her love," Mary whispered as she cradled her in her arms.

"She's beautiful, just like you," Dick corrected. "Thank you lass, thank you very much." He kissed her forehead. He felt like he was going to burst with happiness.

Life wasn't easy for Mary or Dick in the first few weeks of Josie's life. Beth was four and a half and still needed lots of attention. They were making ends meet, but only just and could not afford to let the shop or the gardens slip, if they wanted to enjoy life, as Mary had put it. Mary therefore returned to running the shop the very next week, taking Beth and the baby with her.

It was very hard for Mary. She had to walk to Upton and back three days a week, pushing the pram, and Dick was very grateful for the tremendous effort that he knew it must be for her. He made sure that he got home first every evening and cooked the dinner. As soon as dinner was over, he got the tin bath in front of the fire and gave Josie her evening wash and put her to bed. He loved it, and he loved Mary for her dedication.

"Put your feet up love," he insisted, as soon as dinner was cleared away. "I'll see to the kids."

It worked very well and the weather was kind, so Mary didn't mind the work. They had discussed it, sitting by the fire one evening.

"I will give up the garden," Dick had suggested. "The shop is doing well enough. We can manage on what we make from that."

"I don't want to manage though," Mary had insisted. "It was nice to have a car and enjoy days out, as well as holidays. I want to carry on enjoying my life. I can manage for a while."

"Alright, if you are sure," Dick finally agreed. "It won't be for long love," he assured her. "Once I've got the winter crops settled, I will be able to keep the garden ticking over with just a couple of hours a week."

"I can manage," Mary insisted, "and once you take over the shop for the winter, I can rest a bit. Anyway, by the spring Beth will be at school and Josie won't a problem on her own." Dick kissed her. She was a marvellous women.

As it happened Mary did not continue with the shop for as long as they had intended. Josie was just two months old when the health visitor called to check her out.

"She is doing just fine Mrs Ripley." She gathered up her records. "A word of warning though. There is a measles epidemic spreading at the moment. Keeping Josie in that shop could be exposing her to a very grave danger. Think on now." She picked up her gloves. "I've just lost two babies to the thing and even when the children survive, they can be left blind or damaged in some other way. I've just been to see a little lad who has come down with it and he is really poorly."

Mary had not heard of any such cases in Campsall or Upton but she told Dick of her fears.

"Right lass, you keep Josie and Beth at home from now on." He smiled reassuringly. "Most of the heavy work in the garden is done now. I'll run the shop and keep the garden going on Wednesdays and Sundays when the shop is shut." He put his arm round her. "Don't worry lass, we'll manage."

Despite asking around, Mary could not find any report of any cases of measles in their neighbourhood and, after a week, began to relax, feeling rather silly at the over protective reaction to the health visitor's warning.

"Don't be silly love," Dick reassured her, when she admitted to her feelings. "Josie is our only one. We can't be too careful. Better to be safe than sorry!"

Three days later Dick was to find that they had locked the stable door, after the horse had bolted. First Josie developed a dry, irritating cough.

"It's nothing," Mary insisted. "She's caught a little chill, that's all." She hurried on, the fear entering her voice.

"There's no temperature and she is sucking well." She laughed half heartedly. "I should know!" Dick agreed but hardly slept that night for checking the cot.

"Be well Josie," he whispered as he tucked the blankets more firmly around her. The coughing started again and she started to cry. Dick gathered her into his arms, hoping not to wake Mary. She needed her sleep. Softly he walked down stairs with the baby in his arms. He stirred up the fire and sat in the big armchair that was always pulled right up to the hearth. Josie had snuggled into his chest and was sleeping again but within minutes the coughing stirred her again.

"It's not good enough, little lass." Dick stroked her cheek. "You and I are off to the doctors first thing in the morning."

The doctor was optimistic.

"Well, her temperature is up a bit but her chest sounds clear enough." He smiled at Dick reassuringly. "I understand your worry Mr Ripley, but measles is an infectious disease. To catch it Josie must have been in contact with someone who has the disease. I can assure you that I have no patients around here with measles at the moment. True there is quite an epidemic of it in Doncaster, but it would be pretty unlikely that it would spread to these villages." He stood up, helping Dick gather up Josie's things. "Give me a call if she gets any worse. For now, just keep her warm."

It was the next night that the temperature developed and Josie started pawing at her eyes and crying, particularly when the light was on. Mary was frightened, and so was Dick but he did not dare to show it.

"It's a cold," he reassured Mary. "The doctor said there was no chance of her catching measles here."

Another night passed and Josie seemed much worse the next day. Her eyes were red and heavy and her chest seemed to heave with every breath she took. Dick sent Patrick to get the doctor.

Dick could see by the doctor's face that he was surprised at how badly Josie had deteriorated. He felt panic rising in his throat.

"Not Josie. Oh God no!" Dick thought, as he struggled to marshal his thoughts. He turned to where Mary was standing, white as a sheet. She had sensed the doctor's surprise as well. He put his arm around her.

"Well, Doctor?" Dick asked urgently, as the doctor removed his stethoscope from his ears.

"I'm afraid it is measles," the doctor replied. He gently turned Josie's head and showed Dick a rash of brownish-pink spots, spreading down her neck, from behind her tiny ears.

"There's no doubt about it."

"Well do something!" Mary screeched hysterically. "She's only two months old. The health visitor told me that babies die from this." She clutched at the doctor's arm. He gently unwound her fingers.

"Take it easy, Mrs Ripley." He turned to Dick. "Josie is avery healthy baby but we must watch her very carefully." He turned very gently back towards Mary. "Try to make sure she drinks plenty of liquid. If she won't feed from you, try boiled, cool water in a bottle." He picked up his bag. "I'm afraid all we can do is wait." He raised his hat and turned to leave. "I will call in again later."

Dick busied himself boiling water, first to cool for Josie, then to make tea for Mary. He felt surprisingly calm.

"Come on lass," he said to Mary, as he handed her the mug of sweetened tea. "Josie needs us, we can't give in." Mary smiled weakly.

"She can't die Dick, we can't let her."

The doctor called later, as he promised. Josie was breathing very rapidly and the rash was starting to spread in blotches over her whole body. She looked grey and very ill.

After sounding her chest the doctor drew Dick out of the room. "I didn't want to worry your wife, but I'm afraid that Josie has now developed pneumonia. It had developed very rapidly, as it often does in such small children." He put his hand on Dick's shoulder. "Before the war I would have said that there was no hope and just advised you to pray." He paused to make sure that Dick was listening. "And since the war?" Dick was grasping at anything now.

"Since the war we have a new drug called penicillin." The doctor paused again. "It has been very successful in the treatment of pneumonia, but I have to make you understand that there are risks."

"What are they?" Dick looked the doctor straight in the eye. "I need to know."

"Well, some people have developed allergies to the drug and they do die." He spread his hands out and looked at them. "Then, as well, Josie is very young and it is a very powerful drug."

"What will happen without it?" Dick wanted to be clear that he understood.

"Well, if she survives the night," he paused and took a deep breath, "and it is a big "IF", then she could recover."

"We have to try the drug," Dick insisted. "Please, give her it now. We have no choice." Dick did not hesitate. He had read of penicillin and the wonder cures during the war. He would take the chance.

Josie did survive the night and quickly started to recover, part from a persistent cough, which the doctor felt sure would subside with time.

"I am afraid though," he decided that honesty was the best policy, "that Josie may have a weak chest for the rest of her life." He smiled at Mary. "When I came to see Josie that second time, when I realised that she had pneumonia," he paused as though unsure whether or not to continue. "I doubted that she had any chance at all, but I am Polish and in my country we believe that the next person that a doctor treats, after attending a suicide, will be very lucky." He paused again. "I should not really tell you this, but I believe it and hope that you will take hope from it. Just before I came to Josie that second time, I had been called to cut down a man that had hanged himself." He stood up to leave. "I am sure that Josie will live a long and lucky life, weak chest or not." He raised his hat and grinned as he turned to leave. "Not a very sound medical diagnosis I know, but good day to you and good luck!"

"What an unusual doctor." Dick remarked after he had seen him to the door.

"Unusual or not, I believe him." Mary smiled, picking Josie up. "You are a very lucky young lady." She said as she handed Josie to Dick.

"Very much so, and guess what?" Dick said, "it was the health visitor that brought that dreadful disease here. Our doctor has just told me." He looked Mary straight in the eye. "Do not ever let a health visitor near our baby again. Do you hear?"

Dick liked nothing better than to take little Josie to the gardens with him. She was toddling about now and getting into everything but he didn't mind. Life had settled down quite nicely again. Beth was at school, taken each morning by a very disgruntled Patrick.

"What do you think I look like turning up at school with a brat in tow?" He had complained bitterly. Dick did sympathise, but it made life so much easier for Mary and him, knowing that Beth was being safely delivered. Mrs Dyson, a kindly lady from the village, picked her up and looked after her until Mary came home, or Dick finished in the garden.

Yes, apart from Patrick's complaints, things were looking up again. They had not managed to get another car yet but Mary had a bike with a little seat on the back for Josie. Mary and Dick shared the care of Josie but Dick never complained if he had the lion's share. This morning had been quite typical really. Mary had been in a hurry to get to the shop for opening time and Josie just would not eat her breakfast.

"Don't fret lass," Dick had reassured her. "She'll eat when she's ready."

"Yes but that's usually when I'm rushed off my feet." Mary grumbled.

"Leave her with me today," Dick had insisted. "The weather is good and I've got some planting to do. She can make mud pies all day."

"Well, as you wish," Mary agreed, "just so long as you bath her when she comes in caked in it tonight." She kissed Dick and hurried to get her bike out of the shed.

"Take care lass, see you tonight." Dick waved as she peddled off up the bank.

It had been a lovely day. Josie had potted about, jabbering away and Dick had got all his digging done.

"Nearly time to get off home and get Mammy's tea ready." Dick called to Josie.

"Go home to Mammy." Josie replied clearly, running up and hugging Dick's legs. He swung her on to his shoulders and they set off past the church and down the hill for home.

The local policeman was coming up towards him. "Hello Jim, lovely day?" Dick waved.

"Hold on Dick, I was just coming to find you." It was then that Dick noticed Beth and Janet Dyson hurrying a few yards behind him. Janet flew past Jim and threw her arms round Dick.

257

"Oh yer poor lamb. I'm so sorry." She started to cry.

Dick lowered Josie to the ground and once again felt a chill crawl up his spine.

"What has happened?" He looked imploringly at Jim. "Tell me nothing has happened to Patrick."

"It's not Patrick, Dick. I'm afraid it's Mary," Jim said. He hurried on. "Headquarters have just contacted me. Apparently she was in an accident this morning but she had nothing with her name on it, it's taken them all day to identify her."

"Identify her?" Dick slumped against the wall. "She's de...."

"No!" Jim jumped in quickly, "but she was unconscious. She's in Doncaster Royal Infirmary. They want you there as soon as possible." Dick was numb. Mary in an accident. No, nothing could happen to Mary, he needed her.

"It wasn't bad then?" He asked hopefully. "They want me to collect her do they?"

"No Dick, it's worse than that." Janet spoke softly. "I'll look after t' girls and Patrick. You get along wi' Jim now. He'll explain on t' way, but come and 'ave a cuppa whilst Jim gets the car."

Dick allowed himself to be lead down to the Dysons' house, where Grandma Dyson had a hot, sweet mug of tea waiting. Jim went to get the police car.

Jim explained what had happened on the way.

"Apparently Mary was crossing the Great North Road when a lorry hit her." He couldn't think of an easier way to put it. "The driver didn't stop. Whether he didn't know he had hit her or thought he had better get away quickly, we may never know. There does not appear to have been any witnesses."

"She will be alright, won't she?" Dick pleaded.

"I don't know." Jim spoke as kindly as he could. "It appears that, having knocked her off her bike, he dragged her for fifty yards before she fell to the side of the road."

"Oh my God!" Dick was starting to realise just how serious this had been. "You are sure that she is still alive?"

"Well, she was when I was on the radio earlier." Jim assured him. "I don't know all the details but I understand that she owes her life to the policeman that found her." He paused as he negotiated a difficult bend in the road. "The lad was very good at first aid apparently, having been a medic in the war. Anyway he gave her artificial respiration and then stopped the worst of the bleeding with some pressure techniques he had learnt. Tourniquets or something. I'm not too sure about that." He smiled briefly at Dick. "We'll soon be there and you can ask all the questions you need."

Dick was not prepared for the sight that faced him when he arrived at the hospital. Mary was in intensive care and wired up to endless drips and machines. Her nose was covered with a dressing and her head was swathed in bandages. Dick sat down beside her and tried to hold her hand. To his horror her right hand and arm were totally encased in plaster, as was her upper body and her right hip and leg. He leaned forward and kissed her cheek. How could anyone survive such horrific injuries?

"Oh lass, what a mess you're in. Please, please fight. Don't give in lass. I need you so very, very much." Dick couldn't help it, tears coursed down his cheeks. The door behind opened. The doctor had deliberately given Dick a few moments but now he entered to explain the situation.

"Mr Ripley?" He held out his hand. "I am Doctor Henderson."

"Will she be alright doctor?" Dick asked, shaking the proffered hand.

"I am not going to beat about the bush Mr Ripley." The doctor sat down next to Dick. "Your wife has been very seriously injured and is critical at the moment. Until she regains consciousness we cannot be sure whether or not she has sustained any brain damage. Her skull was certainly fractured." Dick took a deep breath.

"What about her other injuries?" He asked "Are they as bad as they look?"

"Again I don't know yet. Her right arm and leg have been broken in numerous places." He paused as Dick looked decidedly faint. "I know this is hard. Would you like a moment?"

"No, please go on. I need to know," Dick insisted.

"Well. I have pinned the bones and set them as best I can. The broken ribs will have to be strapped up for possibly months. He

259

paused. "To be honest, Mr Ripley, even if your wife does regain consciousness and does not have brain damage, I will be very surprised if she ever walks again." The doctor paused while Dick blew his nose. He was trying to keep calm. The doctor continued.

"The one positive thing in her favour though, her spine appears to have come through this totally undamaged." He smiled as he stood up and patted Dick on the shoulder.

"Nothing is certain yet, Mr Ripley, it's too soon. We will just have to wait and see." He started to leave. "I will get the nurse to bring you a cup of tea." He turned back. "I know it does not look like it now, but she has been very lucky. The young man who found her did everything absolutely correctly. There is no doubt that she would have died without his prompt action."

"Thank you," Dick said. "I would really like to meet this man. Is he still here?"

"I don't think so, but I'll ask." He smiled. "How do you like your tea?"

Dick sat for hours holding Mary's hand. He did not accept for a minute that she would not recover.

"You get better soon lass," he whispered. "We'll take the kids to Primrose Valley." He kissed her cheek. "You like that. The sea air will put you right." The door behind opened and Stephen came in.

"Good grief Pop!" Dick could imagine his shock. He had felt it just a few hours before. "What on earth happened?"

"I'll explain exactly what the doctor has said later." Dick felt suddenly very calm and in control. "Where are Patrick and your sisters. I need to sort something out for them."

"They're fine," Stephen reassured him. "Mrs Dyson has Beth and Josie and Patrick is at his friend Ian's."

"Well, I must sort something out." Dick rose to his feet."Will you sit with Mary while I get in touch with her father."

"I can take care of Patrick," Stephen insisted. "We can stay at home. Mary did loads of baking at the weekend so there's plenty to eat." He hugged his Dad. "We've had our differences Pop, but you don't deserve this. I'll help in any way I can."

Dick quickly got everything organised. Beth and Josie went

to Rossington to their grandparents. Josie screamed as Dick started to leave the house.

"Go on with you Dick." His father-in-law smiled. "I'll take the little mite to the shop for a candy bar. She'll be alright." He shook Dick's hand.

"Look after her," Dick begged. "She's special."

"So is my lass," His father-in-law replied. "You care for my daughter and I'll care for yours." Dick started to leave.

"Bring her home safe Dick, please!" Mary's father shouted after him.

"I intend to," Dick replied and raised his hat, as he hurried down the path.

Mary did come round after several days but she did not know Dick and could not remember anything. The doctor feared the worst, especially when she started calling for help and fighting the nurses when they tried to change her dressings.

"I am afraid that her brain has been damaged," Doctor Henderson had called Dick for a meeting in his office. "She is not responding to anything we try.

"No I will not accept that yet," Dick insisted. "Mary pulled me through, when my son died. Now I will help her."

"I don't think you understand," the doctor said firmly, "there is very little chance of a complete recovery." He leaned forward to ensure that Dick was listening. "Even if she recovers physically, she may always be irrational." He leaned back and started playing with his pen.

"To be honest Mr Ripley," he paused and threw the pen down, "once your wife can be moved I suggest that we move her to the mental health ward for assessment."

"Never!" Dick stood up and turned to leave. "I'll look after her myself."

"Please, Mr. Ripley," the doctor continued patiently, "I don't think you understand.."

"No!" Dick retorted angrily. "You don't understand! I have lost a wife and a son, as well as an uncle that was more of a father to me than my own father. My daughter was almost taken away from me and I took a risk to save her." He returned to the desk and pointed at the doctor. "Understand this. I will not give up on Mary!" He turned and walked to the door, and then looked back. "I cannot lose my Mary." He walked out and slammed the door behind him.

As he headed for her room a nurse came walking quickly towards him.

"Ah, Mr. Ripley," she smiled. "I was coming to fetch you, your wife has just asked for you."

"Really?" Dick grabbed her hand. "She really asked for me?"

"Yes," the nurse confirmed. "She awoke from her nap and asked where you were. I am going to tell the doctor."

Dick ran to Mary's room and she smiled at him as he entered.

"Oh Dick," she started to cry. "I thought you had put me into one of those awful Nazi hospitals and they were doing experiments on me." Dick smiled and hugged her.

"No Mary, you're safe." Dick stroked her hair. "No-one will ever take you away from me." Mary looked up into his face. Her eyes were still frightened.

Promise?" She asked, trying to cling to him with her good hand.

"I promise!" He kissed her forehead.

Mary did recover her memory but she had terrible rages for quite a while after. The doctor still warned of brain damage and spoke of possible paranoia, but Dick would have none of it.

Mary, herself, was determined to get back to a normal life and was impatient to return to her girls.

"How are they?" She asked every time Dick arrived. "I'll get home soon," she always promised. The doctor was still uncertain that she would walk again but, as Dick said later when talking to her father. "He hadn't allowed for Mary's dogged determination." Dick took a puff from his pipe. The two had taken a break at the local hostelry, and were enjoying a well earned pint. Dick had come to Rossington to take Josie home. He had agreed to Beth staying on longer, as she enjoyed the company of her cousins.

"It was so funny," he continued. "The doctor told Mary and I on Sunday that she may have to spend the rest of her life in a wheelchair and, when I arrived on Monday, she was standing by her bed, demanding to be discharged." He smiled at the memory. "An incredible woman."

"Always was bloody minded!" He father added, laughing. Mary did fully recover, physically and mentally, although she did have mood swings and rages that Dick had not seen in her before the accident. Dick didn't mind. He had his Mary back and that was all that mattered.

Chapter 38

Dick had survived half a century by the time he took Mary to Primrose Valley, swathed in plaster, as promised. No-one had noticed his fiftieth birthday pass, although he did have a card from Stephen and Patrick. He didn't care. He sat on a deck chair with Mary propped up beside him, Beth and Josie making sand pies near by and Patrick playing football with a bunch of lads along the beach. The sun was shining and Dick felt that he was a lucky man. He reached across and squeezed Mary's hand.

"Life's going to be different now lass." He smiled into her sleepy eyes. "No more worrying about the garden and the shop. We'll do alright. Let's just see that we enjoy our life." He pointed to the girls. "We'll spend more time with them as well." He looked down the beach to where Patrick's game had moved into the sea. He sighed "It's a bit late for Patrick now. Poor lad, I haven't been much of a father to him."

"Don't be silly Pet," Mary squeezed his hand back. "You're a good father and a lovely husband," she smiled.

"You haven't always been around," Dick explained. "After Cecilia died and Wendy robbed me blind, I was not much fun to live with." He sighed and reached into his pocket for his pipe. Once it was going he continued. "I wrecked the lads lives, thinking only of what I needed." Mary started to interrupt but he hurried on. "It's true. When I wasn't working, I found it easier to call into the local pub, than take my lads out. They were alright when Mother and Martha were there, but I even spoilt that and dragged them away from their family and friends, just because of hurt pride."

"Don't be daft." Mary tried to turn and face him and nearly fell off the chair. She burst into laughter and Dick straightened her up again. "The way I heard it, your family robbed you and then turned their backs on you. Still Harry is nice and the lads do still love their grandmother. Perhaps you should bury the hatchet? Go and see them."

"It's no good lass," Dick replied, "they don't approve of you and Beth, and I'm not going to West Hartlepool without you. So forget that!" Dick relit his pipe. "Do you fancy an ice cream, I do?" He turned to the girls. "Who's for ice cream?" The subject was not mentioned again for two years.

Josie was almost four when Dick had a letter from his mother.

"I have had a slight heart attack and it has made me realise that I may not be much longer in this world," She wrote. "I would really like to see my little grand-daughter before I die... ."

There was no mention of Mary or Beth and Dick was furious. He flung the letter on to the table.

"Says she's dying and wants to make the peace but she still ignores you," he fumed.

"Calm down luv." Mary picked up the letter. "She's a very old lady now you know. If you don't take Josie to see her soon, they may never meet." She got hold of his hand. "Go Dick, please."

A week later Dick and Josie were standing in Doncaster station waiting for the York train, to make a connection for West Hartlepool. Josie looked very smart in a new coat with a black velvet collar.

"I'm not having your mother thinking that we haven't got standards." Mary had insisted, when she blew most of the housekeeping on the coat. It did look fine though and Dick was very proud of his little girl.

The weekend visit went well and Dick was pleased that Mary had made him go. He had never dared to admit to himself how much he had missed his family.

Martha was still tending her mistress, even though she was hardly able to look after herself. She had never married. "Your family was all I ever needed Master Dick," she had said simply, when Dick had asked why she was still there. "I wish I'd seen more of this one though, she is adorable!" She asked Josie if she would like to help her get the tea tray. Josie nodded shyly but skipped off quite merrily beside her. Both the old ladies made a real fuss of her. Mother had given her a rag doll and a cuddly leopard that had been her own when she was a child.

"They are very old, like me! So you must take care of them," she had smiled as she handed them to Josie.

"Thank you very much," Josie had replied politely, as she reached to take them.

Josie had been delighted with the present, but was still a little afraid of her grandmother and Martha. "Why do they dress so funny Daddy?" She had whispered when they had a moment alone. Both still dressed in very dated, though smart, black dresses and Martha still sported a lace apron and cap.

Dick smiled to himself. He had been instantly reminded of pictures of Queen Victoria, when he saw his mother seated in her high backed chair.

"They are Victorians," he explained to Josie.

"Oh, I see," Josie nodded, as though she understood perfectly. "They are very nice ladies anyway." Dick nodded in agreement. He had been surprised at how badly his mother had aged since he had last seen her. Now she was a very frail but still proud shadow of her former self. Dick admitted that he was sorry that he had ever fallen out with his mother, he had always had a soft spot for her, and Martha for that matter.

Later that evening, once Josie was sound asleep, Dick went to join his mother, by the fire in the drawing room. He was unsure what to say but he did not need to worry. His mother rose very stiffly from the chair, as he entered the room, and held out her arms. Suddenly Dick was five again, running in from a fall in the street. He couldn't explain why but he clung tightly to her and wept, just like that five year old would have done.

"Oh Richard, I have been so silly." The old lady broke down herself and slid back into her chair, mopping her eyes with a scrap of lace handkerchief. "I was so terribly indoctrinated by your father, that I just did not realise how much pride can get in the way of happiness." She reached out her hands. "Sit by me and tell me how you are coping. Is Mary fully well again? Patrick told me that she has been rather difficult since the accident."

"Mary wouldn't know how to be difficult," Dick insisted. "You would know if you would meet her."

"I know, I am sure she is a good woman," Winifred sighed. "I have been incredibly stupid. I was terrified that she was some sort of money grabbing Jezebel. Silly really."

"Very silly," Dick agreed, "especially as I don't have any money to grab, in case you have forgotten."

"That is something else that I have asked you here for." Winifred leaned forward and took his hands. "I do not approve of what your father did to you..."

"It wasn't Father, in the end." Dick interrupted. "It was those thieving sisters of mine. Father made another will, I am sure of it."

"Well Dear," Winifred sighed, "you must believe what you will, but I knew your Father, better than you think, and I believe that he never intended to restore you in his will. He had that sort of perverted humour. It was probably his intention to leave everything to the girls, you know he doted on them."

"That's true," Dick remembered that only too well. "But what about the cottage? Did he really hate me so much that he not only disregarded his brother's final request but also lied to me about selling it?" The old resentment started to creep back into Dick's voice.

"I don't think he hated you at all," Winifred explained. "He needed to be in control and to believe himself to be the centre of the universe. He could never fully control you, even as a child you stood up to him." A small smile flickered across her face as she recalled Dick's outburst at Aunt Mary's tea party. "Then there was your success. He was jealous of your experiences, dinner with the prince, appearing on newsreels." She paused to sip her sherry. "Oh he loved bathing in the glory of your success, particularly after the Olympics, but that did not stop him resenting you. To keep face with his cronies he knew he had to keep you sweet somehow." Winifred looked down at her hands, as though ashamed. "I never knew anything for certain, but I should have stood up to him more."

"It wasn't your fault mother." Dick started to object but she held up her hand and looked into his eyes.

"I am truly sorry Richard. I know you won't believe me, but

you were always my favourite. If I had had the courage to leave, that day when you asked me to, things could have been very different." She started to cry. "I was brought up in a world where men ruled and women accepted. I just accepted everything, but I should not have accepted what happened to you." Dick stood up and put his arms around her. "You should have been wealthy and happy now."

"Everything is fine Mother, I am happy," Dick reassured her, "and I don't think that I was ever cut out to be wealthy." He laughed, "I hated being cooped up, behind a desk in Father's office. If I get any money, I just spend it anyway. I think you did me a favour. I just would not fit in with the pin-stripe brigade."

"Well, listen son," Winifred hurried on, "I don't have a lot of money myself, most of it was in trust and goes to the girls when I die." She hurried on breathlessly. "I do have an account in my own name though," she giggled. "I salted a little away each week from the housekeeping. It will be all yours when I go. There must be over a thousand pounds in there now." She rose again holding her aching back as she felt her way across the room to her desk. "My will is in here and my solicitor has a copy, so there can be no confusion this time!" Dick rose and helped her back to her chair. "I have left small legacies to each of the boys and little Josie as well." She sat down heavily. "I am sorry Richard, but the other little girl is not of my blood and, like it or not, she will not be included. However, I do hope you will bring her and Mary up to see me soon. I would like to meet all your family before I die."

"No talk of dying Mother, there's years in you yet," Dick insisted.

"Well be a good lad and get me another sherry and tell me about your shop." Winifred rested back in the chair, exhausted by her efforts. Dick sat talking to her until the early hours. It felt so good to be back with his family again. He finally helped his mother to her room and bid her goodnight with a kiss on the cheek.

"Come home Richard." Winifred grasped his hand tightly. "Come home soon, I have missed you so much."

"I will," he promised, and he really meant it. West Hartlepool was where he belonged and he felt certain that one day he would return. Back to the town that he had always loved, the place where he would really feel peace and contentment. The only place that he could really call home.

Mary and Beth never accompanied Dick back to visit his mother, as she died shortly after the visit. True to her word Winifred left Dick, not one but two thousand pounds. A fortune in those days. Mary wanted to buy a nice house and invest some for the future but Dick would not hear of it.

"I am not going to be caught in that trap," he insisted, as they sat beside the fire one evening, shortly after the funeral.

"Once you own a house the troubles start. First there's the repairs, then it's too small, or not in the right area." He took a long pull at his pipe. " No lass, that's not for us. It's a rat race. We'll just enjoy the money, as long as it lasts and then carry on as before." Mary argued but to no avail. She had to admit that they did enjoy it though. They bought a television, one of the first in the village, an electric washing machine with a motor to operate the mangle, an upright piano and, the love of Dick's life, a Wolseley motor car. A beautiful big shiny, black car with running boards and real leather seats. Mary even had a fur coat, genuine mink. She had to admit that spending the money was fun, but still insisted that a house would have been more sensible.

"Well Mary lass," Dick explained one evening. "We've both had "sensible" pushed down our throats for most of our lives. Perhaps we should, just this once, remember that we only live once and enjoy it while we can."

And that is exactly how Dick lived the rest of his ninety-five years. He did eventually return to West Hartlepool, but not until many years later. Mary and he were together for almost fifty years. They were never rich, rarely sensible but always happy.

Dick had explained his philosophy on life quite simply to Josie. It was the evening of his ninetieth birthday and they had been seated in Josie's garden, reminiscing.

"I've had a good life Josie," Dick had insisted. "Oh yes, there can be no denying that there have been some bad times," a slight shadow passed over his face, "and some really bad times for that matter, but you learn from those. Life is a bit like one of those shuggy boat rides I used to take you on when you were little. Great fun when you are flying high, then someone applies the brake and you come down to earth with an awful bump. The secret is knowing how to handle the bumps!" He winked, puffing contentedly on his pipe.

To Josie her Dad had been a hero. Thanks to Dick she had had a fairytale childhood, even though she had suffered constantly with chest problems and bronchitis. It had been a childhood of laughter and fun, but that is another story...

THE END

Author's note (1)
Harold M Abrahams

During the course of producing my book, I had the very great privilege of meeting Mrs Betty Levinson, a relative of the late Harold Abrahams, who currently resides in Hartlepool. My father had the greatest regard for Harold Abrahams and I don't doubt that there would have been some affinity between them, as they both had to overcome some degree of prejudice in order to obtain their places in the British Olympic team. They both also had Hartlepool connections and both suffered from injuries that cut short their athletic ambitions.

Harold Maurice Abrahams was born in Bedford on the 15th December 1899. The family name was originally Klonimus but this was changed by his father, in recognition of his father, Abraham Klonimus. The family originated from Lithuania and came to Britain as refugees, probably on the timber ships from Russia. Mrs Levinson explained to me that many of these ships landed in West Hartlepool docks, bringing timber to the saw mills here, for the pit props they made. There are no records of the names of those refugees that landed in Hartlepool and, although it is extremely unlikely, it could be possible that the Klonimus family could have passed through here.

Sport was in the Abrahams blood. Harold had two brothers, older than himself, Sidney and Adolf, both connected with athletics. Sidney represented Cambridge from 1904 to 1906 as a sprinter and long jumper. He competed, unsuccessfully, in the 1920 Olympics, whilst Adolf's interest in athletics led to him being appointed doctor to the Olympic team. It was Harold himself, however, who was the true Olympic hero.

Harold Abrahams

271

Harold's career started while he was studying to be a lawyer at college. He had three athletics wins in the Freshman's sports at Fenners and then won eight times in the 100yards, 400 yards and the long jump, in contests between Cambridge and Oxford Universities.

In 1924 he was selected for the Olympics and trained for 9 months with his Arabian coach, Sam Mussabini. Mussabini made small but vital changes to Harold's style, including a new method of leaving the starting block and a cross arm action when running. As explained in this novel, Mussabini also played a significant part in Dick Ripley's career.

Abrahams is best known for his part in the Paris Olympics, immortalised in the film *Chariots of Fire*. Paris was his greatest triumph and here he became the first European and only Britain ever to win the 100 metre gold medal. In the second round of this event he established a new record time of 10.6 seconds, then in a magnificent run against 5 men said to be the fastest in the world, Paddock, Scholz, Murchinson and Bowman for America and Porritt of New Zealand, Abrahams took the gold in a time of 10.52. It was the first time the Americans had been beaten.

Abrahams became Captain of the British Olympic team. One of his best performances was the downhill100 yards, when he got a time of 9.6 seconds. He also set four British long jump records, 7.19 in 1919 to 7.38 in 1924. This last record was not beaten for more than 30 years.

In May 1925 disaster struck when Abrahams badly injured his leg whilst attempting to improve his long jump record. His athletic career was effectively over. This did not stop his continued interest in athletics and he was a very active member of the Amateur Athletic Association and the BAAB throughout his life. His dedication to athletics was renowned. As a member of the IAAF he was described as "the architect of the modern laws of athletics."

He married Sybil Marjone in 1936 and was awarded the CBE in 1957 for his work as Secretary of the National Parks Commission. He died on the 14th January 1978 at the age of 79.

Author's Note (2)
Eric H Liddell

Eric Liddell was undoubtedly one of the most successful and inspired British athletes of all time. His talent for athletics and rugby were only surpassed by the strength and depth of his religious convictions. My father admired Liddell's talents and acknowledged that he was one of the sporting greats, but he was never able to identify with him on a personal level. The film *Chariots of Fire* covered Liddell's unprecedented decision not to run in the 100 yards race, but what was not featured was the fact that he also declined to run as part of the team selected to run the 4 x 400 metres relay, for the same reason. Dick Ripley was part of that team and they did win a bronze medal. That was a disappointment to Dick, especially as the same team, but with Liddell as a member, beat the American team that had taken the gold at the Olympics, two weeks later in the Empire Games.

Eric Henry Liddell was born in Tientsin, Northern China on 16th January 1902. His parents were Scottish missionaries. Eric was educated in "The School for the Sons of Missionaries", Blackheath,

London, later called Eltham College. It was at Eltham College that his love of sport developed. By the age of 15, Eric had played cricket for the School First X1, rugby for the First XV and three years later was captain of both teams. Eric and his brother, Robert, also dominated various athletics events including 100 yards, quarter mile, long jump, high jump and hurdles.

Liddell entered Edinburgh University in 1921, studying Pure Science. Here he initially made his mark on the rugby field and was selected to play rugby for Scotland in 1922. However by 1923 he had abandoned rugby in favour of athletics. In July 1923 he won the 220 yards and the 100 yards in the Amateur Athletics Association Championships in London. In 1924 Liddell joined the Olympic team intending to run the 100 metres, 4 x 100 metres relay and 4 x 400 metres but it was not meant to be as the heats for all these races were run on Sunday. Liddell's integrity would not allow him to run on the Sabbath and he therefore changed to the 200 metres and 400 metres races. Liddell's won a bronze in the 200 metres.

The final of the 400 metres was run on Friday 11th July and Liddell's winning performance of 47.6 seconds beat not only Olympic but World records. The American, Meredith, who was world record holder for the quarter mile, said of Liddell's race: "It was the most wonderful 400 metre race that has ever been run, it was nothing short of marvellous as Liddell had to make his own pace from the crack of the pistol to the tape." An American masseur had handed Liddell a note, prior to the race. It read "Them that honour Me I will honour." (1 Samuel ii.30). No man deserved to reap the reward of this prophecy more than Liddell.

Liddell returned to Edinburgh University on 17th July 1924 to attend his graduation ceremony. The other students carried him shoulder-high to St. Giles Cathedral for the service and he was honoured, not only for his athletic achievements but also for the strength of principle in upholding his religious beliefs. At a public dinner held on the 18th July, Liddell made it clear that his future did not lie in athletics. It was his intention to devote his life to evangelical work.

In the summer of 1925 Liddell left the UK for China to become a Protestant Christian missionary. He was ordained as a minister in 1932. He married Florence Mackenzie, a Canadian nurse, in 1934 and became a father to three daughters, Patricia, Heather and Maureen.

At the beginning of World War 2, Florence returned to Canada and Liddell was interned in a Japanese prisoner of war camp at Weihsien, where he died of a brain tumour on 21st February 1945.

Author's Note (3)

It is interesting to note that Great Britain won no fewer than 60 medals in the 1924 Olympics. Of these 22 were for athletics events. Details of these are as follows:

Name	Events	Medal
Harold Abrahams	100 Metres 4 x 100 Metre Relay	Gold Silver
Guy M Butler	400 Metres 4 x 400 Metres Relay	Bronze Bronze
A Clark	3000 Metre Team Race	Silver
Gordon R Goodwin	10000 Metre Walk	Silver
H A Johnston	3000 Metre Team Race	Silver
Eric H Liddell	200 Metres 400 Metres	Bronze Gold
Douglas G A Lowe	800 Metres	Gold
B H MacDonald	3000 Metre Team Race	Silver
W P Nichol	4 x 100 Metre Relay	Silver
Malcolm C Noakes	Hammer	Bronze
W H Porter	3000 Metre Team Race	Silver
W Rangeley	4 x 100 Metre Relay	Silver
G R Renwick	4 x 400 Metre Relay	Bronze
Richard N Ripley (Dick)	4 x 400 Metre Relay	Bronze
L C Royle	4 x 100 Metre Relay	Silver
W R Seagrove	3000 Metre Team Race	Silver
Philip B Stallard	1500 Metres	Bronze
E J Toms	4 x 400 Metres Relay	Bronze
G J Webber	3000 Metre Team Race	Silver

Living with FrED

By SHARON BIRCH

One family's perspective on living in the shadow of the heriditable genetic condition known as Ehlers-Danlos Syndrome (type III -Hypermobility)

An informative, knowledgeable view of the effects of EDS, relevant to all affected by this often disabling condition – families, medics and professionals alike. It is told with practicality and the unassuming humour of a mother, wife and fellow sufferer.

To order this book:
Email: **shazzabirch@aol.com**
By post to: **13 The Green,**
Seaton Carew, Hartlepool,
TS25 1AS

The book is priced at £7.99 plus £2 postage and is produced by
Cormorant Publishing Hartlepool
<u>www.riddlewrites.co.uk</u>

BAR
ELCINE

"They deserve an
Oscar for their food"

Galloping Gourmet 1997

Pescado Fresco
Jamoncitos
de Pollo

C/. Juan Bariajo, nº 8.
Tfno: 609 10 77 58
LOS CRISTIANOS - ARONA - TENERIFE

Hartlepool Marina is the venue for the 2010 Tall Ships Race when an estimated one million visitors will come to Hartlepool for the biggest sailing event in the Tall Ships calendar. In addition to the spectacle of seeing the old sailing ships enter the Marina visitors can take in the Historic Quay, Maritime Museum, and the two resident ships the "Wingfield Castle" and HMS Trincomalee. For a unique dining experience visitors will be able to dine at Krimo's, Portofino and Casa del Mar - part of the Krimo triangle on the Marina.

Krimos

Krimo's opened on 4th May 1985 with a mere £250 at the seaside resort of Seaton Carew (Hartlepool) in the North-East of England. The restaurant was put on the map with the help of immensely dedicated staff, a few of whom are still with us. From the very start, we realised that Krimo's was a runaway success because we were booked up weeks in advance due to the format of "your table for the night" At one time, there wasn't one free table on Saturdays for 16 weeks. In July 1990, we moved out of the first-floor flat and doubled the seating. In April 2000, we opened the new **Krimo's**, our new self-designed 80 -seater restaurant on Hartlepool Marina. Whilst retaining quite a few of the old menu's favourites, we encourage the chefs to experiment with new dishes and as a result the menu now contains some exciting additions. Over the last two years we have added also a few Algerian dishes. These have been proved very popular. **Krimo's** has remained as popular as ever and, although we may now have the odd free table mid-week, we still refuse people on Saturdays. The same format remains and so does the quality of ingredients. A truly delightful oasis now offering superb Mediterranean and Algerian cuisine in the idyllic setting of Hartlepool Marina.. We have built this restaurant by listening to our customers and therefore your views and comments are greatly valued; please take the time to send us an email with your comments and suggestions. Hartlepool Marina has brought a new breath of fresh air to the town. The Historic Quay, the replica of an 18th century port was voted best tourist attraction in 2000. HMS Trincomalee, attracts thousands of visitors.

Portofino

In October 1998 Portofino was opened and its reputation has grown rapidly due to its beautifully prepared meals, mainly of Mediterranean style. **Krimo** places considerable emphasis on customer care and service ensuring that the recipes are produced exactly as they should by an energetic young team. Visitors to this happy bistro cannot help but be thrilled by the buzzing atmosphere created by the décor and carefully compiled music. The restaurant is placed in a pleasant setting overlooking the **Historic Quay** and **Hartlepool Marina.**

Casa del Mar

Is the latest addition to the Krimo "triangle" on Hartlepool Marina. Offering more than 50 authentic tapas dishes.

Consistency

The common ingredient in all our restaurants is consistency.

www.krimos.co.uk 01429 266120
www.portofino.co.uk 01429 266166
www.casabar.co.uk 01429 222223

Krimo's Blog

For all the latest news from Krimo log onto his blog at
www.krimosrestaurant.blogspot.com